CULTURALLY
CONTESTED
PEDAGOGY

SUNY series, Power, Social Identity, and Education
Lois Weis, editor

CULTURALLY CONTESTED PEDAGOGY

Battles of Literacy and Schooling
between Mainstream Teachers
and Asian Immigrant Parents

Guofang Li

With a Foreword by Lee Gunderson

STATE UNIVERSITY OF NEW YORK PRESS

Published by
State University of New York Press, Albany

For information, address State University of New York Press,
194 Washington Avenue, Suite 305, Albany, NY 12210-2384

Production by Marilyn P. Semerad
Marketing by Anne M. Valentine

Library of Congress Cataloging in Publication Data

Li, Guofang, 1972–
  Culturally contested pedagogy : battles of literacy and schooling between mainstream
teachers and Asian immigrant parents / Guofang Li ; with a foreword by Lee
Gunderson.
    p. cm. — (SUNY series, power, social identity, and education)
  Includes bibliographical references and index.
  ISBN 0-7914-6593-4 (hardcover : alk. paper) — ISBN 0-7914-6594-2 (pbk. : alk. paper)
  1. Asian Americans—Education—United States. 2. Asians—Education—Canada.
  3. Children of immigrants—Education—United States. 4. Children of immigrants—
Education—Canada. 5. Literacy—Social aspects—United States. 6. Literacy—Social
aspects—Canada. 7. Parent-teacher relationships—United States. 8. Parent-teacher
relationships—Canada. I. Title. II. Series.

LC2632.L52 2005
371.829'95'073—dc22

                                                                    2004030459

10 9 8 7 6 5 4 3 2 1

To the loving memory of my brother, Li You-guo,
who always lived with big dreams

Contents

Illustrations

Figures

Table

Foreword

Guofang Li presents a fascinating study in this book, one that describes and analyzes the interactions, communications, and difficulties occurring among teachers, immigrant students, and their parents. It is not, however, a typical immigrant study that explores the plight of poor families interacting with schools and teachers. Li's study includes white middle-class teachers in the school who are a racial minority in the community and Chinese immigrants who are a racial majority and who are not poor but middle-class or higher socioeconomically than the teachers. The Chinese families have economic power and they are enthusiastic about using it to improve their children's chances for success. The difficulty is that there are significant cultural differences between teachers' and parents' views of what students should learn and how they should be taught (J. Anderson, 1995a; J. Anderson & Gunderson, 1997; Gunderson & J. Anderson, 2003; Gunderson, 2000). Teachers, parents, and other interested individuals all seem to want the best for children. The difficulty is agreeing on what constitutes the best. This is as true for literacy teachers and researchers as it is for parents and other community groups. Over the years what is considered the best in reading instruction has varied dramatically.

Gunderson (2001) writes, "Schools and teachers are in many respects the instruments by which governments both national and local inculcate in their citizens the set of beliefs deemed correct and appropriate" (p. 264). Dick and Jane in the United States and in Canada represented mainstream societal views of family, gender, work ethic, and family structures to students, regardless of their backgrounds. In the 1960s the civil rights movement and the immigration of hundreds of thousands of Spanish-speaking students helped to focus attention on the needs, abilities, and backgrounds of students who differed from the individuals found in reading textbooks. Considerable efforts were made to include minority students in reading materials and through busing in the United States to assure that they were distributed equally across schools in ways that were representative of the diversity of the overall community. Basal reading programs were designed to systematize the teaching and learning of reading involving materials that represented the diversity of students. Basal reading series were based on the notion that students should learn discrete, separate reading skills in a systematic and orderly fashion. In the 1960s and 1970s, basal reading series were used widely across North America to teach students to read. They were considered to be essential and, even better, to be based on scientific principles (Shannon, 1989).

A number of revolutions in the way educators view the teaching and learning of reading began in the 1960s. Meaning, many such as Goodman (1967) argued, does not occur in any transcendental sense in text, but is a result of the interaction of a human being and a text. These and other researchers argued strongly that "real literature" was essential to learning, not the artificially constructed and stilted discourse found in basal readers. Others, like Read (1971), showed that reading and writing are not separate processes, but that they occur naturally in an integrated and interactive way. The educational approach referred to as "whole language" was in large part a result of these views. Whole language educators were convinced that children should be encouraged to explore language in meaningful ways, to read authentic literature, and to invent spellings. Delpit (1988, 1991) argued that whole language involves a focus on process, one that benefits students from the middle class but denies minority students access to the "power" code. Whole language as an early instructional approach became the focus of criticism in the 1990s from individuals who believed that early reading instruction should focus on systematic phonics instruction since phonemic awareness was found to be a predictor of reading achievement. The No Child Left Behind Act of 2001 (U.S. Department of Education, 2002) mandated the teaching of phonics and phonics-based reading programs. It represents a politically conservative or traditional view of reading and reading instruction.

The literacy research community has interestingly different views and approaches. Individuals such as Pressley (1998) have proposed "balanced" approaches, while others have developed views of literacy that situate it more broadly as comprising ways of thinking that are tied to different sets of values, cultural norms, and literacies (Gee, 1996). Some speak of multiliteracies or critical literacies existing within a multilayered context varying from the reading and writing of icons to the reading and writing of hypertext. The "New London" group met in 1994 "to consider the future of literacy teaching: to discuss what would need to be taught in a rapidly changing near future, and how this should be taught" (Cope & Kalantzis, 2000, p. 3). They speak of "mere literacy" centered on language only and argue, "A pedagogy of Multiliteracies, by contrast, focuses on modes of representation much broader than language alone" (p. 5). Teachers in Li's study appear to be theoretically situated within a whole-language orientation, while parents are firmly focused on "mere literacy" and on the teaching and learning of the skills they believe constitute literacy and its promise of success in a broad sense in society. Their view is a conservative or traditional view of the teaching and learning of literacy.

Li's goal in this book is to describe and analyze the cultural conflicts occurring between teachers and parents. She wants to develop a careful description of teacher and parental views, not to empower one over the other, but to discover ways to resolve them. The immigrant families in this study were part of the influx of immigrants from Hong Kong just prior to its return to the People's Republic of China. Unlike many immigrants they are economically affluent and have strong educational aspirations for their children. Li carefully describes the many ways in which this disparity in views creates conflict: views about homework, worksheets, "down time," skills instruction, meaning as centered in a book rather than as a feature of top-down processing, rote learning, special education, phonics instruction, student-centered learning, teacher-parent communication and respect, discipline, class work time, personal responsibility, individual choice, and the roles and responsibilities of teachers and their students. Parents use their economic power to compensate for the shortcomings they perceive in their children's classrooms. Li describes in detail the many ways in which the teachers' educational beliefs and practices are in direct conflict with parents' views. She also describes what she calls the "dark side" of parental involvement.

Li considers the role of critical pedagogy, or how teachers and education in general can provide students with the tools to better themselves and to strengthen democracy. The basic notion behind critical pedagogy is that it should result in progressive social change.

In most studies the school is seen as a conservative force that attempts to maintain the privileged status of the mainstream majority, and the purpose of critical pedagogy is to privilege all students. Li's study has interesting implications for understanding the dynamics of the struggles between homes and schools. In the case of Li's study the Chinese families are the majority in the community and their views of teaching and learning are conservative views normally associated with the mainstream. On the other hand, the white teachers are from the minority group in the community, and their views are uncomfortably nonconservative in the eyes of the majority group. The political struggles and their outcomes that Li observes help us understand more about the complexity and relativity of the notions of minority and majority.

Li concludes the book with recommendations for ways to resolve what seem like irreconcilable differences. I believe you will find this to be an interesting study, one that will challenge many mainstream views of teaching and learning. It will provoke both conversations and arguments about teaching and learning and about multicultural education. It will challenge teachers to evaluate their views of inclusion in significant ways. With no further comment, I invite you to begin your journey to meet the teachers, students, and parents of Richmond's Taylor elementary school as chronicled by Guofang Li.

Lee Gunderson
The University of British Columbia

Acknowledgments

I am indebted to many individuals for helping me with the researching and writing of this book. The teachers, students, and parents at Taylor Elementary, who cannot be named for reasons of confidentiality, generously invested their time and interest in the research project and shared much of their lives with me. I remain deeply appreciative of their support and participation that had made this book possible.

The project began in 2000 at the University of British Columbia where I was a postdoctoral fellow funded by the Social Sciences and Humanities Research Council of Canada (SSHRC). I am deeply indebted to Dr. Marilyn Chapman, my postdoctoral sponsor at UBC who played an important role in the research project from the very start. She not only supported me in many concrete ways (such as arranging office space, helping me find a place to live, and making contact with the schools), but also offered me professional guidance and wisdom and analytical insight as the research project progressed and evolved. She read and commented on an earlier version of the manuscript and provided invaluable suggestions. Her enthusiasm and dedication to research and teaching continues to inspire me to become a better scholar. I thank also Dr. Lee Gunderson for his support as chair when I was at UBC and for his wonderful foreword for the book.

I am also indebted to many of my colleagues and friends in the Graduate School of Education, University at Buffalo where I completed the writing of this project. I am thankful to Dean Mary Gresham and Department of Learning and Instruction for granting me a much needed course release in the Spring 2003 semester to focus on writing. I owe a special thanks to Dr. Greg Dimitriadis for consistently providing me with good advice, for keeping me focused on the big picture, and for commenting on an early version of the manuscript. He challenged me to go beyond the cultural lens to include more critical analysis. I benefited much from his intellectual mind and deep commitment to research. I also thank Dr. Lois Weis, my series editor, for her support and faith in my scholarship and research in the past several years. I am grateful to have such a fine role model as my colleague.

My appreciation is also extended to a number of people who have been a very important part of the process. Special thanks to Dr. Sam Robinson at the University of Saskatchewan who has offered me continuous support over the years and who also read and provided insightful comments on the early draft of this book. I also thank the two anonymous reviewers for their important suggestions that have strengthened the book. I would also like to thank several graduate students Jason Deane, Xiaojun Hu, and Kelly Spring who helped me with transcription, translation, editing, and data entry—their work on the project was invaluable.

My gratitude also goes to the staff at the SUNY Press. I am deeply indebted to Priscilla Ross who took a strong interest in the book when I first presented her with the project. I am grateful to her faith and belief in me. I would also like to thank Lisa Chesnel and Marilyn Semerad for providing constant feedback and prompt replies to my e-mails and questions. They have made the production process a pleasant experience.

I thank also my friends in Canada, Barry, Yvonne, and Roberta for being my constant support throughout the years. My final appreciation goes to my family in China, especially my elder brother, Li Ming, and sister-in-law, Cao Xinyuan. Their endurance, strength, and dedication to our family during the difficult times of our lives in the past several years have encouraged me to be many ways strong.

Introduction

Literacy Learning and Teaching in a
New Socioeconomic Context

[Mainstream] educators are being tested by [the Chinese]
parents' views, different views about education. And [the
Chinese] parents are being tested because our educational
systems are different and it's hard not to be judgmental.
Both groups come from different backgrounds, different
beliefs.

—Ms. Dawson, Taylor Elementary School

In 2000, upon the completion of my doctoral research on Chinese
immigrant families' bicultural literacy practices and socialization in
Saskatoon, a small city in Western Canada, I moved to Vancouver,
British Columbia, to continue my research on Chinese immigrant children's school-home literacy connections at the University of British
Columbia. When I landed in Vancouver, I found myself in a state of
cultural shock. In Saskatoon, there were only about 4,000 Chinese residents; they were mostly manual laborers and were often scattered in
the city without forming a solid ethnic community. The Asians were at
the periphery of the heated racial and educational tensions between
whites and native peoples. I was a member of an "invisible minority."
However, in Vancouver where Asians had become the majority,
numerically surpassing the whites, I became part of a "visible majority." Since more than one-third of its population is Chinese, Vancouver
has been nicknamed "Hongcouver," and the University of British
Columbia (UBC) is called "University of Billion Chinese." I was

1

surprised that local media such as the *Vancouver Sun* and *Vancouver Courier* were flooded with news about new middle-class Chinese immigrants and communities, especially issues such as their campaign for the legitimacy of the Chinese language in university admissions, their critical attitudes toward K–12 public school education, and their push for traditional teacher-centered schools.

I was quite intrigued by the power the Chinese community exhibited and even shocked to learn that in several school districts traditional schools had been established due to the Chinese parents' efforts. Later in my interviews with the Chinese parents in the Vancouver suburb of Richmond, all of them responded that if they had a choice in their district, they would send their children to such schools. Their critique of Canadian schools, however, was perceived as their unwillingness to make efforts to adapt to the new world. Later when I discussed this issue with a white female colleague, a professor of education, she commented, "I'm sorry. This is Canada, not Hong Kong. If [the Chinese] don't like the schools here, they should not have come here." This view (though not necessarily shared among the faculty at UBC), as I learned, was unfortunately the common sentiment of the mainstream. In return, the Chinese perceived that the Canadians simply refused to face reality and accept change.

"To change" or "not to change" became the on-going battle between the Chinese and the mainstream Canadians. As a Chinese immigrant to Canada, educated both in Canada and in China, I found myself puzzled by the two competing paradigms, unable to take sides. The question to me is not whether we should change, but more changing *to what and how much*. If we believe in multiculturalism and in building a democratic society, then we should respect ethnic groups' and parents' choices regarding their children's education. After all, the Chinese, as a historically marginalized group, seem to be fighting against the dominance of the Eurocentric hegemonic practices by demanding that their ways of knowing be legitimized. However, if we believe that the Chinese should change and accept mainstream practices, then we endorse the dominance of the mainstream and the marginalization of the minority. The responsibility of schools, as I understand it, is to serve the needs of the students and their community, rather than vice versa. These battles between the two parties, therefore, have gone beyond an educational and pedagogical debate to become social and political.

Is it possible that both camps can learn from each other and a middle ground can be achieved between the two orientations? How are the two dichotomous orientations played out in school settings? In order to better understand the dynamics and complexities of teaching and learning in an increasingly complex situation in which literacy, culture, race, and social class intertwine to make an impact on teachers, students, and parents, in this book I provide a descriptive account of cultural clashes and symbolic struggles between Canadian teachers and Chinese immigrant parents and the experiences of their children who live through these cultural conflicts in their intersecting worlds of school, home, and community. I explore the experiences and perspectives of the teachers, parents, and students who were at the heart of these cultural conflicts and contradictions, and I examine the inter-institutional linkages between school and home and how pedagogy was culturally and politically contested between mainstream teachers and Chinese parents.

Teaching and Learning in a New Time

The recent mass immigration has resulted in the emergence of many middle-class immigrant and ethnic enclaves in many cities in North America. Although they have enriched the cultural diversity of the society, these ethnic enclaves at the same time have also created a sense of cultural separateness. This perceived separateness often leads to social and cultural conflicts that are inherent within a multicultural society with a range of discordant values and beliefs. Schooling and education often become sites of embodiment of such social and cultural conflicts. Ms. Dawson's words quoted at the beginning of this chapter, for example, are an example of such embodiment. Indeed, as Ms. Dawson's words suggest, diversity and differences have put educators to the test. This test is not simply about understanding cultural differences, but about reconceptualizing the power differences and the changing structural relations between mainstream schools and immigrant families.

Since the focus of minority education has been concerned with students of lower socioeconomic backgrounds, the education of children of these new middle-class immigrant minority communities remains unexamined. The emerging voice of a middle-class immigrant group, rising from their historically marginalized position to challenge mainstream schooling practices, has added yet another dimension of challenge to the education of minority children in the current post-modern reality. As countries such as Canada and the United States become increasingly multicultural and multilingual, more and more mainstream classroom teachers, like Ms. Dawson, are facing the challenge of dealing with cultural and social conflicts between immigrant families' and schools' values and beliefs.

According to the U.S. Census Bureau's 2001 population survey, the U.S. population grew by 33 million during the 1990s; about one-third of new residents were immigrants. The survey projected that in 2050, the total U.S. population will exceed 400 million, and the greatest increase in population will be Hispanic (from 12.6% in 2000 to 24.3% in 2050), and Asian/Pacific Islander (from 3.7% in 2000 to 8.9% in 2050). In Canada, Asia and the Pacific region have been the leading source of immigrants since the 1990s (53.01% in 2001), with China (including Hong Kong) being the number one source country (Citizenship and Immigration Canada, 2002). In the Province of British Columbia alone, immigrants accounted for 87.2% of its population growth from 1993 to 2000. According to British Columbia Statistics 2002, 81% of the immigrant population came from Asia (mostly Hong Kong and mainland China).

The increased immigration of families of Asian and Pacific Islander and Hispanic backgrounds has also changed the landscape of communities in many cities such as Vancouver, Toronto, San Francisco, and New York. The new Chinese immigrants since the 1980s have often come with resources—financial capital, training, and education. Unlike Asian immigrants prior to the 1980s, who settled in urban ethnic enclaves (Chinatown), the majority of these new immigrants settled in concentrated suburban areas and established new middle-class ethnic communities. In Vancouver and Toronto, for example, many new Asian immigrants settled mostly in ethnically concentrated areas in the suburbs (e.g., Richmond, British Columbia and Richmond Hill, Ontario), and changed the originally white middle-class neighborhoods into predominantly Asian middle-class communities (P. S. Li, 1998). In the United States, Asian-born populations are concentrated in a handful of metropolitan areas. Close to half (45%) of the nation's new Asian-born population live in Los Angeles, New York, or San Francisco. Within the San Francisco area, Asians make up more than half of the foreign born population (U. S. Census Bureau, 2001).

The shifted landscapes in these communities have also changed the landscapes of the classrooms in the public schools. Many regular classroom teachers used to teach in a setting in which subject matter and literacy skills were taught entirely in English and the majority of the students were native speakers of English; and they often had no training in how to deal with ESL students (Penfield, 1987; Valenzuela, 1999). These teachers are now teaching students with limited English proficiency who are primarily from one ethnic background such as the Chinese. Since language and literacy practices—their functions, meanings, and methods of transmission, shaped by different social and cultural norms—vary from one cultural group to another (Au, 1998; Langer, 1987), this classroom landscape shift has added unprecedented challenges to mainstream classroom teachers' pedagogical practices. These mainstream teachers, who are naturally transformed into immigrant teachers due to the dramatic demographic change, need to deal with not only linguistic barriers, content, and interaction around instruction, but also different sociocultural values of the immigrant students' ethnic community, as well as different types of parental involvement within the particular ethnic community (Huss-Keeler, 1997; G. Li, 2002; Valdés, 1996; Valenzuela, 1999).

To overcome these linguistic and sociocultural barriers and maximize the learning experience of the minority students, teachers not only have to learn about students' cultures and backgrounds, but also need the ability to interpret and make pedagogical decisions based on the socialcultural data collected (Davidman & Davidman, 1997; G. Li 1998). Researchers on minority education suggest that pedagogical models that make teaching relevant to students' diverse backgrounds can help mainstream teachers overcome the barriers. For example, Ladson-Billings' (1990, 1994) "culturally relevant teaching" and Au's (1993) "culturally responsive teaching" maintain that teachers should include students' cultures and adapt instruction to the interactional, linguistic, and cognitive styles of the minority students (e.g., African Americans and native Hawaiian children) so as to transcend the negative effects (cultural assimilation, loss of ethnic culture and language, low self-esteem) and empower students intellectually, emotionally, and politically.

These pedagogical approaches are problematic for this study. First, these models assume that classroom teachers are familiar with minority students' cultures and their interactional, linguistic, and cognitive styles. In reality, with the sudden influx of ESL students, many teachers were not prepared to take on the role of teaching these students, and many did not have much contact with the minority students' culture outside school (Clair, 1995; Huss-Keeler, 1997). Although there is much talk about building teacher-parent partnerships, there has been very limited implementation of a true partnership (Fine, 1993; Epstein,

2001). Also, many of the practices involving parents have been geared toward resocializing immigrant and minority parents into mainstream parenting styles rather than understanding their own practices as a source of knowledge.

Second, these models operate on the premise of middle-class educators teaching and responding to lower-class students from minority backgrounds. These models do not address the challenges teachers face when class status between teachers and students' communities is reversed (that is, middle-class teachers of minority children from upper-middle-class homes). Researchers in sociology and anthropology of education (Heath, 1983; Lareau, 2000; P. E. Willis, 1977; Weis, 1990) have concluded that social class affects minority schooling in many ways. It shapes the resources parents can have at their disposal to comply with teachers' requests for assistance, and influences their expectations, strategies, and investment in their children's education (Lareau, 2000; Louie, 2001). More importantly, social class determines who controls what is taught, who has access to what, and whose literacy is legitimized in schools. Since mainstream schooling has been dominated by Eurocentric practices (Giroux, 1991; Corson, 1992b), a change of class structure will affect immigrant minority's social positioning in society, and therefore their interactions with mainstream society. Immigrant minorities, such as the Chinese in this study, may challenge the mainstream status quo, resist and reject the mainstream practices, and demand the legitimization of their own literacy practices.

Third, these models are teacher centered; they neglect the autonomy of students and their families regarding what they can contribute to instruction and curriculum. Minority children bring to school a repository of knowledge from their homes and communities. However, this knowledge is often not recognized in the school milieu (Moll, 1994). Research on minority family literacy practices has shown that minority families have very different cultural beliefs and practices of literacy and different ways of parental involvement from mainstream practices (Compton-Lilly, 2003; Delgado-Gaitan, 1990; Heath, 1983; G. Li, 2002; Taylor & Dorsey-Gaines, 1988; Valdés, 1996). Yet current models assume that the teachers' own cultural and literacy beliefs are not in conflict with those of the minority students. Furthermore, these models assume that the minority community welcomes and accepts the teachers' pedagogical approaches. What happens when teachers hold fundamentally different beliefs from those of students' cultures and when the minority parents challenge the teachers' practices and demand that teachers teach in ways they do not believe in? How responsive should teachers be to the minority culture? Can they teach what they do not know or do not believe in? What about the parents? Should they accept practices that they do not believe in? Who decides what is the best for the children?

To answer these questions, we need to take a closer look at the linkages between school and home. We need to understand not only classroom practices, school structures, and practices in children's homes and wider communities, but also the interactions and relationships between school and home/community (Hull & Schultz, 2002; Lareau, 2000). We also need to understand teachers' own cultural beliefs and pedagogical practices and how minority communities actually respond to their beliefs and practices. As McCarthey (1997) documents, although many teachers have employed a variety of methods to welcome diversity, their efforts may inadvertently reinforce oppressive practices and ignore or even devalue home literacy practices. Therefore, it is imperative not only to uncover the "hidden literacies" (Voss, 1996) in the homes and communities of immigrant children in order to provide insights into their education in the schools, but also to examine teachers' cultural beliefs and their pedagogical approaches to minority children's home/community and school connections, as well as minority perspectives on their beliefs and instruction. Furthermore, it is necessary to examine the interplay of power relationships between teachers' and minority discourses to shed light on minority students' education in a changing sociocultural climate.

This book is such a critical examination of teachers' beliefs and pedagogical practices and the minority community's response to their beliefs and practices. It is based on the findings of my year-long ethnographic research on Chinese immigrant children's home and school literacy connections at Taylor Elementary School (pseudonym) in Richmond, a predominantly middle-class Chinese neighborhood in the greater Vancouver area. It documents two Euro-Canadian teachers' beliefs and pedagogical approaches and eight Chinese families' beliefs and uses of literacy, their reaction to school practices, and their children's home-school literacy connections (and disconnections). These are examined in a new socioeconomic context in which the Chinese surpass the white community numerically and socioeconomically, but not politically.

Prior to this research, I had conducted an ethnographic study that focused on the home literacy practices of Chinese immigrant children and had learned much about the Chinese cultural beliefs about literacy and education and how their beliefs shape their literacy practices and parental involvement in the home milieu (G. Li, 2002). My intent for this study, then, was to move beyond the home milieu to examine how Chinese immigrant children bring their families' cultural values to the school setting and make connections between home, community, and school literacy practices, and how teachers foster such connections. I was interested in understanding the Chinese families' cultural beliefs and the students' literacy experiences in and out of school and how they translated school and home differences. I was also interested in the teachers' cultural beliefs and pedagogical practices and how they perceived and accommodated the students' cultural differences.

During the course of the research I learned more about the teachers, the students, and the parents, and discovered that disconnections and miscommunications were evident in their lived reality of teaching, learning, and parenting in a cross-cultural context. Instead of finding harmonious and happy pictures of school and home connections, I uncovered disturbing collisions of discourses and silent power struggles between school and home. These cultural collisions and symbolic struggles are the focus of this book. Thus, this book is not about home-school cultural connections, but about cultural disconnections, disagreements, and disarticulations. It is about the battles of literacy and culture between Euro-Canadian teachers and middle-class Chinese immigrant parents regarding their children's education. It is about the battles "between home language and school language, home values and school values, home discourses and school discourses" (Lopez, 1999, p. 4).

To talk about cultural conflicts and battles of literacy and schooling concerning the Chinese in North America is a novel concept as they are often associated with the image of "model minority" who can (and willingly do) assimilate into the mainstream society, and who can "make it" within socioeconomic constraints without much support or questioning the status quo (Lee, 1996; Suzuki, 1995). These model minority images have become a destructive myth for those Chinese children whom the schools are failing. They have led attention away from the problems many Chinese children face in and out of school (sociocultural barriers, language differences, and socioeconomic factors), and have prevented us from unraveling the social realities of those who are facing problems in our educational system, for example, schools' misconceptions and negligence to immigrant families' pleas for help, insensitivity to parental expectations, and insufficient resources (G. Li, 2003; Olsen, 1997).

As the stories of the students will demonstrate, contrary to the popular model minority myth that all Asian students are high academic achievers who are joyfully initiated into North American life and English literacy practices (Lee, 1996; Townsend and Fu, 1998), many of the Chinese students at Taylor Elementary experienced difficulties not only in learning English, but also in achieving academic success. For example, the 2001 results of the British Columbia Foundations Skills Assessment indicated that nearly 37% of the fourth graders (in addition to the 21% of students who were excused from taking the test due to their limited English proficiency) in the school had not yet reached the provincial standards in reading comprehension (BC Ministry of Education, 2001). Unlike the model minority image that Chinese parents are docile and nonconfrontational to the mainstream society (Chun, 1995), the middle-class Chinese families reported here not only actively challenged Canadian school practices, but also demanded that Canadian schools follow pedagogical practices similar to the traditional practices in their home country. When their demands were not met, the Chinese parents took action at home to remedy what they considered to be lacking in the mainstream schools.

The raising of the Chinese voice concerning their children's education in Canadian public schools has posed unprecedented challenges to the Euro-Canadian teachers who hold different beliefs about literacy practices and education in general. Cultural conflicts and educational dissensions have often arisen between the teachers and the Chinese parents. The teachers of Taylor Elementary faced not only the challenge of dealing with cultural differences, but also the challenge of adjusting to a changing socioeconomic structure in which the Chinese middle class is challenging the status quo of the dominant white society (P. S. Li, 1998).

This study examines the cultural conflicts and clashes in literacy beliefs and pedagogical practices of two mainstream teachers and eight Chinese parents within this new power structure, and the meaning of these clashes for the students who were at the heart of these cultural conflicts and educational dissensions. By offering a rich, descriptive account of the challenges and difficulties faced by the teachers as well as the Chinese parents and students, I hope to provide:

1. understandings of mainstream teachers' experiences and perspectives on teaching middle-class minority children in a concentrated ethnic community to inform teacher professional development and teacher education;
2. understandings of minority parents and students' experiences and perspectives of learning in a cross-cultural context to suggest recommendations for successful accommodation and adaptation to the cultural differences in schooling;
3. understandings of the extent to which cultural differences between teachers and parents/communities play a role in the education of minority children in order to build effective school-community partnerships within a new sociocultural and socioeconomic context.

This Study

The study on which this book is based took place over a one-year period during 2000–2001, and was funded by a postdoctoral grant from the Social Science and Humanities Research Council of Canada (SSHRCC). It involved one elementary school (Taylor Elementary), two combined classes (grade 1/2 and grade 4/5), and their respective teachers (Mrs. Haines* and Ms. Dawson), eight focal Chinese children from these four grades (Anthony Chan, Alana Tang, Sandy Chung, and Kevin Ma in grade 1/2, and Andy Lou, Billy Chung, Jake Wong, and Tina Wei in grade 4/5), and the students' parents. It also involved interviews with one teacher assistant (Mrs. Yep) and one ESL/resource teacher (Mrs. Smith), and informal discussions with school personnel and administrators such as the principal. All the Chinese parents were first-generation immigrants. Among the eight focal children, Alana Tang and Tina Wei were foreign born, and all other children were born in Canada.

When designing this research project on Asian students' home and school literacy connections at the University of British Columbia, I was looking for teachers to participate in the study. When presented with the project, Mrs. Haines and Ms. Dawson volunteered to participate in the study because they both had large numbers of Chinese

---

*All names used in this study are pseudonyms. English first names were chosen for the children who used English names in school.

students in their classrooms and were both frustrated by the resistance of Chinese parents to cooperating with the school, and eager to find out more about Chinese parents and their educational values. They hoped that my research would help facilitate communication and understanding between the school and the Chinese parents.

As my goal was to gain an understanding of the participants' literacy practices, values, perspectives, and meanings in their sociocultural contexts, I used educational ethnography as the research method (Spindler & Spindler, 1982). This method allowed me, the researcher, to have direct and prolonged engagement with the participants in and out of the classroom, and to explore their beliefs, actions, and interactions in these settings (Goetz & LeCompte, 1984). In order to provide rich descriptive data about the contexts, activities, and beliefs of participants, I gathered data from multiple sources using a variety of methods including direct observation, participant observation, interviewing, and artifact collection. My key modes of data collection included participant observation resulting in extensive field notes; semistructured interviews with teachers, parents, and students; and focus-group discussion with students and teachers.

My fieldwork entailed weekly visits (two school days per week) to the two classes during the 2000–2001 academic year. During the school visits, I observed the students' activities and interactions with teachers and peers, as well as the teachers' instruction and their interactions with students in and outside their classrooms. I paid particular attention to the literacy activities in which the students participated, their language use and choices in different settings, their interactional patterns with teachers and peers, and the ways they used or talked about their home literacy experiences. I also collected, read, and photocopied samples of the students' written work. As a participant observer, I took part in some classroom activities and field trips. My observations and thoughts in the field were recorded in my field notes.

During my visits I also had numerous informal conversations with the teachers about language, culture, and teaching. The two teachers were interviewed twice during the research process. The first interviews took place at the beginning period of the research project. I asked the teachers about their understanding and beliefs regarding literacy and its instruction, their experiences and perceptions of teaching Chinese students, and their understanding of cultural differences. The second set of interviews occurred at the end of the fieldwork, when I followed up with some questions that emerged from my field observations. I asked the teachers to comment on the focal students in the larger study, some specific classroom literacy activities, school policies, and their interaction with the parents and their perceptions of the parents' involvement in their children's learning. An ESL/resource teacher, Mrs. Smith, and the Chinese teacher aid, Mrs. Yep, were also interviewed on similar issues. These interviews, all semistructured, lasted one to two hours.

Semistructured interviews were also conducted with parents of the students (one parent per family, and eight parents in total). These interviews took place in the parents' homes towards the end of the research project. To understand the parents' cultural beliefs, their perspectives on their children's schooling, and their children's literacy practices at home, I asked the parents about their understanding of language learning, the children's home literacy activities, and their perceptions of and involvement with the school system.

Toward the end of the project, I also conducted three focus group discussions (in English) with the focal children. Discussions with grade 1/2 students were conducted with the whole class, while discussions with grade 4/5 students were conducted in small groups with the focal students only. For each focus group session, the students were asked to discuss their literacy experiences in and out of school; to explain their perceptions of reading, writing, and learning; and to illustrate with pictures and write a paragraph about what literacy meant to them. Each focus group discussion was half an hour long and was audio recorded. These pictures and focus-group discussions provided in-depth insight into the children's perceptions of literacy learning in both English and Chinese.

Over the course of the research, as I came to know more about the teachers, the parents, and the students in classrooms, over dinner tables, in the hallway, on the playground, and at their homes, I became more familiar with their concerns, questions, beliefs, and practices. My knowledge of these people as cultural agents, combined with the analytical and comparative analyses of the data collected, convinced me that the battles between the culturally different understandings of literacy and its instruction had become a risk factor in the Chinese children's academic learning—a wall erected between the two groups.

Researcher's Roles

A researcher's positioning and role are critical to the design, implementation, and interpretation of an ethnographic study (Goetz &

LeCompte, 1984; Alvermann, Dillon, & O'Brien, 1996). I am a Chinese/English bilingual and bicultural researcher who had educational experiences in both China and Canada. I began the process of becoming literate in Chinese through traditional, teacher-centered, code-emphasis instruction in an impoverished elementary school in rural China. Starting in grade 6, I began to study English as a foreign language also through a teacher-centered, basal-text approach. My success with English allowed me to pass the competitive college entrance examination and become an English-as-a-foreign-language (EFL) major in a teacher's university. I continued to refine my English and apprenticed under my Chinese professors through teacher-centered instruction in my undergraduate and graduate studies in China. Although I was successful in learning English through the traditional skill-based methods, like many others, I also observed that the traditional methods produced some students with strong grammatical knowledge, but with weaker abilities in reading, writing, and speaking. Despite many years of training, many students were unable to communicate in the language. To critique what I called this "static" teaching, I published an article in a local journal to promote a more dynamic approach to foreign language teaching (G. Li, 1995).

My dynamic approach to EFL teaching, as I learned later in my graduate studies in Canada, was similar to a student-centered, meaning-based literacy instruction. In graduate school in Canada, I learned more about the top-down approach to reading instruction and the process-writing strategies. I embraced the progressive, holistic approaches to language and literacy education, and came to a new understanding that people learned to read and write not by being taught skills and grammar, but by reading and writing in meaningful contexts.

Prior to this research project, I worked as a research assistant on a number of studies relating to the professional development of in-service teachers of minority children, and conducted independent research projects with Chinese immigrant families and students in Canada. During the time of this study, I was a postdoctoral fellow in literacy education at the University of British Columbia, as well as a university instructor of preservice teachers who worked with elementary students from diverse backgrounds. Through these experiences, I learned that many teachers faced pedagogical challenges in trying to help learners become fluent readers and writers, while many Chinese parents wanted to make sure their children acquire good English skills (that they themselves lacked) in a totally different educational system. I also learned that while many teachers wanted to implement more progressive, student-centered approaches, many Chinese parents preferred more traditional, teacher-led instruction. Like Lisa Delpit (1995), I was puzzled by these conflicting demands and challenges from teachers and parents (that is, progressive, student-centered versus traditional, teacher-centered approaches) and wondered whether there was much to be gained from the interactions of the two orientations. This research study provided me with much insight into an understanding of such interactions between the two parties. It represents my own inner battles in coming to terms with the two different pedagogical approaches and the underlying belief systems that accompany them.

My bilingual and bicultural background enabled me to have easy access to the field and to quickly establish rapport with both the teachers and the Chinese families. I was perceived by the teachers as a resource person to help them understand the Chinese parents and their communities, and to discuss cultural and educational issues they encountered while working with the Chinese students. The Chinese parents were willing to share with me answers to questions regarding education, and at times approached me with questions and concerns about their children's education or Canadian schooling in general.

I had the additional advantage of not being an official school teacher or a parent in the community. Making visits regularly to the classrooms, I became familiar with classroom activities and was available to help students in need. I also became familiar with the parents' concerns. My "nonmember" status allowed me to understand and communicate the issues from both the parents' and the teachers' perspectives. In this sense, I served as a communication channel between the teachers and the parents.

My background and experiences helped to shape my understanding of the teachers and the parents. I saw how the different cultural beliefs of literacy and literacy instruction played a key role in the tensions and dissensions between the teachers and the parents, as well as how the success or failure of educating the children was anchored in communicating and overcoming these different cultural beliefs.

Outline of the Book

This book is primarily concerned with the different cultural beliefs and perspectives of the mainstream teachers and the Chinese immigrant parents and how the power play between these beliefs and perspectives has shaped the literacy experiences of the Chinese children in and out of school. In order to understand the depth and complexity of the teachers', the parents', and the students' varied literacy experiences and viewpoints, I will begin the book with a theoretical understanding of literacy and culture, and in the chapters that follow, I will provide "thick descriptions" (Geertz, 1973) of the context, the teachers' and the parents' perspectives on literacy instruction, and the respective experiences of each focal child in the school and home milieu. The paragraphs that follow provide more detailed descriptions of each of these chapters.

Chapter 1 situates this research within a theoretical framework that emphasizes both sociocultural and sociopolitical perspectives on literacy and education. The chapter begins with a definition of literacy as a sociocultural discourse, and is followed by a discussion of cultural conflict on methods of education within the larger context of the on-going debate between two competing discourses: the progressive, meaning-emphasis versus traditional, code-emphasis education. This chapter also explores the politics of school discourses, with a focus on teacher perspectives of student cultural differences, and the politics of home discourses, with a focus on cultural differences in parental involvement. Finally, a section is presented on literacy and educational practices of Chinese immigrants in North America.

Chapter 2 presents a historical perspective on Chinese immigrants in British Columbia with a focus on the racial, economic, and educational tensions between the Chinese and the mainstream society. This chapter provides detailed descriptions of the community, the school, the teachers, the students, and their families who are the foci of this study.

Chapter 3 examines the different perspectives on literacy and education of the teachers and parents. It explores differences in their perceptions and understandings of the sociocultural contexts in which they were situated, first-language (L1) Chinese use at school, second-language (L2) English literacy instruction, students' home literacy practices, and parental involvement at school. These different perspectives suggest that the teachers and parents were engaged in literacy and culture battles between school and home.

Chapter 4 brings readers into the worlds of four first and second graders who have just embarked on the journey amidst the battles between school and home literacy practices. It provides a detailed description of the students' home and school literacy practices. The children's differential experiences at home and in school suggest serious misconceptions and misunderstandings between the teachers and the parents regarding the barriers in students' learning and development. These barriers experienced by the children demonstrate that the battles between teachers and parents over educational beliefs can have an impact on these learners as early as the beginning grades.

Chapter 5 describes the home and school literacy experiences of four grade 4/5 learners. In each description, separate sections on the teachers' and the parents' perspectives on the children's struggle with schooling are also included. These children's separate worlds of literacy and the different perspectives between the parents and teachers mirrored increased tensions and discords between the school's cultural values and those of the Chinese families. The heated battles between school and home resulted in greater cultural mismatch between school and home, and were detrimental to the academic success of the students.

Chapter 6 examines the meaning of the battles over literacy and culture in relation to the school-parent relations and the children's school achievement. It discusses the cultural conflicts over literacy and its instruction, parental involvement, and the politics of difference underlining the battles between school and home. The chapter also discusses the complexities that contributed to the children's learning difficulties. These complexities included negative effects of such factors as well-intentioned parental involvement, modes of incorporation and integration into host communities, school policies, school and home responses to students' underachievement, and the lack of school and home communications.

Chapter 7 presents the implications and conclusions of this study. In light of the cultural conflicts between school and home, I propose a "pedagogy of cultural reciprocity" model for bridging the differences and working toward equitable education for immigrant students. The chapter elaborates on this model by revisiting the broader issues of difference discussed in the first two chapters of this book: (1) culturally responsive teaching; (2) the great debate between teacher-centered, code-emphasis education and progressive, student-centered, meaning-emphasis education; (3) parental involvement and parent-school relations, and (4) understanding the actual experiences of Chinese minority learners in the process of change.

CHAPTER ONE

Literacy Instruction and Cross-cultural Discourses

Literacy is a discursive practice in which difference
becomes crucial for understanding not simply how to read,
write, or develop aural skills, but also to recognize that the
identities of "others" matter as part of a broader set of politics and practice aimed at the reconstruction of democratic
public life.

—Henry Giroux,"Literacy, Difference,
and the Politics of Border Crossing"

Literacy achievement has become one of the most critical issues for
immigrant and minority education. For the theoretical framework
in which this study is situated, I turn to research that examines the
social effects of literacy practices across the various social institutions
such as school, home, and communities. I look at literacy as a sociocultural construction through interactions among the members of
these social institutions. To address the cultural conflicts involved in
the teaching and learning of Chinese immigrants, I first embed my
understanding of literacy education within the larger context of the
on-going debate between progressive and traditional pedagogy. I also
draw on minority literacy research to examine the impact of teacher
perspectives on minority students' learning and development, the
interrelationships between cultural diversity and parental involvement, and the influence of modes of immigration and assimilation on
English literacy acquisition. Each perspective helps me to look at the
experiences of cultural conflicts and their impact on the focal children
from a different angle. The combined perspectives bring to light ways

different cultural values have shaped the literacy experiences of immigrant children and influenced their success with social integration and academic achievement. Thus, I begin by examining the definition of literacy and its practices, and then I explain the different theoretical perspectives that inform my research on battles over literacies and cultures in immigrant children's schooling.

Literacy as Sociocultural Discourse

Over the last four decades, literacy researchers have developed a view of literacy as multiple and situated within social and cultural practices and discourses (Gee, 1996; B. Street, 1993). Literacy is no longer thought of as the technical ability to read and write, nor the ability of individuals to function within social contexts associated with daily living. Rather, beyond these capacities, it is an ability to think and reason, a way of living, a means of looking at the world we know and how we behave in the world (Langer, 1987; Schieffelin, 1986). In Gee's words, literacy constitutes ways of behaving, interacting, valuing, thinking, believing, speaking, and often reading and writing that are embedded within particular discourses and are tied to particular sets of values and norms (Gee, 1996).

Literacy is therefore inseparable from culture. In this book, I adopt McLaren's (1998) critical concept of culture to signify "the particular ways in which a social group lives out and makes sense of its given circumstances and conditions of life" (p. 175). As a set of practices, ideologies, and values from which different groups draw to make sense of the world, culture is deeply rooted in the nexus of power relations. According to McLaren, the link between culture and power is embodied in three aspects: (1) culture is intimately connected with the structure of social relations that produce forms of oppression and dependency; (2) culture is analyzed as a form of production through which different groups in either their dominant or subordinate social relations define or realize their aspirations through unequal relations of power; and (3) culture is viewed as a field of struggle in which production, legitimation, and circulation of particular forms of knowledge and experience are central arenas of conflict (McLaren, 1998, p. 176). The negotiation of these power relations, that is, the definition of who has power and how it is reproduced, is dependent on the ability of individuals (as well as the collective) to express their culture through their particular language and literacy practices.

Bakhtin's (1981) dialogic perspective maintains that language and literacy are the means by which people position themselves in their social worlds and that learning to use language involves learning the truths of human relationships. In order to understand these truths about human relationships, it is necessary that members of this dialogic learning community locate their understanding in the contemporary as well as historical social locations of the participants in literacy events. Therefore, literacy is an interactive sociocultural process, a process of different voices coming into contact (Toohey, 2000; Wertsch, 1991). These different voices are members of the learners' particular sociocultural contexts—teachers, peers, parents, and community members. Each of these members represents a voice of learning and knowing, and together they form a "dialogized heteroglossia," or multivoicedness in which multiple layers of values of knowing and learning are embodied (Bakhtin, 1981, p. 272).

According to Gee (1989), learners' dialogized heteroglossia can be categorized into two overarching domains: the primary Discourse of the home and community, and the secondary Discourse of the public sphere—institutions such as the public schools. Nested in these two sociocultural Discourses are different social languages—concrete literacy belief systems that define distinct identities within the boundaries of the Discourses (Bakhtin, 1981). These social languages or sets of social beliefs intersect and interact with one another in a multitude of ways, and shape what the individual member's voice can say (Wertsch, 1991). For example, power struggles between the social languages in primary and secondary Discourses may affect an individual learner's choices of appropriating or speaking a particular social language and becoming a member of that social community. In some cases, learners are capable of repositioning themselves in the contesting social languages, and recreating their own social languages such as counterword (Bahktin, 1981) or counterscript (Gutierrez, Rymes, & Larson, 1995). In this sense, these different literacy belief systems become "zones of contest" in which cultural borders and Discourse boundaries are negotiated and defined (Sleeter & McLaren, 1995).

Literacy learning as a sociocultural practice emphasizes the relational interdependency of agent and world, persons-in-activity, and situated action, and learners' participation in learning is inherently "situated negotiation and renegotiation of meaning in the world"

(Lave & Wenger, 1991, p. 51). McKay and Wong (1996) explored the multiple identities of a group of Chinese immigrant students in a junior high school in California. They conceptualize minority students such as English language learners as complex social beings who actively exercise their agencies in their particular learning environment. By exercising their agencies, children take ownership of language and literacy (Pierce, 1995). Au (1998) defines ownership of literacy as "students' valuing of literacy, including holding positive attitudes toward literacy and having the habit of using literacy in everyday life. Students display positive attitudes by willingly engaging in reading and writing, showing confidence and pride in their own literacy and taking an interest in the literacy of others" (p. 169).

Literacy researchers have discovered that children can develop an understanding of what literacy is and what it means from a young age (Wells, 1986; 1989). Children can acquire not only the conventions of reading and writing, but also the sociocultural values that are attached to their particular literacy practices (Teale & Sulzby, 1986). However, motivation theorists point out that children's continuous development of literacy is related to their motivation to learn and that learners' beliefs, values, and goals for learning are crucial to their school achievement (Guthrie, McGouch, Bennet, & Rice, 1996; Pintrich & Schrauben, 1992). Wigfield (1997) further argues from a socioconstructivist perspective that learners' continuing engagement in learning depends on their intrinsic motivation, that is, their on-going participation in learning is motivated by the thoughts and feelings that emerge from their meaning making processes. Therefore, learners' continuous engagement in learning involves personal investment in that learners not only exchange information with others, but they also constantly reread, reflect, and revisit a sense of who they are and how they are related in their complex social relationships with others in their everyday lives (Pierce, 1995). In this sense, language learning is not simply a matter of the individual learner's mental functioning; it is also a mediated action situated in the cultural, historical, and institutional settings in which learning occurs (Bakhtin, 1981; Wertsch, 1991).

Literacy learning and teaching as a dynamic social process is also highly political. It is not static, nor always harmonious. Many tensions and dissensions are inherent in the discourses of literacy learning and schooling in the contexts of home, school, and community. In the apprenticeship of new social practices, minority learners have to become complicit with a new set of values and norms that may not match their initial enculturation and socialization within their primary discourses (Gee, 1989). Their cultural and personal knowledge is often in conflict with the schools' ways of validating knowledge, the nature of school, or main tenets and assumptions of mainstream academic knowledge (Banks, 2002; Gay, 2000). Indeed, home and school discourses often collide because of the sociocultural (and linguistic) incongruencies, especially when one discourse maintains its dominant status over the other (Lopez, 1999). These tensions and collisions often result in the surface of minority groups' antagonistic voice, resistance, and opposition that counteract the hegemony of mainstream pedagogy (Giroux, 1991). These counterhegemonic actions are often related to ways in which our discourses (both local and public or authorized) surrounding the pedagogical practices are connected or disconnected, and ways in which the issues of power, class, race, and identity within and across communities are interplayed (Rogers, Tyson, & Marshall, 2000).

In this book, the concept of pedagogy connotes both a professional or teaching activity and a political activity that shapes students' learning experiences. It is not just an act of teaching and instruction, but a deliberate attempt to influence how and what knowledge and identities are produced within and among particular sets of social relations (Giroux & Simon, 1989, p. 239). In Simon's (1987) words, "pedagogy" refers to

> the integration in practice of particular curriculum content and design, classroom strategies and techniques, a time and space for the practice of those strategies and evaluation purposes and methods. All these aspects of educational practice come together in the realities of what happens in the classrooms. Together they organize a view of how a teacher's work within an institutional context specifies a particular version of what knowledge is of most worth, what it means to know something, and how we might construct representations of ourselves, others, and our physical and social environment. In other words, talk about pedagogy is simultaneously talk about the details of what students and others might do together and the cultural politics of such practices support. (p. 371)

The concepts of literacy as a sociocultural discourse and pedagogy as a form of cultural politics are important to the present study as its emphasis on historical situatedness, multiplicity of voice, and dynamic human agency is embedded in the battles of literacy and schooling between mainstream schools and Chinese immigrant parents. The interplay of these three elements is reflected in the parents' and the teachers' different sets of beliefs about pedagogical practices. In the next section, I examine these contested pedagogies.

Competing Discourses of Literacy Education

At the forefront of the cultural conflicts between the Chinese parents and Canadian teachers were the methods of literacy instruction. The Chinese parents preferred traditional, teacher-centered, code-emphasis education while the Canadian teachers believed in progressive, student-centered, meaning-emphasis education. What is the best practice for literacy instruction? Is there a best method? In order to better understand these cultural conflicts, I situate the battles at Taylor Elementary within the larger context of the on-going debate in the field of literacy education in North America.

The debate about the best method to help students achieve high levels of literacy has lasted for over one hundred years in North America and is still alive today at the peak of the push for standardized testing. At the center of this disagreement is whole language (meaning-emphasis) versus phonics (code-emphasis) debate. Proponents of the whole language approach believe that learning to read and write are natural to human development, and language is best learned when students are provided with opportunities to learn for real purposes using real examples of language; therefore, direct, systematic instruction of skills and grammar is not necessary (Goodman, 1977, 1986). Phonics, defined as an approach to teach children about the orthographic code of the language and the relationships of spelling patterns to sound patterns (Stahl, 1992), is based on the philosophy that education is not a natural act, but consists of imparting certain information and skills revered in the past to a new generation of learners (Chall, 2000). Proponents of the phonics approach believe that direct, systematic instruction is not only necessary, but also essential for more effective learning, especially for early literacy instruction.

Chall (2000) extended the original debate on reading instruction methods to other subject areas such as math, science, and social studies. She summarizes the main aspects of this great debate as follows:

1. Curriculum: The progressive, student-centered approach integrates materials across subject areas, bases learning as much as possible in students' interests, and follows students' individual development pace. On the other hand, the teacher-centered approach has standards established for each grade level and specific subject areas are taught separately.
2. Materials: The progressive, student-centered approach uses a rich variety of materials including manipulatives, different trade books and authentic literature; and it permits students' choices. The teacher-centered approach uses commercial textbooks such as basal readers that focus on building phonemic awareness and systematic, sequential progression of knowledge and skills in language.
3. The role of the teacher: From a progressive, student-centered perspective, the teacher is a facilitator of learning who provides resources and helps students plan and follow their own interests. The teacher's role involves "constant planning, continuous innovation, and a sensitive system of monitoring students' performance, and well-developed skills in maintaining order without being authoritarian" (Gage & Berliner, 1992, p. 486). In a traditional approach, the teacher is a class leader and is responsible for content, learning lessons, recitation, skills, seatwork, and assigning homework. In this approach, learning is seen as the responsibility of both students and teachers. Facilitating in and of itself is not enough, and interests alone cannot be relied upon. Teachers are seen as the knowledge source from whom students can learn.
4. Evaluation: Evaluation of student performance in a progressive, student-centered approach is based on comparisons of learners with themselves rather than with their classmates or grade standards. Diagnostic rather than norm-referenced evaluation is preferred, and formal testing is deemphasized. In a traditional approach, evaluation is based on norm-referenced tests and grade standards, and both informal and formal testing is emphasized.

After reviewing research findings over the last several decades, Chall (1967, 1983, 1996, 2000) concludes that phonics and teacher-centered instruction are more effective for beginning reading instruction than various progressive, student-centered methods because they result in higher achievement in word recognition, reading comprehension, and reading speed. These three skills are predictors of students' later literacy achievement. She also concludes that traditional approaches are particularly more effective for at-risk children who are from lower socioeconomic status and different cultural and ethnic backgrounds, bilingual children, and children with learning disabilities, and the more progressive approach only benefits children from families where children are well socialized into English literacy before school. She also explains that traditional phonics programs appeal to many well-educated, upper-middle-class parents as well as to culturally disadvantaged parents such as immigrants. Based on these findings, Chall points to a need to change beginning literacy instruction from a meaning-emphasis, student-centered approach to a code-emphasis, teacher-centered method, especially for children of disadvantaged backgrounds. Furthermore, Chall and her associates suggest the code-emphasis, teacher-centered approach should be used at all elementary levels, especially given the research evidence that many students' literacy achievement begins to slump at grade 4 and this slump continues to intensify through grade 7 (Chall, 2000; Chall, Jacobs, & Baldwin, 1990; Snow, Barnes, Chandler, Goodman, & Hemphill, 1991). The factors that result in this slump mainly include the students' lack of phonemic awareness, spelling-sound knowledge, lexical knowledge in early grades, and skills which can be improved through systematic phonics instruction (Juel, 1988; Juel, Griffith, & Gough, 1986).

However, phonics instruction has often been protested and even rejected by many educators due to a perceived dichotomy created by the media. Proponents of phonics attribute the confusion over phonics to the politics of the debate in that phonics is often misunderstood as devaluing or rejecting meaning-based instruction. Many phonics proponents emphasize that advocacy for traditional, teacher-led direct instruction does not mean that whole language instruction is of no value, and they warn against ignoring meaning-emphasis in literacy instruction (Delpit, 1995; Stahl, 1992; Stanovich, 1990). Many literacy educators propose an eclectic approach combining both methods— they maintain that these approaches should complement each other to achieve optimal results for literacy instruction. Adams (1990) takes the position that systematic phonics instruction is most productive when it is conceived as "a support activity, carefully covered but largely subordinated to the reading and writing of connected text" (p. 416). She points out that "children must learn to think not just the letters and their sounds; rather they must understand the basic nature and purpose of the system and reflectively use that understanding to contextualize the letter-sound parings productively" (p. 255).

Meaning-emphasis instruction can benefit children in many ways: it gives students freedom to experiment with and explore literacy and to become members of a community of readers and writers, and exposes students to the rich resources of children's literature, especially trade books (Spiegel, 1992). Therefore, in addition to traditional phonics instruction, children should be exposed to meaningful written text as soon as possible so that they will begin to notice and develop an interest in the many things around them that there are to read, and to sense the utility of their phonics lessons as soon as possible (Adams, 1990). The goal is to ensure that students can use phonics with new, authentic materials for authentic purposes (Spiegel, 1992). Adams (1990) argues that phonics without connected reading amounts to useless mechanics: "Connected reading provides the meaningful exercise necessary for linking the spelling patterns to the rest of the cognitive system, for ensuring that they are understood and learned in a way that is useful and usable toward the tasks for which they were taught" (p. 286).

Adams concludes that phonological awareness, letter-recognition facility, familiarity with spelling patterns, spelling-sound relations, and individual words must be developed in concert with real reading and real writing and with a deliberate reflection on the forms, functions, and meaning of texts (p. 422). Recent research on effective early-grade literacy instruction provides evidence that excellent early literacy instruction does not support theory that emphasizes only one approach such as phonics or whole language; rather, it involves multiple instructional components articulated with one another. This exemplary instruction is characterized by an integrated and comprehensive teaching of skills, literature, and writing; scaffolding and matching of task demands to student competence; encouragement of student self-regulation; and strong cross-curricular connections (British Columbia Ministry of Education, 2000; Pressley et al., 2001). This infusion of different approaches is also found in expert instruction for language minority students (Gersten & Jiménez, 1994; Gersten & Woodward, 1992; Jiménez & Gersten, 1999).

The questions remaining are: What is the right balance between code and meaning instruction and what should be taught? What is considered "best practice"? Though there are no definite answers to these questions, many researchers believe that it depends on teachers' solid understanding of the principles and goals of the approaches and their ability to be conceptually selective in combining practices that work well in order to address the needs of students of diverse backgrounds (Adams, 1990; Gersten & Jiménez , 1994; Gersten & Woodward, 1992; Pressley et al., 2001). That is, effective teachers use a continuum of instructional approaches (rather than one single approach) to ensure students' high academic engagement and competence.

In light of the on-going battle between the Chinese parents and Canadian teachers in this study, the debate seems to suggest that it is necessary for the Canadian teachers to have a solid understanding of their own beliefs and practices as well as the Chinese parents' traditional, teacher-centered approach. Such a solid understanding may help them better communicate with the parents and make decisions on what aspects of traditional instruction can be included in their meaning-emphasis instruction. It is, however, equally important for the Chinese parents to have a solid understanding of the teachers' meaning-emphasis instruction because it may help them recognize the limitations of their own beliefs and practices and become more aware of the benefits of student-centered instruction. This kind of mutual understanding, however, as the data in the study will show, is hard to achieve due to profound power imbalances and cultural differences between the two groups.

The traditional and progressive binary has focused narrowly on instructional dimensions and sees these dimensions as culturally neutral and nonideological. It has neglected the social and political dimensions of literacy education (Cummins & Sayers, 1995). The battles over literacy instruction between Chinese parents and mainstream teachers have gone beyond being simply about the methods of teaching, but are about the legitimacy of a particular set of cultural knowledge in schooling. While the mainstream teachers tried to maintain the progressive pedagogy, the Chinese parents actively fought for their preferred traditional pedagogy. The parents' struggle for voice suggests that the pedagogical divide between the teachers and the parents has gone beyond the binary to become a political activity that attempts to redefine the power structure between school and home. In this sense, the teachers' and the parents' particular cultural knowledge and preferences become sites of multiple and heterogeneous borders where relations of power and privilege are negotiated. To make sense of the instructional as well as the political nature of the battles between school and home, it is necessary to look at not only how literacy is taught, but also how cultural borders are negotiated and defined through underlying social assumptions (Cummins, 1996; Giroux, 1992). In the next section, I discuss the relationship between cultural differences and teacher perceptions and how other school discourses may have an impact on minority schooling.

Cultural Differences, Teacher Perspectives, and School Discourses

Culture is seen as a vital source for developing an understanding of minority schooling. Cultural differences are often seen as a risk factor in the school experiences of minority children (Erickson, 1993; Trueba, Jacobs, & Kirton, 1990). Educational anthropologists argue that how teachers perceive cultural differences plays a key role in the success or failure of minority students in overcoming the discontinuities between school and home. Teachers who have a deficit view of minority cultural differences often assume that minority students lack ability in learning or have inadequate parenting or both (Pang & Sablan, 1998). Teachers with this perspective often attempt to change minority students through instruction so that they will better fit into mainstream schools (King, 1994). This type of instruction does not build on students' skills and knowledge or affirm their cultural identity and often results in "subtractive schooling" that reinforces the existing home/school dichotomy, and limits children's access to school literacy learning and achievement (Valenzuela, 1999).

On the other hand, teachers who view minority cultural differences not as barriers to overcome but as resources usually have a positive attitude toward students' ability to achieve and often see students' background knowledge as funds of knowledge (Moll, 1994). Teachers with this perspective often develop culturally relevant and linguistically congruent instructional approaches to translate school and home differences for minority students, for example, adapting their speech patterns, interaction styles, and participation structures to adhere more to those of minority students', or using cultural referents to impart knowledge, skills, and attitudes (Au & Jordan, 1981; Banks, 2002; Gay, 2000). These equity pedagogical approaches build on students' strengths, affirm their cultural identity, and help them make meaningful connections between school and home.

How teachers perceive students' cultures can have significant implications for minority students' academic success as it is often translated into their instructional practices. Many instructional factors can contribute to students' success or failure with literacy (Snow, Burns, & Griffin, 1998). One key factor is whether the teachers' instructional approaches incorporate the language and culture of minority students (Au, 1998; Cummins, 1996; Moll, 1994). These approaches include factors such as goal of instruction, instructional materials and methods, classroom management and interaction with students, the role of the home language, and assessment.

Research has suggested that literacy instruction that is not made personally meaningful to minority students will likely impede their reading development. Also, inappropriate teaching materials and content such as isolated, formalized worksheets or culturally irrelevant materials have adverse effects on students' reading development (Snow, Burns, & Griffin, 1998). Use of such materials rather than multicultural literature that accurately depicts the experiences of diverse groups will decrease students' motivation to read and devalue their own life experiences as topics for writing (Au, 1998; Banks, 2002). Besides instructional materials and content, ineffective or insufficient instruction can also cause reading difficulty for students. If teachers of minority students do not provide them with authentic literacy activities and a considerable amount of instruction on specific literacy skills needed for gaining a command of the mainstream discourse, their literacy development will likely suffer (Delpit, 1995).

Another important aspect of pedagogical influence is whether teachers are culturally responsive in their management of and interaction with minority students. Students from diverse backgrounds exhibit culturally different learning styles, and instruction that caters to different learning styles can enhance their academic achievement (Banks, 2002; Irvine & York, 1995). Chinese students who come from families that emphasize skill-based instruction and rote-memorization tend to be structure-oriented learners who are more accustomed to definite goals and specific tasks. Because of this, they may require more reinforcement rather than subjective questioning or opinion-based instruction from teachers; they may also perform poorly on creative writing and analytical commentary tasks (Yao; 1985; S. Y. Zhang & Carrasquillo, 1995). Classroom instruction that does not build on these learning characteristics will have adverse effects on the learning of many Chinese students.

Teachers' attitudes toward students' home language in the classroom is also a significant causal factor in students' underachievement. Most teachers in regular classrooms perceive that using English exclusively in a classroom with students of different languages is a natural and commonsense practice, and if other languages were to be used in the classroom, the standards of English would drop (Auerbach, 1993; Phillipson, 1988; Valdés, 1998). These attitudes often prevent teachers from utilizing students' literacy skills from their first language in order to facilitate learning of English and knowledge of content (Freeman & Freeman, 1992). Research has demonstrated that schools who value students' languages and cultures have higher rates of academic success with ESL students (Lucas, Henze, & Donato, 1990; Moll & Diaz, 1993). Contrarily, the exclusive use of English often prevents low English proficiency students from understanding teachers as they explain and present material or from comprehending the content materials that they are expected to learn (Wong Fillmore, 1982). Lack of understanding instruction and material often results in nonparticipation, frustration, negative attitudes toward learning, low self-esteem, and even dropping-out among many ESL students (Auerbach, 1993; Skutnabb-Kangas, 1983).

In addressing the impact of cultural differences on teaching and learning, scholars and educators have proposed to incorporate multicultural education into the basic school curriculum (Banks, 1993; Fillmore & Meyer, 1992; Nieto, 2002). This will require teachers and schools to transform their curriculum in five dimensions (see Banks, 1993, 2002, 2004):

- *Content integration:* Teachers use content from diverse cultures to illustrate key concepts, principles, generalizations, and theories in their subject area.
- *An equity pedagogy:* Teachers modify their teaching in ways that will facilitate the academic achievement of students from diverse social, cultural, and social class groups (for example, use a variety of teaching styles to match students' learning styles within various cultural groups).
- *The knowledge construction process:* Teachers help students understand and investigate implicit cultural assumptions, frames of reference, perspectives, and bias and how these

influence individuals' and groups' social positioning and identity.

- *Prejudice reduction:* Teachers modify teaching methods and materials to help students develop more positive racial and ethnic attitudes.
- *An empowering school culture and social structure:* Teachers and schools establish a school environment that empowers minority students. For example, teachers can establish fair and culturally sensitive assessment procedures, show respect for students' first languages and dialects, set high expectations, and help students realize positive career goals.

In sum, many pedagogical factors may have an impact on minority learners' motivation and investment in learning. These factors suggest that we need to contextualize learners' literacy experiences not only in their sociocultural contexts, but also through their particular schooling and pedagogical experiences that may or may not connect with their cultural backgrounds.

Cultural Diversity, Parental Involvement, and Home Discourses

It is widely recognized that parental active interest in and continuing support of children's learning have a positive impact on school effectiveness and students' academic achievement. Epstein (1992, 1995) theorizes that there are different levels of parental involvement, ranging from involvement in the home, to participation in activities and events at school, and to participation in the schools' decision-making process. Parental involvement at home includes attending to children's basic needs, discipline, preparing for school, and supporting school learning or engaging actively in homework. However, the degree and the ways of involvement vary from family to family and from culture to culture as families of different races, classes, and religions have different ways of transmitting and socializing literacy, different perceptions of families' and schools' roles in their children's education, and different ways of involvement in their children's academic learning.

The influence of social class on parental involvement has been well documented. Research shows that parents of higher socioeconomic status place more emphasis on education, feel more confident of their right to be involved in the school, and consistently take a more active role in their children's schooling than parents of lower socioeconomic status (Heath, 1983; Hoover-Dempsey, Bassler, & Brissie, 1987; Lightfoot, 1978). Parents of different social classes also differ in their patterns of involvement in their children's schooling. Lareau (2000) found that parents in both working-class and upper-middle-class communities wanted their children to achieve academic success, but they took very different steps to try to ensure that success. In the working-class community of Colton in the San Francisco Bay area of northern California, parents perceived education as something that took place at school and as the responsibility of teachers. At home, they helped to prepare their children for school by teaching them manners and rudimentary educational skills, but they did not supervise, compensate for, or attempt to intervene in their children's program. In contrast, parents in the upper-middle-class community of Prescott in the same district demonstrated much more proactive involvement: "Rather than preparing children for schooling and helping to support the teacher, parents actively supervised, supplemented, and intervened in their children's schooling. When faced with a weak teacher, some parents compensated with additional tutoring. Parents also hired additional educational consultants, particularly during the summer. While not always successful, upper-middle-class parents sought a more individualized education for their children" (Lareau, 2000, p. 169).

Social class, however, is not the only variable that affects the degree of parental involvement. For immigrant and minority families, active involvement is also influenced by parents' educational background, their English proficiency, their knowledge of and familiarity with mainstream schooling, and their socioeconomic status (G. Li, 2002). For example, immigrant parents who have limited education or lack fluency in English would be seriously handicapped in supporting their children's education as those factors not only restrict employment and interaction in the mainstream society, but also impede their effective interaction with teachers, understanding of schoolwork, and ability to assist their children academically at home (Moles, 1993).

Parental educational experience in both the country of origin and the host society is also an important factor. Parents who are more highly educated tend to be more familiar with how the educational system works in the culture in which they were educated, and it becomes easier for them to follow the educational patterns. Immigrant parents who have more education in their home country would likely

find it easier to draw on their own educational experiences and repli-
cate some of those instructional approaches to support their children's
learning. This phenomenon is especially common among Chinese
immigrant families. Moreover, parents who have educational experiences in the host culture will likely have a better understanding of the
educational system and therefore can better work with teachers to
help their children to adapt to the culture of mainstream literacy (G.
Li, 2002; Purcell-Gates, 1996). Immigrant parents of limited educational experiences often do not understand their children's school
experiences, nor do they know how to facilitate their children's school
success. Some examples of this are the Juarez family in Carger's (1996)
study, the Liu family in G. Li's (2003) study, the Ye family in G. Li's
(2001) study, and the Hmong families in Trueba, Jacobs, & Kirton's
(1990) study.

Because literacy is a cultural practice, parents from different cultures have different beliefs about what it means to be literate, how to
acquire literacy, and the role of schooling in achieving literacy. For
example, several studies on Hispanic families in the United States
have documented how their ways of learning and familial values are
distinctively different from other cultures such as white and Asian.
Parental involvement in these Hispanic families often includes providing opportunities for children to learn through observation, to achieve
gradual mastery of skills, to cooperate in tasks, and to collaborate in
negotiating life's everyday trials (Carger, 1996; Valdés, 1996). These
practices are different from the white middle-class families' emphasis
on independent learning (as described previously), and from the
Asian families' preference for a direct instructional approach (Anderson & Gunderson, 1997).

Social class and cultural differences also shape how families view
their involvement in school settings. White working-class parents, for
example, view education as the school's responsibility and often resist
parental participation in school settings. Many immigrants from other
cultures such as Hispanics and Southeast Asians also share similar
perceptions that teachers are the authority and specialists and that
parents are to avoid trespassing on those territories. For example, in
Huss-Keeler's (1997) study of the mainstream teachers' perceptions of
Pakistani parental involvement, many Pakistani parents demonstrated
their interest in their children's education by supporting and assisting
their children's studies at home and not by being actively involved at
school. Their culturally different expectations, however, were perceived by teachers as disinterest in their children's education, and

consequently, their children's learning and achievement were frequently undermined.

These different patterns of parental involvement have a profound influence on family-school relations since they may affect how parents and teachers view each other's roles and hence their attitudes and communication to each other. Schools' communications and actions can convey positive, family-oriented attitudes that show concern for family needs and perspectives as well as negative attitudes, for example, viewing differences as deficiencies or parents' active participation as overinvolved or intrusive (Christenson & Sheridan, 2001). The latter attitude, which often places families in a powerless position, is detrimental to healthy family-school relationships and might increase the potential for conflict between school and parents (Fine, 1993). As Moles (1993) points out, "Disadvantaged parents and teachers may be entangled by various psychological obstacles to mutual involvement such as misperceptions and misunderstandings, negative expectations, stereotypes, intimidation, and distrust. They may also be victims of cultural barriers reflecting differences in language, values, goals, methods of education, and definitions of appropriate roles" (p. 33).

These cultural and social barriers are important for understanding the conflict between the Canadian teachers and Chinese families in this study. The Chinese parents and their children at Taylor Elementary were influenced by social class, racial, and cultural factors. Social class shaped the parents' confidence to challenge the schools' performance in educating their children, and influenced the resources the parents could invest in their children's learning outside school. Race and cultural backgrounds have determined their ways of parental involvement, resulting in child-rearing and value systems that are different from Canadian mainstream practices. How the teachers responded and understood these differences significantly affected their communications, attitudes, and actions toward the Chinese parents and students, and ultimately the parent-school relationships.

Literacy, Education, and Chinese Immigrants in North America

As familiarity with schooled literacy discourses is the mark of school success, students from nonmainstream cultural backgrounds have to learn a different set of literacy conventions and often experience difficulties with schooling (McCarthey 1997; Lopez 1999). Cultural differences between Chinese home practices and mainstream practices have been well documented largely to explain the "model minority" myth. Chinese parents' cultural values on education (high expectations, parental sacrifice for their children's education, and emphasis on obedience and close-knit family relations) are reported to have determining effects on their children's academic performance (Peng & Wright, 1994; Siu, 1994; Xu, 1999; S. Y. Zhang & Carrasquillo, 1995). However, within Chinese ethnic groups, parents' expectations, strategies, and investment in their children's education are influenced by their social class, their educational backgrounds, and their level of English proficiency (Louie, 2001; G. Li, 2002, 2003). Middle-class parents with more educational background and more access to mainstream resources are likely to be more actively involved in their children's learning, by either teaching their children themselves or hiring tutors, than are parents of lower socioeconomic background and little educational experience.

Despite the within-ethnic differences, there are some generalizations that can be made about the Chinese, especially middle-class Chinese immigrants. Several comparative studies have found that many middle-class Chinese parents hold cultural beliefs that are fundamentally different from their mainstream counterparts. For example, they are more likely to engage their children in varying literacy activities every day or at least provide a nurturing literacy environment; they also provide more structured and formal educational experiences after school and on weekends than their white counterparts (Yao, 1985; Xu, 1999). Chinese parents (especially mothers) also have different beliefs from Caucasian parents about their specific roles in their children's education. They place greater value on education and are willing to invest more in their children's education, and they also use a more direct intervention approach to their children's schooling and learning and therefore convey a much stronger belief that they can play a significant role in their children's school success (Chao, 1996). Furthermore, different from other ethnic parents, Chinese parents are more likely to take an active part in remedying the shortcomings of the school at home if they lack confidence in the school (Pang, 1990).

Chinese parents also hold different beliefs about specific literacy instruction and practices from mainstream parents. Chinese parents are reported to favor traditional, skill-based approaches over holistic principles of literacy learning (J. Anderson, 1995b; G. Li, 2002). They are more concerned with basic literacy skills and with monitoring and correcting performance such as teaching a child to print and write properly, checking for reading comprehension, teaching a child how to spell correctly, and having a child recite a story that the child has read. They also appear not to recognize the effects sociocultural dimensions of literacy (such as providing role models and encouragement to their children) may have on their child's literacy development.

These beliefs are antithetical to the emergent literacy perspective that is commonly adopted in Canadian and American mainstream classrooms (J. Anderson & Gunderson, 1997, p. 514). Anderson & Gunderson (1997) conclude that Chinese parents diametrically oppose many aspects of mainstream literacy instruction. For example, Chinese parents believe that accuracy and precision are important from the beginning and see little value in children's early attempts at reading or invented spelling; they view the teacher as the authority in the classroom rather than as a facilitator of learning; and they expect large amounts of homework from school and emphasize rote memorization.

Pai (1990) posits that the effectiveness with which a child can learn in school depends on the degree of continuity between the school and the learner's family environment. The cultural differences between Chinese parents' beliefs and mainstream schooling suggest that to many Chinese children, going to school requires students to function in two divergent and sometimes contradictory arenas of literacy learning. Unless teachers are aware of these cultural differences and are able to transform mainstream discourses, these cultural differences and discontinuities often become a source of misunderstanding and conflict. This may in turn result in inappropriate educational evaluation and planning for these children (Delpit, 1995; Pai, 1990).

Immigration, Integration, and English Literacy Acquisition

From a sociocultural perspective, the practices of literacy, what they are and what they mean for a given society, depend on the social and cultural contexts. These contexts have an overwhelming influence on literacy purposes, demands, and processes (Mikulecky, 1990). The outcomes of an individual's literacy learning are shaped by the social contexts in which the learning is embedded, and can only be fully understood in relation to these social contexts (Langer, 1987). These contexts are particular "modes of incorporation," that is, the immigrants' particular social context in the host society (Portes & Rumbaut 1990, 1996). Three modes of incorporation can shape their downward or upward assimilation and hence their educational success or failure:

strength of ethnic solidarity, socioeconomic level of their schools, and societal reception (Portes & Rumbaut 1990, 1996). Immigrant children who are positioned in favorable social contexts and receive positive societal reception are likely to succeed in their socioeconomic mobility and integration in their community. This social capital will in turn have a positive effect on the children's educational attainment. Conversely, unfavorable social contexts and negative societal reception (such as racism) will result in negative educational attainment (Gibson, 1988; Portes & McCleod, 1995; Zhou & Bankston III, 1996). Moreover, as Portes and McCleod (1995) found, the contextual advantages and disadvantages are often transmitted to the second generation.

The Chinese immigrant children in this study are favorably situated in a higher socioeconomic status school, but unfavorably in a racially divided social environment (this aspect will be discussed in detail in the next chapter). British Columbia has had a strong antioriental sentiment since the mid-nineteenth century, and historical racial stereotypes continue to exist in the contemporary social structure (K. J. Anderson, 1991; Chow, 2000; P. S. Li, 1998; Ward, 1978). Many of the parents in this study expressed the view that racism existed and was affecting their children's future social and educational attainment. These perceptions were passed on to the children through the Chinese parents' strong emphasis on education.

The Chinese immigrants' ethnic solidarity, though favorable for preserving their first language, was not favorable for their acquisition of English literacy—a vital skill necessary for "making it" in the mainstream society. In research literature, ethnic solidarity is usually considered favorable for immigrants to preserve ethnic cultures and traditional values, and for accumulating social capital through ethnic networks (Zhou & Bankston III, 1996). However, ethnic solidarity, in my view, can also have negative effects on immigrant children's schooling in that it prohibits immigrant children from having frequent contact with the culture of power. This lack of contact often prevents the children from effectively acquiring the "codes of power," such as mainstream language and literacy that are the gateway to the upward social mobility in the mainstream society (Delpit, 1995).

Several studies on Asian immigrant youths have indicated that living and learning in highly ethnically concentrated schools and communities have also made it difficult for Chinese immigrant students to acquire English literacy. First, ethnic solidarity means that there are fewer speakers of the target language (English) who know it well enough to provide ESL learners with access to the language, and few social settings which bring learners and target language speakers into frequent enough contact to make language learning possible (Wong Fillmore, 1991a). Second, ethnic solidarity also influences ESL learners' choice of language. ESL students often choose the comfort and familiarity of their home language and culture rather than acquiring new ones. For example, in studying Cantonese-speaking students' language choice in a school with a large Chinese population in Toronto, Goldstein (2003) found that many Cantonese-speaking students chose to use only Cantonese with other Cantonese speakers and therefore limited their opportunities to use and practice English. In a similar study situated in Vancouver, Minichiello (2001) also found that the large numbers of Chinese students in one school exacerbated their adjustment difficulties and slowed their English development. Third, high ethnic solidarity can also lower the students' motivation to acquire a new language and culture, as they do not see the immediate need to achieve high levels of English literacy (Wong Fillmore, 1991a). Similar findings on the negative effects of ethnic concentration on immigrant and minority children's academic achievement were also reported in studies of other ethnic groups in ethnically concentrated communities in the United States, for example, Hmong students (Trueba, Jacobs, & Kirton, 1990), Latino students (Valdés, 2001), and Vietnamese students (Zhou & Bankston III, 1996).

In the current study, although the majority of the students were Canadian born, they also faced similar problems when acquiring English literacy. Furthermore, these students also faced the challenge of acquiring first language literacy in Chinese. Though many of them are fluent in oral language, many struggle with reading and writing in their first language. Due to the limited time to learn reading and writing and to practice literacy, many immigrant parents have much lower expectations for their children to learn native language literacy than to acquire English literacy, which is necessary for educational advancement in the host society. Many parents only expect that their children will be able to speak the language and communicate with family members. This factor, combined with schools' and society's push for monolingualism, often results in rapid first language and literacy loss in immigrant children (Portes & Hao, 1998; Portes & Schauffler, 1996; Wong Fillmore, 1991b). Thus, if these children fail to learn English literacy, they may become doubly disadvantaged in both literacies and cultures.

A View from Both Sides

In the chapters that follow, I bring into focus the perspectives and beliefs of two Canadian teachers and eight Chinese parents who were engaged in on-going battles over literacy and culture concerning the education of the children they shared. I will also provide a detailed description of the lives of the eight children amid the paradigm war on literacy instruction between school and home. In exploring the conflicts between the teachers' and the parents' values and beliefs as well as the impact these differences have upon the education of immigrant children, my objective is to raise serious questions about the current educational practices that may constrain the learning of immigrant children inside and outside school in a new socioeconomic context.

As the stories and experiences of the teachers, parents, and children will demonstrate, the new Chinese immigrants, empowered by their socioeconomic capital and their collective power, challenged the mainstream schooled literacy practices in direct and indirect ways. And the teachers, shaped by their own class, culture, and experiences, tried to maintain their ways of knowing and practices. The power struggle between school and home had a profound influence on immigrant children's literacy development and identity formation. By offering a view from both sides, my intention is not to show the superiority of one set of cultural beliefs over another, or one set of literacy practices over another; rather, by providing "hetereoglossic voices" from both home and school, I hope to shed light on how to resolve the cultural conflicts, build a bridge between school and home, and make recommendations for future theory and practices of teaching immigrant children in a new social climate.

CHAPTER TWO

The City, the School, and the Families

The City: Richmond

The city in which this study was carried out is called Richmond. It is in the lower mainland of Vancouver, British Columbia. Before 1980, it was a quiet farming and fishing community. It is now a significant suburb of the Greater Vancouver area. The high influx of Asian immigrants since 1980, particularly from Hong Kong and Mainland China since 1997, has significantly changed the demographics of the city. Statistics Canada 2001 Census reports that 101,765 Chinese immigrants came to settle in Greater Vancouver, an increase of more than 42% since 1991. According to the 2001 Census, more than half of them (65,325) chose to settle in Richmond. This number comprises more than one third of the total Richmond population (164,345). After 1997, with the rapid economic growth and more opening up of Mainland China, the number of Mandarin-speaking Chinese was also increasing in Richmond. Since 1998, Mainland China has become a leading source of British Columbia immigrants, representing 16% of the total landing in British Columbia and 11% in Canada (British Columbia STATS, 2001). It is said that Richmond became attractive to Chinese immigrants because of its good "feng shui" (geomantic omen): a map of lower mainland Vancouver looks almost like a dragon's head, and Richmond's location occupies the coveted position in the dragon's mouth.

The drastically changing demographics have had a significant impact on the sociolinguistic, sociocultural, and socioeconomic face of Greater Vancouver, especially in Richmond. The 2001 census results already show that nearly half (46.8%) of the total population in British Columbia speak Chinese as their first language. Chinese has become

English Canada's second language—it has replaced French as the second most common language spoken in homes outside Quebec (Klotz, 1999). Richmond, nicknamed Vancouver's Hong Kong, is unique in its own linguistic representation: the street and business signs are in Chinese and English. In Chinese shopping malls and businesses such as karaoke bars, many signs are monolingual Chinese and very few non-Chinese customers are spotted.

The influx of Chinese immigrants has also changed the economic sector of Vancouver. It was largely the money of the Hong Kong immigrants that helped the province of British Columbia begin an economic recovery while the rest of Canada continued to languish in the late 1980s and early 1990s (Gibbon, 1999). The investment of these new Chinese immigrants has caused the prices of the real estate market to skyrocket. The new Chinese immigrants built many large Chinese shopping malls and businesses as well as mansions that non-Asians call "monster houses." In addition, they penetrated into the city's high-paying white-collar job market. For example, in 1996, more Chinese Vancouverites went into finance, insurance, and real estate (13,585 versus 10,740 Canadians), and more Chinese Vancouverites had a bachelor's degree or higher than Canadians (46,105 versus 35,375) (Gibbon, 1999). The children and their families who are the focus of this study were part of these changes.

Along with the changing economic structure of the city, new racial tensions surfaced (P. S. Li, 1997, 1998). Many local non-Asian residents had been forced to move out of the city due to the socioeconomic changes. These new immigrants were not the stereotypical "railway Chinese," who settled in the ghetto of Chinatown known to many Canadians (K. J. Anderson, 1991; P. S. Li, 1997, 1998). They were relatively well-to-do middle- to upper-middle-class citizens from Hong Kong, Taiwan, and Mainland China, who settled in the suburbs and drove BMWs and Mercedes. Their presence had changed the status quo of the non-Asians in their communities: "In Vancouver, local residents who had considered themselves well off suddenly realized that with the arrival of the newly rich Hong Kong immigrants, and the sky high real estate prices they triggered, their own economic standing had dropped to middle class. 'Immigration is OK when someone comes over to work as a domestic or in a laundry because the local people can feel superior to them,' said Jack Austin, a senator for British Columbia. 'But it's pretty hard to feel superior to someone in a Mercedes'" (DePalma, 1997, p. 3).

In Richmond, Chinese-only signs in some shopping malls and the availability of Chinese books in the libraries have evoked several racial conflicts and controversies. Analyzing the situation from the non-Chinese perspective, Chinese Around the World (CATW), a bimonthly newspaper published by the Chinese Coordination Centre for World Evangelism, reports that much of the racial conflict stems from the perception that Chinese immigrants are reluctant to integrate into the mainstream society, but prefer to establish their own ethnic ghetto (CATW, 1996, p. 1). The news report quotes Dave McCullough, a high-profile publisher of the *Richmond Review*: "We have officially sanctioned the ghettoization of Richmond. We have said to our new citizens that they are not officially required to speak English. We've acknowledged that they don't need it in their daily lives, and we've encouraged them to segregate themselves from the mainstream society" (CATW, 1996, p. 1).

On the other side of the argument, Peter S. Li, a sociologist who specializes in research on Chinese immigrants in Canada, argues that the new controversies and conflicts are a form of covert racism based on an ethnocentric conviction of the encroaching foreign race. Li points out that the historical image of the Chinese as culturally distinct and racially foreign has become a deep-seated cultural stereotype for Canadians; this conviction also explains why some white Canadians see Chinese immigrants' adherence to the Chinese language and their concentration in ethnic markets and residential enclaves as threatening the cultural and racial homogeneity of Canadian society (P. S. Li, 1997, pp. 142–143).

These racial and economic tensions are not new in British Columbia. Historically, the province's primary concern over racial stereotypes and economic tensions has been about the Chinese who preceded other Asians (K. J. Anderson, 1991; Ward, 1978, 1990). In fact, anti-Chinese sentiments have been endemic since the Chinese first arrived on the west coast in the 1850s. They were perceived socially as a "yellow peril" to the homogeneity of "white Canada," racially inferior to whites, and economically a threat to the west coast white workingmen in that the Chinese took away the white men's wages, jobs, and stable status (Ward, 1978, 1990). Moreover, the Chinese have been constructed as a racial category that is "unassimilable"—it had become one of a "fixed, persistent type, alien, beyond any control or chance of change, to everything that concerns western civilization" (Ward, 1978, p. 5). In addition to these racial prejudices, the Chinese also experienced institutional racism expressed through government policies and laws (P. S. Li, 1998). Along with the four consecutive head taxes, the Chinese Immigration Act of 1885, and the Chinese Immigration Act of 1923 imposed by the federal government, the British Columbia legislature passed numerous bills to prevent new Chinese from immigrating to Canada and to restrict their political and social rights (P. S. Li, 1998; Knowles, 1997; Ward, 1978, 1990). These anti-Chinese feelings also extended to the school system (P. S. Li, 1998) and many requested the segregation of Chinese students from white students as it was "necessary to separate at the public schools the children of one portion of the inhabitants from the other for the preservation of the Anglo-Saxon standard of moral and ethical culture" (*Victoria Columnist*, Jan. 26, 1902, as quoted in Ashworth, 1979, p. 58).

Over a century has passed during which the Chinese immigrants have undergone many trials and tribulations. Although the Chinese have gained a much broader acceptance through multicultural awareness, prejudice and discrimination against them continue to this day in different socioeconomic contexts (L. Chow, 2000; Knowles, 1997). As K. J. Anderson (1991) points out, at present "benign perceptions of the resplendent East and the industrious Chinese persist alongside 'Hongcouver's' more classic fears about its wealthy new 'yacht-people'" (p. 249).

In Richmond today, racial tension and the recent economic downturn have shaped another layer of complexity among the Chinese community. Since its handover to China in 1997, Hong Kong has stayed stable and unchanged in its economic structuring, and the expected economic turmoil and drastic social change has not happened. Many Hong Kong residents who moved to Canada have begun to move back to Hong Kong. In many families, the father would travel back to Hong Kong to work and earn money to support the family in Canada. This new phenomenon has also had an impact on their children's education. The parents expect their children to be able to choose where they will settle down in the future and to be prepared for both worlds—East and West. Therefore, they want their children to grow up knowing not only Chinese, but also English.

The changing demographics in Richmond and in the school have posed several challenges for the public school system. Unlike the "railway Chinese" who did not have a voice in public education, the new Chinese immigrants are active advocates of their children's education. Two major issues are worth mentioning here. First, the

Chinese fought for their first language education rights. In 1994, the newly formed Chinese Language Education Advancement Coalition of British Columbia urged the British Columbia government to include Chinese in the provincial examinations for students leaving grade 12, and to allow some Chinese courses to be taught in high school. In addition to these efforts, the Coalition established traditional Chinese schools where children can learn Chinese since no Chinese courses were offered in the public school system. Second, the Chinese have expressed much dissatisfaction with the quality of the Canadian public school system. They have raised concerns about issues related to school discipline, homework, teacher-led instruction, reading instruction and phonics, combined classes (i.e., mixed grades), inclusion, the dress code, reporting and conferencing, and communication between school and home. These concerns resulted in their joint effort to push for a traditional school that emphasized regular assessment and reporting to parents and traditional models of instruction: structured, teacher-centered direct instruction, strict discipline and code of behavior, a dress code, and a school ethos more competitive than cooperative (Coleman, 1998; Miller, 2000). In 1998, Richmond's Asian parents lobbied a second time for a traditional school with a 3,000–signature petition and the local school board trustees passed a motion to approve the proposal (Makhoul, 2000). To communicate the school practices to the Chinese parents, the school district launched a reform initiative called Foundations in 2000 which details the district's commitment to "clarity, consistency, and communication" with parents, teachers, and students at elementary schools to address the issues at the heart of the traditional school request. One of the projects that the district started was to launch a series of discussion papers on the issues raised by the Chinese parents, such as teacher-led instruction, reading instruction and phonics, homework, combined classes, and dress codes. These papers explained the schools' educational philosophies and positions on these issues, citing current research findings. Although the Foundations initiative alleviated the tensions between the Chinese parents and the schools, it did not fully solve the problem between the two parties.

    In order to better understand these tensions, in the next two sections, I provide first a brief summary of schooling practices in Mainland China and Hong Kong, and then a description of the Canadian school context in which this study was situated.

Elementary School Education in
Mainland China and Hong Kong

In China, elementary school lasts six years and is compulsory. All six-year-olds enter elementary school and all primary school graduates meeting local requirements for graduation enter nearby lower secondary schools without taking any entrance examinations. All-day system schools are the predominant form in China and consist of "ordinary" elementary schools and "key" elementary schools. Ordinary schools are open to children in the neighborhood where they are located. Key elementary schools provide high-quality education and have the most experienced teachers and the most advanced teaching equipment and facilities. Entering the key elementary schools does not require taking entrance exams, but students must live in the area in which the school is located. Parents from outside the jurisdiction of a key elementary school usually must pay a donation of more than 30,000 Yuan (about $3,600 U.S.) to gain school placement for their child (Wang, 2003).

A typical elementary school in urban cities may have four or more classes with 40–50 students per class at each grade level. Most often, a single-grade class will have its own room, though students may move to other rooms for art, music, or other special lessons and will go outdoors for sports, exercises, and large meetings. Students normally are seated at rows of desks facing the front of the classroom, where there is a raised platform and perhaps a desk or lectern. Portions of the back blackboard and other blackboards and bulletin boards around the room are often elaborately decorated with designs and calligraphy in colored chalk or decorative displays of student art, poetry, or schoolwork.

The academic year of elementary schools in China is generally divided into two semesters. The first semester begins in the first week of September and the second in the middle of February. Five days a week of six- to seven-hour days is the norm in elementary schools. The school day starts early and ends late. Students are encouraged to arrive at school at least half an hour before classes start (around 7:30 a.m.) so that they have a chance to read and study their texts. Students are also encouraged to do independent study during the lunch break and after school. As a result, it's rare for students to leave school before 4:30 p.m. Homework is normally assigned every day, but recently limits have been placed on the amount of homework assigned, in response to what has come to be seen as excessive student workloads (Wang, 2003).

Class periods last about 45 minutes. The four class periods before lunch are usually devoted to the most rigorous academic subjects such as Chinese and mathematics. After the second morning class, there is a break of about 20 minutes for morning exercises. After the lunch break, which includes time for a midday nap, there are two more class periods in the afternoon plus time for extracurricular activities and independent study.

The curriculum of the lower grades is devoted mostly to Chinese literacy and mathematics education. In grades 3, 4, 5, and 6, the curriculum branches out to include two hours per week each of natural science, history, and geography (collectively called "common knowledge"). Throughout the course of compulsory education, students must take end-of-term examinations as well as writing tests or checkups at the end of each semester, each school year, and before graduation respectively. Chinese language and mathematics are the required examination subjects for graduation.

The curriculum for China's elementary schools is guided by a teaching plan formulated and promulgated at the national level (Hawkins & Stites, 1991). The national curriculum ensures a high degree of uniformity in elementary schools throughout China. The teaching style is often characterized as traditional, centered on the teacher, and fairly rigid or even authoritarian (Carron & Châu, 1996). According to several cross-cultural comparative studies (Carron & Châu, 1996; Stevenson & Stigler, 1992), contrary to common negative assumptions, this teaching style often proves to be effective and engaging. As Carron & Châu (1996) described, "The pedagogical process is structured and effective: The teacher and the pupils are rarely absent, and the teacher knows the subject matter and how to present it, he/she teaches according to a precise plan, presents the lessons in a structured manner, has the pupils participate actively, frequently uses the blackboard and other didactic means, gives examples, alternates explanations and exercises, often assigns homework and corrects it individually, gives regular written tests, and communicates their results to pupils and parents" (p. 202).

The time-consuming and difficult process of gaining basic literacy in Chinese characters dominates the first three years of elementary school in China. Because Chinese characters are logographic rather than alphabetic, children typically must spend a great deal of time and effort simply memorizing several hundred of them before they can begin to acquire the most rudimentary level of literacy (Hawkins & Stites, 1991; Hudson-Ross & Dong, 1990). Chinese literacy educators have made continuous effort to reform the language as well as methods of teaching it. Since 1982, a new literacy instructional method, a phonetic-symbol-based method, was developed and adopted by Chinese schools. This method seeks to promote character acquisition through the use of phonetic symbols, facilitating reading and writing; it teaches students first to read and write in pinyin (writing of Chinese in the Roman alphabet) and then gradually switch over to Chinese characters as they are acquired (Dai & Lu, 1985; Hawkins & Stites, 1991).

Besides Chinese, mathematics is another important part of the elementary education. The teaching of mathematics is also guided by a national curriculum and standardized textbook series. Comparative studies on international mathematics education have discovered that the difficulty level of the curriculum, the rate of progress, and the complexity of calculations that Chinese students are expected to do are much greater than those comparable age groups in many Western countries including the United States and Canada (Hawkins & Stites, 1991; Stevenson & Stigler, 1992).

The most important characteristic of Chinese elementary education is its academic orientation. Assisting students to succeed in their provincial unified entrance examinations so as to get into an outstanding higher-level key school or an elite university seems to be the goal of teaching (Hawkins & Stites, 1991; Wang, 2003). Since the competition to get into a university is very fierce and each family has only one child, all parents want their children to start preparing for post-secondary education from the outset of their primary schooling. Meanwhile, all the primary schools compete with each other for better enrollment rates to outstanding secondary schools. Students themselves also take school seriously and work very hard toward the objectives of entering an ideal key school.

There are many similarities between elementary schooling in Hong Kong and Mainland China. For example, schooling in Hong Kong also begins at the age of six and lasts six years, is free for all students, and focuses on academic achievement and testing in core subjects such as Chinese literacy and mathematics. The primary school curriculum in Hong Kong also aims to provide a coherent and well-balanced program to promote the all-around development of the child. All public-sector primary schools adopt a core curriculum together with general studies which integrates social studies, science and health education, music, physical education, and arts and crafts.

Other learning programs such as citizen education and environmental education are offered on a cross-curricular basis or as separate optional subjects. Children's progress in Chinese, English, and mathematics, the core curriculum subjects, is evaluated yearly with the standardized Hong Kong Attainment Tests. And similar to the schools in China, children's academic results are the key criterion for secondary school admission and this creates a lot of pressure on children and parents.

However, because of Hong Kong's unique history as a British colony and unique context as a Special Administrative Region with a special economic status, elementary schooling in Hong Kong also differs from Mainland China in many ways. For example, different from Mainland China's whole-day schools, most Hong Kong primary schools operate bisessionally. That is, primary students can go to either a morning session or an afternoon session. Recently, the Hong Kong government has been pushing for whole-day primary schooling by 2009. Another significant difference is that besides its focus on Chinese literacy and mathematics education, English as a Second Language is also a key subject in the Hong Kong primary curriculum. One of the main goals of Hong Kong primary education is to foster "two literacies (Chinese and English) and three languages (Mandarin, Cantonese, and English)" (B. Chow, 2004).

In Hong Kong, Chinese is the medium of instruction in most primary schools and most schools offer Mandarin (the official Chinese language) classes. With Hong Kong's return to China in 1997 and the economic growth in Mainland China in recent years, Mandarin has been intensively promoted in the school curriculum (Adamson & Lai, 1997) and positively endorsed by the public (Pierson, 1998). Even though Chinese is the language of instruction, English education is also viewed as having paramount significance as it is a key element in assessment for placement in secondary education and entry to tertiary education (Adamson & Lai, 1997). In fact, because English ability is associated with better jobs in the economic sector in Hong Kong, it remains a high-status subject in the primary curriculum and academic results of English testing are used by schools to vie for the best students (Morris, 1997).

Although classrooms in Hong Kong has been primarily portrayed as teacher-centered with a tense atmosphere stressing mechanical or rote learning (Mok & Morris, 2001), the instructional approaches in Hong Kong primary schools have gone through some changes in the past several decades. For the Chinese parents who obtained education in the 1970s and 1980s, instruction in literacy (both Chinese and English) and mathematics was based on a transmissive model in a whole class style as the teaching styles in Mainland Chinese schools described above. Paine (1990) described this teaching as a "virtuoso" style in which the role of the teacher is mainly demonstrating while students are expected to follow the teacher's model.

In 1995, based on "international good practice" (that is, the progressive approach in the West), the Hong Kong educational council introduced the Target-Oriented Curriculum (TOC) initiative in the three core primary subjects (Carless, 1998, p. 356). TOC consists of three main conceptual elements: targets (common directions for learning for all schools), tasks (purposeful and contextual learning activities), and task-based assessment (criterion-referenced assessment). Under TOC, students are encouraged to be involved in pair work, group work, and individual work on projects and tasks. In terms of English language teaching, TOC has much in common with communicative methodologies (Carless, 1998). Because of its student-centered, communicative nature, TOC signified a major departure from the traditional teacher-centered, whole-class teaching styles. According to Morris & Lo (2000), "The career of the TOC could simply be portrayed as a clash between an innovation based on Western cultural precepts and a Chinese/Confucian culture, but the process was more complex and fragmented and was characterized by the competition between groups that operated within distinct arenas" (p. 176).

Because of its cultural and philosophical differences, this new pedagogy has encountered tremendous resistance among teachers whose background and experience are often in alignment with more traditional teacher-centered methods (Carless, 1998; Morris & Lo, 2000). As a result, even after several years of implementation of TOC, whole-class instruction is still the dominant mode of pedagogy in many classrooms in Hong Kong (Mok & Morris, 2001).

In sum, Chinese and Hong Kong elementary schooling can be characterized as teacher centered, academic oriented, and test driven. Core subjects such as Chinese, mathematics, (and English for Hong Kong) are accorded high importance in education. These characteristics of schooling were well reflected in Richmond Chinese parents' political struggles and their views on Canadian schooling. In the next section, I introduce the Canadian school context in which this study is situated.

The Canadian School: Taylor Elementary

Richmond's sociolinguistic, socioeconomic, and sociocultural changes are well reflected in the local school system. According to Makhoul (2000), the Richmond school district educates 24,500 students in 50 public schools (including 10 secondary schools, grade 8–12). Approximately 10,000 of these students are ESL students of Chinese background, a threefold increase since 1990.

The school in this study, Taylor Elementary, is one of the elementary schools (K–7) among the 50 schools in Richmond. It is a multiethnic school with a total of 241 students. The school's 2001 demographics indicated that 151 students were considered ESL students; 158 students' home language was Chinese; 32 students' home language was English; and 51 students spoke other languages at home. Altogether the school had students who spoke 20 different languages.

The school has 10 divisions. Each division (except for kindergarten) consists of one combined class of two grade levels (grades 1/2, 2/3, 3/4, and so on). Mostly, each teacher is responsible for one combined class with the exception that two pairs of teachers co-teach two classes. Combined classes are very common, comprising two thirds of the elementary classes in Richmond. Combined classes are established for administrative reasons (maximum number of students in fewer classrooms, and less costly), practical reasons (more choices for student placements), and philosophical reasons (more accommodating to individual differences and their needs). At Taylor Elementary, according to the two focal teachers, combined classes were philosophical choices of the teachers. The choice, however, was not understood or supported by the Chinese parents, who preferred single-grade classes.

The school is located in the middle of a quiet middle-class neighborhood. Many students live just minutes away from the school. This is very different from a Chinatown elementary school I visited where the school was fenced with wires and had no playground. Taylor Elementary is unfenced and boasts a large open playground the size of a soccer field. The well-maintained green grass fosters a peaceful atmosphere. Here many physical education classes are held during the school year. Likewise, the inside of Taylor Elementary is also different from the Chinatown school. Whereas the Chinatown school has signs that are bilingual Chinese and English, signs inside Taylor Elementary are monolingual English. In the Chinatown school library, there are many books in the Chinese language, and community members can come and read in the library. At Taylor Elementary there are no such books and the library is not open to community members. At the Chinatown school, photographs of some Chinese-Canadian role models, such as the well-known journalist Jan Wong of *The Globe and Mail,* are displayed. At Taylor Elementary, many copies of the school's code of conduct, STAR (Safe, Thoughtful, and Responsible) are displayed to remind students of proper behaviors at school. Along with the STAR posters, there hangs student artwork on the hallway walls. Compared to the Chinatown school, Taylor Elementary feels much safer since it is not open to the community. No security code is needed, as opposed to the Chinatown school, which communicates to students the potential for unsafe people inside the school through a secret code. Comparatively speaking, the Taylor Elementary atmosphere is very relaxed and all the teachers are extremely friendly and welcoming.

In contrast to its multiethnic student population, the teachers and staff in the school were homogenously white. At the time of the study, the school had 12 regular classroom teachers and three ESL/resource teachers; all of them were English-speaking Caucasians. The school had one Chinese employee, Mrs. Yep, who was a classroom assistant. Most of the regular classroom teachers, such as Mrs. Haines and Ms. Dawson, did not have formal training in teaching ESL. They were trained as English Language Arts teachers, and were naturally transitioned to teaching ESL students due to the change of student population in Richmond over the years. However, in the Taylor Elementary Handbook, they were considered ESL teachers: "At Taylor Elementary every teacher is an ESL teacher and works carefully with students to include all students in the regular program. Some students will work with the ESL/resource teachers outside the class. Other students will receive extra support in the class. The goal of the ESL program is to have every student working within the regular class program as closely as possible."

These ESL programs are actually based on a resource model. A resource model is a combined model in which ESL/resource specialists are members of the teaching team in the school who serve both ESL and special needs students to reinforce regular classroom instruction. The ESL/resource specialists' main role is to provide services to special needs and ESL students who require extra support in their learning and in developing their competencies in oral and written English so that the students are able to integrate into and work in their regular classes. These services are provided both within the regular classroom setting as in-class support and to smaller groups of individuals in the resource room setting as pullout programs. Under this model, ESL students are often pulled out of the regular classroom together with cognitively delayed special needs children to receive small group instruction.

According to British Columbia Ministry of Education Special Programs Branch (2001), ESL students are those whose primary language(s), or language(s) of the home, is other than English and who may therefore require additional services in order to develop their individual potential within British Columbia's school system. These additional services are usually funded by the British Columbia Ministry of Education. The ESL support needed for students comes under two broad categories. There are those who require Basic Interpersonal Communications Skills (BICS) and those who require Cognitive Academic Language Proficiency (CALP). Students who are acquiring conversational fluency receive pullout support outside the regular classroom. When students are ready to acquire language proficiency, in-class support from the teacher is required. Levels of support have been divided into five categories ranging from Level 1 (beginner) to Level 5 (near fluent). In Richmond School District, students in levels 1–4 receive direct support from an ESL teacher in their classroom or in the ESL teachers' room. In Taylor Elementary, due to limited government funding, there were only three ESL/resource teachers who had to serve 158 ESL students as well as all the special needs students in the school. Most ESL students remained in the mainstream classroom to receive in-class ESL support, and only a smaller number of lower level ESL students were pulled out of their regular classrooms to receive group instruction from ESL/resource specialists.

ESL students who are new to the country are initially assessed and assigned a level by the district school board office. Each spring, the ESL teachers conduct an assessment of the students' progress and adjust their placement. Classroom teachers collaborate with ESL teachers to determine the appropriate support that ESL learners will need. Grade 1 students take an oral and written assessment while students in grades 2–7 are required to have a reading, writing, and oral assessment.

In addition to these ESL assessments, each spring students in grades 4 and 7 (and 10 in secondary school) are also required to take part in the provincial Foundation Skills Assessment (FSA). This involves testing students in three areas: reading comprehension, writing, and numeracy. Students assessed as unable to respond meaningfully to the assessment instrument are excused and do not participate in the testing (British Columbia Foundation Skills Assessment, 2001).

The main purpose of the assessment is to help the province, school district, and schools evaluate existing programs and make plans for improvement. The results for individual students are mailed to parents, and the interpretation of the school-wide results in relation to provincial standards is usually published in school newsletters. Although the results provide a snapshot of where a student is in relation to provincial standards, they do not count toward student report card results. Instead, teachers use a variety of evaluation and assessment tools on an on-going basis to ascertain the progress of their students and to plan curriculum and instruction. Among the range of evaluation and assessment tools used are teacher observations, conferences with students, and collections of written work products over time, such as journals and portfolios.

In addition to English, the school also offers classes in Canada's second official language, French. Beginning in grade 5, it is mandatory that all students in Richmond take French twice a week (two 40–minute periods). In a 4/5 combined class, the grade 4 students can take French as well, but it is not mandatory for grade 4. French is usually taught by the classroom teacher.

The school has a Parent Advisory Council (PAC), a group composed of school administrators and parent executives who support school programs and advise the school administration through different fund-raising activities during the year. Every parent or guardian of the Taylor Elementary students is a member of the PAC. PAC activities include the monthly hot-lunch program (in which hot dogs or pizza are sold) and Scholastic Books sales to raise funds for school programs. They also arrange guest speakers from the school board to talk about Internet safety and give tips to parents on how to monitor students' use of the Internet at home. This group also organizes family barbecue nights where families can come to school and meet the teachers. Though PAC (and the teachers) have spent much time and effort on these activities, attendance by the parents was reported to be low. If 15–20 parents attended, it was considered a good turnout.

Since none of the teachers could speak Chinese, communication with the new students and their families could be very difficult. Many students were given English names by the ESL teachers upon their arrival at school. An ESL/resource teacher said that sometimes it took the students several weeks to identify with their new English names. In other circumstances, it was hard for the teachers to understand the happenings in the students' lives. For example, two students (who were sisters) suddenly decided to transfer to another school. One ESL

teacher was trying to explain to them that they did not need to transfer to other schools, but the sisters insisted on doing so. Unable to
understand what was happening with the students and communicate
with them, the teacher asked me to translate for them so that he could
explain to the two sisters about the transfer.

Many students referred to the school as the "English school" to
differentiate it from the "Chinese school" that they attended on weekends. No Chinese courses were offered in the school. Speaking Chinese was also discouraged in school setting. It was widely believed by
the regular classroom teachers and the ESL/resource teachers that
many students failed to learn English because they often spoke Chinese. To be accountable to the Chinese parents, Taylor Elementary had
adopted an unwritten policy—the "English-only policy." The teachers
or staff members, when hearing Chinese in the hallway in the school,
would sometimes remind students, "English please! No Chinese in
school." In some classes, such as Ms. Dawson's, if students repeatedly
spoke Chinese in class, they might be detained after class. Despite the
school's effort to get the students to speak only English in school,
many students, especially those in the higher grades, continued to
ignore this school policy and speak Chinese whenever they wanted to.
Mrs. Smith, the ESL/resource teacher said, "It is not that we really can
enforce it. We just asked them to speak more English, 'Try to speak
English, speak English as much as you can.' But if you go outside at
lunch time, they all speak Chinese."

The Focal Teachers

The two teachers who generously supported this research study were
Mrs. Haines and Ms. Dawson. Although both were senior teachers,
they were eager to learn more about current issues in education. As
mentioned in the introduction, both teachers were aware of the dissen-
sion among the Chinese parents and were eager to find out more about
the parents' thoughts on education through this research project.

Mrs. Haines was a white, middle-class woman in her fifties. I was
impressed with her caring manner and concern for the well-being of
the students. When I first met her, she appeared to be a very outspoken person who was very passionate about teaching and about teaching philosophies. She was teaching a grade 1/2 combined class and
she had been teaching in the school district for 29 years. Although she
did not have any training in ESL, she taught English in an elementary

school in Japan for one year about 10 years ago. At the time of the study she was enrolled in a master's degree program in the Department of Language and Literacy Education at a local university. She was married to a former high school teacher who was retired and stayed home. They had a son who was a freshman in the same university Mrs. Haines was attending for her master's degree.

Mrs. Haines's classroom was divided into different centers and areas by a couple of bookshelves with different children's books and music cassettes. The open area consisted of three round tables and chairs where students did most of their writing and drawing, an art center where students could paint, and a play center with different games and toys, such as Legos. At the corner of the play center there was a rocking chair where Mrs. Haines usually sat and did the morning routine and read stories to the whole class.

One side of the classroom was a huge window that overlooked a courtyard. In the courtyard, the class raised a small rabbit. Along the top of the walls, Mrs. Haines displayed the alphabet and examples of words that began with the different letters of the alphabet, as well as students' drawings and artwork such as big paper trees, valentines, and greeting cards. There was also a chart of the students' "Home Reading Stars" which indicated how many books each student had read at home. Beside the Home Reading Stars, there were two rules: the "ABK" rule (Always Be Kind) and the "Three L" rule (Look, Learn, Leave It Alone). On top of the Three L rule was a "Parking Lot Safety" rule (Stop, Eye Contact, Hand Signal, Walk). On the other side of the wall, there were calendars and cards with the days of the week and different numbers. Close to the corner, there was a respect chart which said: "Respect—self, others, property, and environment." Underneath the respect sign was a list of school tasks:

1. Compost
2. Recycle
3. Clean up
4. Be kind
5. Talk/answer politely
6. Listen politely
7. Do your school work
8. Do your homework
9. Take care of your things

In Mrs. Haines' grade 1/2 combined class, there were 23 students: 18 were Chinese, 3 were of East Asian origin, 1 was Caucasian, and 1 was a student of African origin adopted by Caucasian parents. Two of the Chinese students came into the classroom without any prior knowledge of English. The classroom assistant, Mrs. Yep, was a quiet, hard-working, and caring Chinese woman in her late forties. Her major responsibility was to help with a special needs student. She was also a teacher in the local Chinese language school.

Ms. Dawson, a teacher of a grade 4/5 combined class, was in her late forties. Like Mrs. Haines, Ms. Dawson also had a bachelor's degree in education, and had been teaching in the district for 22 years, including 8 years of experience teaching special education. At the time of the study, she was in her first year at Taylor Elementary. She did not have training in ESL either, but had one year of overseas teaching experience in the United Kingdom. Mrs. Smith, a white woman in her fifties, was the ESL/resource teacher for Ms. Dawson's students. Ms. Dawson did not have a classroom assistant, but Mrs. Smith came into the classroom to help her occasionally.

Ms. Dawson's classroom was on the other side of the building from Mrs. Haines's class. It was a larger room with a big window looking out on a basketball court. Under the window was a row of built-in bookshelves with different textbooks, dictionaries, and students' project boxes. On top of the shelf stood a small globe, and on the wall beside the window hung a map of the world. In the front of the room beside the teacher's workstation were a blackboard and an overhead projector. Beside the overhead projector was a desk with a small computer, which was rarely used, except for a few times by a new student who was assigned to play word games. The front wall displayed posters of the alphabet and a list of classroom helper tasks (such as messenger, cleaning chalkboard and sink, and so on). Beside the helper tasks were directions for classroom discussion:

Second Step: Discussion
- Raise your hand
- Keep your hands to yourself and sit still
- Use "power talk" and "I" statement
- Control your temper
- Be an active listener
- One speaker at a time.

In the back of the classroom were two bookshelves with different trade books. These books were for students to choose for their daily silent readings in the morning. The back wall displayed some students' work, such as writings about Taylor Elementary community care on heart-shaped papers. In the center of the room, the children's desks were arranged in small groups of four or five. Later, when one parent complained about the small-group seating, Ms. Dawson changed to rows as in a traditional classroom.

Ms. Dawson had 28 students: 21 Chinese, 3 East Asian, 3 Caucasian, and 1 African Canadian. Out of the 28 students, only 4 (3 Caucasian students, and 1 Chinese student who withdrew from the ESL program) were not considered ESL. Among the 24 ESL students, 3 recently came from China and did not speak any English.

Over the course of the research, I developed a personal relationship with Mrs. Haines. She invited me to her home for Christmas and for other family events such as her son's football games. Together we had numerous conversations about teaching and education and many other subjects. Ms. Dawson appeared to be a more private person. We had several dinners together, but our relationship remained largely professional. Our conversations centered mostly around the education of the focal children in her class.

The Focal Children and their Families

Eight children from seven families (two students were brother and sister) participated in the study. There were four children from each classroom. The children were selected based on their family backgrounds, interests, and English literacy levels, and whether their varied experiences would provide a rich understanding of the lived reality of learners in the sociocultural context of a highly concentrated ethnic Chinese suburban community.

In the grade 1/2 combined class, the focal children and their families were recommended by Mrs. Haines because she wanted to know more about the children's parents and their home practices, and these children met the criterion of being children of Chinese immigrant families. Originally, six students were selected. Unfortunately, two students' parents declined to participate, so I finally decided to focus on the four students whose families agreed to be part of the study. The children were:

- Sandy Chung, age 6, grade 1, born in Canada.
- Anthony Chan, age 7, grade 2, born in Canada
- Alana Tang, age 6, grade 1, born in China
- Kevin Ma, age 6, grade 1, born in Canada

In the grade 4/5 combined class, 16 Chinese students who met the criteria were originally selected and consent letters were sent to the families in both English and Chinese. However, only four consent forms were signed and returned. I made phone contacts with two other parents to further explain the study. One parent, Mrs. Ling, who was the only guardian in Canada, declined her son Xiao-min's participation (her husband was in Taiwan), but agreed to be interviewed herself. Communication with the other parent was extremely difficult and I eventually dropped this parent from the study. The four focal students who agreed to take part in the study were:

- Billy Chung, age 10, grade 4, born in Canada
- Andy Lou, age 10, grade 4, born in Canada
- Jake Wong, age 11, grade 5, born in Canada
- Tina Wei, age 12, grade 5, born in China

I interviewed one parent from each family, except for Tina Wei's mother whom I only briefly interviewed on the phone. Table 2.1 is a sketch of the families' profiles.

Sandy and Billy Chung. Six-year-old Sandy was in grade 1 and her 10-year-old bother Billy was in grade 4. Their parents emigrated from Hong Kong to Canada in 1990 together with their extended families who now lived just a few blocks away from them. Both parents had high school education in Hong Kong. Their father operated his own landscaping business while their mother stayed home to take care of the two children. Sometimes when Mr. Chung's business became busy, Mrs. Chung would help. I never met Mr. Chung in person, but I talked with him on the phone a few times. I met Mrs. Chung several times through school field trips. She was the only parent who volunteered to come to school activities.

Anthony Chan. Seven-year-old Anthony, who was in second grade, was the only child in his family. His family immigrated to Canada in 1987. His mother had post-secondary education in Hong Kong and was an executive secretary before moving to Canada. She was now working as an executive assistant in a children's hospital, and was also taking courses in alternative medicine. Anthony's father

Table 2.1. Family Profiles

Focal Children	Parental Education and English Proficiency	Parental Occupation	Immigration	Focal Parent
Sandy Chung, 6, grade 1, born in Canada **Billy Chung**, 10, grade 4, born in Canada	Both parents had high school education in Hong Kong. No additional training in Canada. Not fluent in English.	Father: landscape designer Mother: homemaker	Immigrated from Hong Kong in 1990	Mother
Anthony Chan, 7, grade 2, born in Canada, only child	Father: master's degree in business in U.S. Mother: post-secondary in Hong Kong, had taken courses in management and alternative medicine. Fluent in English.	Father: print marketer Mother: executive assistant in a hospital	Immigrated from Hong Kong in 1987	Mother
Alana Tang, 6, grade 1, born in China, with a brother, 14, born in China	Father: college diploma in China. Mother: college diploma in China. No additional training in Canada. No English.	Father: investor working from home Mother: technician in a biochemical company	Immigrated from Mainland China in 1999	Father
Kevin Ma, 6, grade 1, born in Canada, with a brother, 15, grade 9, born in Hong Kong	Father: high school education in Hong Kong. Mother: polytechnic college in Hong Kong. No additional training in Canada. Fluent in English.	Father: investment, working from home Mother: sales representative in a telecommunication company	Immigrated from Hong Kong in 1994	Father
Andy Lou, 10, grade 4, born in Canada, with a sister, 17, born in Canada	Father: bachelor's degree in Hong Kong. Mother: high school in Hong Kong, and college degree in Canada. Fluent in English.	Father: sign business Mother: housewife	Immigrated in 1982	Mother
Jake Wong, 11, grade 5, born in Canada, with 2 sisters, 18 and 16, born in Canada	Mother: high school education in China; Father: elementary education in Hong Kong. No additional training in Canada. Not fluent in English.	Father and Mother: restaurant owners	Immigrated from Hong Kong in 1981	Mother

Table 2.1. (continued)

Focal Children	Parental Education and English Proficiency	Parental Occupation	Immigration	Focal Parent
Tina Wei, 12, grade 5, born in China, only child	Unknown Not fluent in English.	Father: Chinese restaurant employee Mother: ESL student	Immigrated from Mainland China in 1999	Mother
Xiao-min Ling, grade 5, born in Taiwan, only child	Father: master's degree in Taiwan. Mother: college diploma in Taiwan. Not fluent in English.	Father: college professor in Taiwan. Mother: homemaker in Canada	Immigrated from Taiwan in 1995	Mother

* Xiao-min's mother declined to have him in the study, but agreed to participate herself. Xiao-min is not a focal child.

had received an undergraduate degree in Hong Kong and a master's degree in the United States. Before moving to Canada, he worked as an advertising agent, first in New York and then in Hong Kong, for a few years. Now he worked as a print marketer in Richmond. I did not have a chance to meet Mr. Chan, but had a long formal interview with Mrs. Chan about Anthony at their house, which was only minutes from the school. The interview took place shortly after Mrs. Chan's mother passed away from Alzheimer's disease in a nursing home.

Alana Tang. Six-year-old Alana was the second child of the family. Her 14–year-old brother was in the seventh grade. She came to Canada with her family in March 1999. Prior to moving to Canada, Mr. Tang had his own real estate business and was a multimillionaire. Alana's mother worked in business management. Both parents had associate degrees from colleges in China. They came to Canada as investors. Although she did not need to work for money, Mrs. Tang worked part time as a technician for a biochemical company in the area (operated by Chinese-speaking people). Mr. Tang stayed home, buying and selling stocks on-line and researching new ideas for businesses in Canada and in China. He told me that his new life style in Canada was an early retirement for him, and this change was a challenge for him as he did not work and use his talents as he did in China. "I feel that I am wasting my time here," he told me, "but it also gives me a chance to spend more time with my children. I was too busy in China." Neither he nor his wife could speak any English when they arrived. Both went to study English in government-sponsored ESL classes for a few months. They decided to quit the classes because they felt that they could not learn very well because of their age and they were not yet sure how long their family would stay in Canada. Mr. Tang told me, "We will definitely learn English if we decide to stay here long term."

Kevin Ma. Six-year-old Kevin was also the second child in his family. He had a 15-year-old brother who was in the ninth grade in high school. His brother, who came to Canada when he was nine, was struggling with English reading and writing, and because of his English he also fell behind in other core subjects such as math and science. His parents hoped that Kevin would not have difficulty with English reading and writing since he was born and schooled here in Canada. Both his parents were in the trading business in Hong Kong, and became investors after immigrating to Canada in 1994. They were educated in Hong Kong—Kevin's father had a high school education while his mother had a diploma from a polytechnic institute. Now Mr. Ma worked from home and took care of the two children while Mrs. Ma was a busy sales representative in a telecommunication company. I did not meet Mrs. Ma but I met and chatted informally with Mr. Ma many times at school when he came to pick up Kevin.

Andy Lou. Ten-year-old Andy was the second child of his family. His parents immigrated to Canada in the late 1980s. His father, who had a bachelor's degree from Hong Kong, was in the sign business; his mother, who completed a college degree in Canada, had been an accountant for a large firm, but had recently quit her job so that she could have time to supervise her children's study. Andy's sister was 17 years old and was in grade 12 in a nearby high school. Facing graduation and the provincial tests, she was struggling to get by in school, especially in English writing and Math. Her academic skills were far behind those of students who were partially educated in Hong Kong before immigrating to Canada. Her academic failure had made her parents lose their confidence in the public school system. They believed that the public school system had failed to educate their daughter in academic subjects such as writing and math. Both parents were very worried about her future, and were trying to do the right thing for Andy so that he would not have the same fate as his sister.

Jake Wong. Jake was the youngest of the three children. He had two sisters who were in grades 10 and 12. Although his eldest sister was doing well in school, his second sister was struggling. His parents emigrated from Hong Kong in 1981. His mother had a high school education in Canton, China, while his father only had an elementary education from Hong Kong. They now operated a large Chinese restaurant in the busiest business area in Richmond. I met Mr. Wong briefly at the restaurant, and interviewed Mrs. Wong in their family mah jong room at home. Though they had been in Canada for about 20 years, they had not learned English. They had to rely on their children, especially their daughters, to read and translate school documents and newsletters and to represent them at teacher-parent conferences for Jake.

Tina Wei. Tina was a grade 5 student who had been in Canada for 17 months at the time of the study. Different from other Chinese students who were mostly Cantonese speaking and from well-to-do families, Tina's parents were immigrants from Mainland China. Neither of her parents was proficient in English. Her father was working in the kitchen of a Chinese restaurant, and her mother was studying English in a college ESL program. I did not have a chance to interview her parents face-to-face, but was able to have a brief conversation with them on the phone. What I learned about Tina mostly came through my informal conversations with her during my classroom visits.

Xiao-min Ling. Similar to Tina Wei, Xiao-min was one of those students who did not belong to the Cantonese circle. His family, who spoke Mandarin, came from Taiwan in 1995 so that he could have a better education in Canada. His father had a master's degree and was a college professor in Taiwan. Mrs. Ling, who had a college diploma from Taiwan, quit her business management job to come to Canada to take care of Xiao-min while Mr. Ling still taught and resided in Taiwan. Because she was the only parent in Canada, she was extremely nervous about Xiao-min's every move. Every day for five years she came to school during lunchtime and recess (and sometimes during gym classes) to watch Xiao-min or to supervise his lunch. I visited their home, went to the local Buddhist temple with Mrs. Ling, and had lunch with her.

As the profiles demonstrate, all parents were first-generation immigrants. The parents' backgrounds represented a wide range of experiences in Canada. Some were recent immigrants and some had been in Canada for almost 20 years. Although a few parents were fluent in English, most were not, even though they had been in Canada for many years. With few exceptions, most parents had received their education in their countries of origin, had no additional schooling experiences in Canada, and were working within their ethnic economy in Richmond. All families lived in comfortable houses (except for Tina Wei's family, who lived in an apartment) within proximity of the school. Some even lived across the street from the school. All parents reported that Chinese (Mandarin or Cantonese) was their language of interaction at home and in the community, and they had little opportunity to interact with non-Chinese people in their lives. For most parents, their life was no different from where they came from because of the Chinese environment in Richmond.

All families were extremely supportive of their children's education. Some parents even quit their jobs in order to have more time to supervise their children's learning. Although their life was similar to that in their home countries, they were aware of the educational differences, and they were learning to deal with them. Their constant comparison with schools in their countries of origin significantly influenced their perceptions of Canadian schools, the differences between Canada and China, and the strategies they developed to deal with the differences. For example, the parents coped with the differences by either teaching their children themselves at home or sending them to tutoring schools. Their direct instructional approaches, however, were not congruent with the schools' philosophy that learning should take place through experiences and through social interactions.

Although the parents all expressed some positive opinions about Canadian schooling, they also offered direct and indirect critique of some of the differences. In the next chapter, I will describe the literacy instruction at Taylor Elementary, mainly the two teachers' literacy beliefs and practices. I will also present the parents' perceptions and response to these school literacy practices. As their different perspectives will demonstrate, a cultural disjuncture existed between the teachers' and the Chinese parents' literacy values, how literacy should be taught, and the role parents should play in and out of school.

CHAPTER THREE

Literacy and Culture Battles

Teacher Beliefs and Parent Perspectives

"It's hard to get to the Chinese parents," Mrs. Haines told me when I first started the research project in the school, "They're polite to us, but I sense that they don't trust us. It's hard to explain." As I spent more time at the school, I finally understood why Mrs. Haines felt the way she did. During lunchtime every school day, many Chinese parents came to deliver hot lunches to their children because Chinese people believe that cold food is harmful to one's health. Some parents nodded to the teachers but many did not even greet the teachers. Instead, they remained distant and watched their children finish eating from far away and then left the school. Many came back in the afternoon to pick up their children. They waited outside the classroom for their children but did not engage in any conversations with teachers. Ms. Dawson was perplexed by the parents' attitudes, "I don't know what it is, but it doesn't take much to say a simple hello."

Why did the Chinese parents remain so distant to the teachers? Is it true that they distrust the teachers? What are their perspectives on the teachers' literacy practices? After interviewing both teachers and parents, I came to realize that indeed in the peaceful friendly environment at Taylor Elementary, there was an undercurrent of tension between the teachers and the parents. This undercurrent was a result of profound differences in their perspectives on schooling and literacy education, and the roles of parents and schools in the children's education.

I use the term "perspectives" to refer to the teachers' and the parents' thoughts, ideas, and actions in dealing with problematic situations, and their ways of thinking, feeling, and acting in such situations (Becker, Geer, Hughes, & Strauss, 1961; Mead, 1938). This chapter emphasizes the different perspectives between teachers and parents on literacy and education. I begin with a description of their perspectives on the sociocultural contexts in which they were situated. I then present the respective understandings of first and second language literacy instruction, literacy practices at home, and parental involvement at school. As their differences will demonstrate, different from other parents who are marginalized in school and society, the middle-class Chinese parents not only disagreed with school practices, but also placed different demands on the school. In addition, their use of community resources to pursue their own beliefs further complicated their conflicts with the school.

Understanding of the New Sociocultural Context

The complexities of racial, economic, and educational tensions were mirrored in the interactions and negotiations between the two teachers and the Chinese parents. Both Mrs. Haines and Ms. Dawson have experienced a demographic change in their teaching careers. They began their careers by teaching predominantly white students and now found themselves teaching predominantly Chinese students. They themselves had become a minority in an Asian community. They understood that the new Asian immigrants differed from earlier immigrants in that "they came to Canada not because they wanted to," but because they were attracted to the political and social environment in Richmond due to Hong Kong's return to China in 1997. These new immigrants, as the teachers observed, were better off than other immigrant groups: "So they came here, they bought their houses in our area, which is quite an expensive area. They buy fancy new cars," Mrs. Haines noted. She also sensed that this new wave of immigrants had a unique characteristic: "With the people from Hong Kong, they were coming here, not because they were fleeing their homeland forever. It was almost like an insurance policy. We had one woman, she got her Canadian citizenship and left the next day, and she came back once for a short visit. It was just the insurance policy."

This "insurance policy," however, had an impact on the Chinese families' education preferences for their children. Many fathers returned to their country of origin to work while their wives remained in Richmond to raise their children. These close ties with their home country had made the maintenance of Chinese one of their children's educational priorities. As one parent explained, "They're Chinese; they have to learn Chinese for they can't predict whether they'll go back to China or Hong Kong when they grow up." Moreover, the Chinese parents believed that learning Chinese was important because in the future it would be an important world language.

Both teachers had realized that the increase in these new middle-class Chinese immigrants had changed the status quo of the racial divide in the community. Reflecting on being a white minority in an Asian-dominated community, Mrs. Haines detected some reverse racism and admitted that she sometimes felt uncomfortable in the Asian community:

> I think it's almost reversed in some ways. I don't know if my perception is warranted or not. But sometimes I almost feel looked down on, or the clientele that I'm working with feel superior, and it's a funny feeling. I'm not saying that I should feel superior but it's just that there doesn't seem to be any corespect. . . . There are a lot of Caucasian people who feel very uncomfortable in parts of Richmond. There are a lot Caucasian people that would not go to Aberdeen and Yohan Center. They would not feel comfortable there, and they feel discriminated against there. I've heard stories from people [who were] treated badly in the parking lot and not treated well in the shops. Personally I've never had any problem.

Ms. Dawson, on the other hand, did not express this kind of feeling and experiences. She viewed media reports that blamed the new Asian immigrants for the social problems in Canadian society as disrespectful to Chinese culture. "We really benefit from all cultures. We've all come from somewhere . . . none of us were originally from here except for the native people." However, she admitted that she was not blind to the challenges the rapid growth of Asian population had created for educators. Both teachers were well aware of the Chinese community's campaign for more rigorous traditional schooling and their challenge to the public schools' educational practices. Mrs. Haines pointed out that the consequence of the parents' campaign was that "it supports a lot of the myths that are out there about education, and the myth about how the students are not learning to read in public school." She held that "the quality of education, the quality of learning in school is improving." Agreeing with Mrs. Haines, Ms. Dawson viewed the change as a test for both mainstream educators and the Chinese parents: "In general I think that [the Chinese parents] really value education. They have a real belief, strong belief that education is a very important benefit, and it gives you all of the things that you'll need. Educators are being tested by parents' views, different views about education. And parents are being tested because our educational systems are different and it's hard not to be judgmental. Both groups come from different backgrounds, different beliefs."

Because they did not share the same cultural backgrounds with the parents, the two teachers considered themselves as windows to Canadian culture for the Chinese students and their families. Ms. Dawson observed, "There are lots of Chinese families here this year. . . . I think that I'm more of an ambassador for the Canadian culture and Canadian lifestyle than I probably would be in another school. Probably the children and families view white teachers as being sort of, okay, this is what they're like. Maybe that's why they don't question me so much about what I'm doing. Maybe it's like, oh, I guess that's the way they do it here. I don't know."

Parent Perspectives

For the Chinese families, the teachers (and the media) had indeed become ambassadors of the Canadian culture. Some parents such as Mrs. Chan even felt that the school should aim to "be multicultural, but more Western, as this is Canada, and this is not Hong Kong." Many parents in the community working within the ethnic economy had little contact with white or other non-Chinese people. As a parent humorously put it, "We have contact with mainstream society through the school and the tax forms." The Chinese parents who worked in the mainstream economy had some contact with other ethnic groups at work, but very little in the community outside of work. Three of the interviewed parents, for example, said that they worked with Caucasians, but never socialized with any. None of the focal children played with children from other cultural groups outside of school. The school, therefore, became the only place where the Chinese children had close contact with peers from other cultures and with Caucasian teachers.

The parents interviewed all considered themselves as sojourners and the Canadian society as "the white people's society," as Mrs.

Chan put it. Her description of the Chinese in Canada was very typical among the Chinese parents: "It's like when you go to a friend's house, you know who is the host and who is the guest. You don't jump in and take over. . . . You don't complain and you don't want to take charge."

The parents commented that discrimination existed in the society. The parents who worked in the mainstream economy observed that for Asians, it was hard to get ahead in companies run by white Canadians, as the mainstream group sought to protect itself from other minority groups. Mr. Ma elaborated this point by comparing Canadian society to Hong Kong society: "In Hong Kong, if you can't do this job, you can do another. Even when I open a small shop, I can still earn more money than here. Here, you have no choices. If you can't do this job, you have to choose the worst one. As I have said just now, there's discrimination from the mainstream society. Asians don't belong to the mainstream society, so it's hard for us to get the same pay as them. Even if you do the same job as them, you can't get the same pay."

Some parents quit their jobs because of perceived racism and discrimination. Like many immigrants reported in previou research studies, these parents also believed that education was their children's ticket to counteract this discrimination (G. Li, 2000; Ogbu, 1978). They believed that the situation was getting better because their children would be educated here in the host society and would be more empowered by their education. Mr. Ma suggested that hope lay in the next generation, such as his son: "I think we have to wait for the next generation to do so. For the next generation who are born here, they will not allow the situation to continue. They will not understand why they do the same jobs while [getting] lower pay. They will not allow such racial discrimination. But for us, we can't ask for more."

Almost all parents expected their children to pursue higher education in the future, and becoming proficient in English was the top priority in their children's education. At the same time, they also wanted their children to be able to speak and become literate in their first language, Chinese. Therefore, the new Chinese immigrants wanted their children to be bilingual and biliterate and to be prepared for both the English and Chinese worlds. These double aspirations posed many challenges for the two teachers, who were held accountable for the children's English instruction.

Dealing with Chinese in School

In talking with the students, Mrs. Haines and Ms. Dawson concluded that the school was the only place where the Chinese children were exposed to English. They observed that outside of school, many of the children got very little exposure to English, or Canadian culture, because, as Mrs. Haines explained, "Everything is in Chinese when they go home—they listen to Chinese radio, watch Chinese TV, and they play Chinese video games." The teachers saw the children's oral and written language experiences in Chinese as detrimental to their learning English. Similar to many mainstream teachers reported in research, both teachers believed the best way was through English immersion (Ashworth, 2001; Fránquiz & Reyes, 1998; Valdés, 1998). As Ms. Dawson states, "Being immersed in English is really the best way. It's how you learn any language the best. I think that children who're learning English as a second language are better immersed when there are not other children who speak their first language."

Mrs. Haines and Ms. Dawson, together with other teachers in the school, believed that too many Chinese-speaking children in one school presented a disadvantage for the Chinese students in learning English. The teachers thought that speaking too much Chinese in and out of school contributed to the students' low performance in English. The ESL/resource teacher, Mrs. Smith, who helped Ms. Dawson's class, explained that "the children who don't speak Chinese learn very quickly. . . . The ones who speak Cantonese can spend forever learning it because they always have somebody to speak Cantonese to." Mrs. Smith also noticed the differences between Cantonese speakers and Mandarin speakers from Taiwan and Mainland China. She observed that many Mandarin speakers often chose not to speak Mandarin to each other and therefore learned English much faster. Giving Tina Wei as an example, she said, "Look at Tina, she made so much progress this year. She just doesn't participate when they talk in Chinese. I think she'll be OK."

To better engage the students in an immersion environment, both teachers enforced the English-only policy in their classrooms. Whenever they heard students speaking their first language in the hallway, the two teachers and others would remind the students that it was an English-only environment, and ask them to try to speak English as much as they could. Both teachers communicated this message to the parents through report cards.

However, in both teachers' classes, the Cantonese-speaking students significantly outnumbered children who did not speak Cantonese, and many students chose to speak Cantonese during unstructured class time, especially in Ms. Dawson's grade 4/5 classroom. This made the teachers feel even more responsible for encouraging the students to use more English in school. Ms. Dawson explained, "Unless teachers or people in their lives really push them, they really don't have to challenge themselves to learn more English or to improve their English because they can communicate well enough with the people who speak English and they got lots of people that they can communicate with in their first language."

Although Mrs. Haines and Ms. Dawson saw the children's constant use of their first language as a hindrance to their acquisition of English, both strongly believed that it was important for the children to maintain their first language. Mrs. Haines noted, "When they go to Chinese school on the weekends, I don't dissuade the parents from taking them to that. If I see the child is really overprogrammed, I would ask them to drop the English classes and the Kuman math classes—sort of rote-learning kinds of things; I know that they'll get it at school. But keeping their own language and keeping their understanding of their own culture, I think that's very important."

Ms. Dawson also stressed the significance of being able to function in two languages and two cultures for the students. However, she was quite aware that the Chinese parents wanted their children to learn English, and if that did not happen she was held accountable for it. She expressed her conflicting thoughts at length:

> I really think that children need to feel comfortable speaking their first language. . . . We need to make sure that that is communicated to the parents and children and that it's really important that you learn your first language. But as an educator who's teaching in an English system where there are a whole variety of children, there has to be a time, I feel, that it's agreed that you speak English. Or at least you try to speak in English, because for some of those children their English is not improving. . . . There are several in my class who had been at an English-speaking school for many years and yet they're not making progress—and I'm accountable for that. I don't want to be construed as being a teacher who punishes children for speaking their first language, because I

really value that first language. But I'm accountable for teaching them English. I'm not accountable for teaching them Chinese or Hindi or whatever language. So I'm torn. I've tried with this class to press upon them the need that they really practice their English, because all of their parents want them to learn English. They all live in an English-speaking country. But when it comes right down to it, a good group of them are just ignoring me in my own class. So it got to the point where I thought, I've got to be taken seriously here. Since I've said that you'll get this detention, I don't have any kids [who] have to stay after school.

Ms. Dawson did not feel good about using detention as a measure for getting the students to use English at school, but she felt that as an English teacher who was responsible for the children's English learning, she had to. She further explained her feelings: "In our school the language that we all have in common is English. But I'm really torn here because I don't want to be punishing children for speaking their first language. But when it comes down to it if they don't learn English, who is going to get blamed? Where is the buck going to stop? Seven years from now when they're graduating from high school and they still can't write fairly well in English and their oral English is not very good. Then of course it's the education system that has failed them."

However, both found it hard to maintain the English-only rule, especially when they had new students with no prior English backgrounds. Mrs. Haines occasionally allowed some students to explain class instruction to new students in Chinese. She explained:

We try to encourage them to speak Chinese in situations where it's educationally beneficial. . . . They need to practice English because I know they need to be fluent enough to understand the concepts and work through those concepts in English. But with Kara and Alicia, and even Alana, sometimes they need to work through those concepts in Chinese because if they don't, they won't get anything out of it if they are forced to speak English. When they don't have any English language yet, and they don't get that English language through the chart work, the stories and songs, they still need to speak in Chinese to each other to clarify it. So, it's constantly a judgment call of whether or not they should be speaking English when they're working at the tables.

In Ms. Dawson's class, for example, two new Chinese students who could not speak any English constantly conversed in Chinese, sometimes loudly, and disrupted the class activities. Ms. Dawson had to constantly separate them and assign them different tasks (for example, one on the computer playing word games and the other one coloring) so that they would not disrupt the class. Ms. Dawson felt the English-only rule was more problematic for her older students: "I think it's a little frustrating for children coming to learn English. The older they are the more frustrating it is for them. . . . The gap is much narrower in a young child learning English, whereas with a 13-year-old, we were trying to modify and adapt what we could in the classroom for him in terms of his ability to understand what we were saying and what we were asking him to do. But there's only so much that you can do within a regular classroom and still have that 13-year-old feel like [he is] a contributing member of the class."

Maybe because of the age difference, I observed that in Mrs. Haines's classroom fewer students spoke their first language during class time. If some students spoke Chinese, other Chinese-speaking students in her class would remind them of the English-only rule. Before I knew about this rule, I talked with Alana, one of the focal children, in Chinese since she was not yet fluent in English. Sandy, another focal student, would come over to remind me, "Miss Li, Chinese is not allowed here. You should speak English." However, in Ms. Dawson's class many Cantonese-speaking students and the new Mandarin-speaking students frequently spoke Chinese, regardless of whether it was structured or unstructured class time, even though they knew the English-only policy. These students were often perceived as slow in learning English. Sometimes some non-Chinese students would protest, especially during some class discussions, "English please! I don't understand what you're saying!"

Parent Perspectives

All the parents agreed with the teachers that students should learn English at school since it was an English school. All parents endorsed the English-only policy in the school and supported the idea that in

English school the children should speak English and in Chinese school they should speak Chinese. As one parent put it, "It's good for teachers to teach and for students to learn English faster." Several families even thought of moving to another area where "they have less Chinese there in school."

As described earlier, the Chinese parents wanted their children to learn both languages. Most of the parents viewed Chinese as important for their children's future as well as for intergenerational communication, and accepted responsibility for maintaining the Chinese language. Most parents sent their children to a weekend Chinese heritage language school if they did not have time to teach them at home. And as the teachers understood it, the parents perceived teaching English as the responsibility of the school.

However, many ESL students did not perform at their grade level in English and other core subject areas (for example, math education was perceived by the parents to be two grades behind students in Asia). The parents often blamed the school system for the students' low performance. For example, the parents believed that the students were given too much freedom to choose what they wanted to do, including speaking Chinese at school. Some blamed the combined class structure, but more often, they questioned the teachers' instructional practices. In the next section, I describe the two teachers' perspectives on their instructional practices for teaching these ESL children, as well as the differences of opinion the parents had about these practices and the actions the parents employed to deal with the differences.

English Literacy and Instruction

In terms of actual language and literacy instruction, the two teachers believed that there was no difference between ESL learning and first language learning because children who learned to read and write in any language followed the same pattern. Therefore, both teachers adopted the same progressive methods they used to teach English to first language children. Mrs. Haines strongly opposed a traditional, structured, back-to-basics approach to language and literacy instruction, and advocated a language-experience approach to literacy. Ms. Dawson adopted a literature-based approach in which she used more challenging novels as a starting point for reading and writing instruction. Since both teachers realized that it took more time for the students to develop vocabulary, they both incorporated phonics and spelling in their instruction to consistently work at vocabulary building.

*Mrs. Haines's Literacy Beliefs and Instruction
in Her Grade 1/2 Classroom*

Mrs. Haines defined literacy as reading, writing, and "verbal literacy in which children are required to be able to communicate." Her language-experience approach to literacy instruction encouraged children to have "a great deal of experience with story, song, and poetry," and "they must dance, sing, and play with words and dwell in stories" (personal communication, Jan. 28, 2003). She believed that this approach was particularly effective for ESL children, "because you're using all sorts of cues: you're using picture cues, a lot of action and dramatization, and in reading and writing, there are lots of patterns and repetition, and they're taking meaning from their knowledge base." Mrs. Haines considered it crucial to learning to be grounded in meaning: "I like the whole-to-parts philosophy rather than the looking at the tiny letter and sound pieces first, because I think research says that most children, about 80%, don't need that little tiny phonetic instruction. For the small number of students that do need it, I think that should be grounded in a meaningful chunk of language so that they can relate to it in a meaningful way rather than just by rote, because if they learn by rote, it's not going to be like embedded learning. That's just going to be surface learning. That's when they forget learning. But in deep learning, meaning-based learning, they really learn it."

Mrs. Haines held that learning should be driven by children's interests and should be facilitated by the teacher rather than the other way around: "I think the program should fit the child rather than the child fit the program." She strongly opposed scripted, structured literacy instructional programs such as "Open Court" and "Reading Mastery" that were used in a few inner-city public schools and received a considerable amount of media attention for their purported success (Steffenhagen, 2001). She believed that such programs "dissolve pedagogy, stifle creativity and turn teachers into technicians" (personal communication, Jan. 28, 2003).

Mrs. Haines told me during our first interview that her belief about experience and meaning was heavily influenced by her own "pioneer background" of growing up in a mining community in northern Canada: "My grandfather on my mother's side was a blacksmith and a farmer. If they didn't have something, he went to the blacksmith shop and made it. My grandfather on my father's side was a Northwestern Mounted Policeman. They had to create what they needed. I guess it was like that in all cultures. That seems to be the stronger core I learned, and it just became a part of an integrated class-room curriculum."

Her beliefs about early literacy education were also shaped by her experiences in her undergraduate education in the early 1970s. "The delivery has evolved but the philosophy has not been changed," said Mrs. Haines during our first interview. In her paper on philosophy of education, an undergraduate paper she produced in 1973, she wrote, "In order to achieve this end, children have to have endless opportunities to think, to interact with their environment, and to solve their own problems." In this paper, she suggested several principles of open classroom instruction including child centeredness, a relaxed setting, establishment of a play atmosphere, and flexibility—a flexible skeletal plan that accommodates different interest and progress, and emphasis on the process of learning rather than isolated facts. These principles were evident in Mrs. Haines's instructional approach in the classroom. Her language experience approach was reflected in three kinds of daily literacy events: the morning routine, story reading and response, and chapter book reading.

The morning routine that began after a daily 15-minute silent reading period included a calendar activity (for students to figure out the date and day of the week), "Question of the Day" answer count (to do addition and subtraction), and a salutation reading (to read and learn vocabulary). During the calendar activity, a student would help carry out the routine in which the students supplied the day and the date for the calendar in front of the class. The activity usually started with a prompt from Mrs. Haines, such as "Yesterday was?" The class supplied the answer, and Mrs. Haines continued with another prompt: "What day is today?" After the correct day and date were identified, the class read together the sentence, "Today is Wednesday, November 22, 2000." At the end of this activity a math problem would be interjected that used sticks that stood for different values. For example, a question might be, "Today is November 22, 2000. If I was born in 1950, how old am I?" The class would work together to figure out the answer using the sticks.

After the calendar routine, the class moved to the "Question of the Day" answer count. The question was usually written on the blackboard with a "yes" and a "no" column under the question. Every day the question varied and might be related to the project they were to do that day, or homework, or a school task. Some examples of the questions include: "Can you name one thing about Richmond?" "Did you bring $7.25 for the field trip today?" "Did you bring some food for the Richmond Food Bank?" "Do you think the gingerbread people will run away today?" Mrs. Haines recorded the students' answers in the respective columns on the blackboard and used them as a basis for math. She asked the class to count the numbers together, figuring out how many said "yes" and how many said "no" and then used addition and subtraction to figure out how many students were in class that day and how many were not.

This math activity was followed by "salutations," an activity that involved reading and writing. Mrs. Haines wrote the message on the blackboard prior to the class, and used it as the planner of the day. I will use an example from November 23, 2000, to illustrate this activity. The salutation was written as follows:

> Yesterday we did a self-portrait of ourselves. Today we will draw another picture for our eco-pals. Some of us will draw a picture of the courtyard. Some will draw a picture of the classroom. Some will draw the playground. Some will draw the school. The portrait will tell them about you, and other pictures will tell them about the school and the *community*.

Mrs. Haines usually asked individual students to read the sentences and explain the new concepts introduced in the message (which were often underlined). In the above message, the new concept was "community." After the students went through the message sentence by sentence, the class read the message chorally several times.

These "salutations" usually encompassed the major reading and writing activities of the day which were most reflective of Mrs. Haines's language-experience approach to instruction. Students usually were presented with a real-life task such as the one presented in the above "salutations"—to write to their eco pals in Saskatchewan about their school. They first listened to a story to enrich their understanding of the task. Mrs. Haines read to the class a story entitled *A Prairie Boy's Summer*, by Kurelek (1998). After reading she discussed concepts about Saskatchewan that the students were unaware of. A student mentioned a wheelbarrow race in the story:

> Mrs. Haines: Has anyone seen any wheelbarrow race?
> Students (laughing): No!
> Lucy: My mom told me a story when she uses a wheelbarrow
>   in her garden.

Lynne: My friend and I took some dirt in the barrow and put the dirt in the garden. That's it.

Mrs. Haines: Life in Saskatchewan is quite different, isn't it? What questions are you going to ask your pen pals?

Anthony: Do you live on a farm?

Kevin: Have you milked a cow?

Lucy: Have you rode on a horse before?

After reading the story and discussing it, Mrs. Haines brainstormed with the class about what they could write to their eco pals regarding their school. Based on the ideas generated by brainstorming, she divided the class into four groups: the classroom, the school, the playground, and the courtyard groups. Each group walked around the school to collect information for their letter to their eco pals. After they came back from their short excursion in the school, they sat down in groups at the round tables to write their letters. Mrs. Haines modeled a letter format on the blackboard for the students. After they finished their writing and drawing, Mrs. Haines and her assistant sat down with each child to discuss the child's drawing and wrote down a description of the pictures. These writings were later mailed to their pen pals.

Mrs. Haines's classes were always conducted around a real-life activity. The students seemed to enjoy these real-life activities and were always very enthusiastic in participating in them. For example, in order to write about the community, Mrs. Haines took the class on a field trip to a historical site in Richmond. To learn about the gingerbread man story, the class baked real gingerbread in the school's kitchen and each student designed a plan for gingerbread man's getaway. To learn about Hanukkah, Mrs. Haines invited a Jewish colleague to the class to dance, demonstrate the Menorah candle lighting, and serve latke. For Christmas, they made Christmas decorations. Mrs. Haines also integrated different genres of readings into these experiences, such as Christmas songs, nursery rhymes, poetry, information books, and storybooks. These activities, which focused mostly on holidays and celebrations, reflected Mrs. Haines's contributions approach to the students' diversity (Banks, 2002).

In the afternoons when several lower-level ESL students were pulled out of class for small group ESL instruction, Mrs. Haines usually read the class a chapter from *Elmer and the Dragon* (Gannett, 1987), a book from the *Blueland Dragon* book series. This was a typical story-reading activity during which Mrs. Haines constantly asked the class many comprehension questions and asked the children to predict what would happen next in the story. Students were then asked to draw and write about the story they had listened to. After each student finished drawing and writing, Mrs. Haines and her assistant again sat down with each student to listen to the description of what the child had drawn or written based on the story reading.

Parent Perspectives

Many parents were especially pleased with the multinational festival, hands-on experiences that Mrs. Haines provided besides the Chinese New Year's festival, such as the Jewish festival. They regarded it important that the school respect other cultures. However, Mrs. Haines's experience-based approach was novel to the Chinese parents, who were more familiar with a traditional teacher-centered instructional approach. The parents interviewed all saw that this "learn it yourself gradually through experience" method had merits for children as it "is very practical. You learn through doing it." However, several parents pointed out that the method might be problematic for many children. Mr. Ma explained, "For example, the kids are required to read the newspaper today. If there's something useful in it, then the kids will learn to speak English gradually. If there's nothing useful or special in it, then they'll not learn to use it. What the teacher teaches is very practical, and the knowledge will enter the kids' mind gradually. If the kid is willing to learn, then such a system is good. But I think the problem with the system is that it can't ensure every kid learn."

Mr. Ma also thought that the method could be limiting because of the lack of direct instruction: "The teaching method here is to teach a child how to manage learning himself, and to master it himself. It's useless if you ask a child to read so much. But if you teach him how and he can go look for the material he needs and is able to search it himself, then what he can read has no limit, because what you can teach him is limited."

Though he thought that encouraging a child to learn independently was good, Mr. Ma cautioned that it might be dangerous for kids who do not have the autonomy to learn: "Here it requires the child to learn by himself. It works if the child wants to learn or someone forces him to learn. But if a child doesn't want to learn or doesn't have the autonomy, then he will not be able to learn. . . . The learning gradually through one's own experience, if the child can absorb the method, it's good. If the child can't adapt to the method, then he will suffer."

For these reasons, the parents, including Mr. Ma, preferred a traditional school if one was available, "While in the traditional school, every kid will be forced to learn, to follow a schedule." Mr. Ma believed that it was more important to use traditional methods in the primary grades so that kids can lay a firm foundation and develop good study habits early on: "I think to develop good habits is very important for the kids. It's not good if the kids are given too much freedom and too little discipline. If the kid is good, then there's no problem with him. But if the kid is naughty, he won't form good study habits."

In addition to traditional teacher-led instruction and discipline, the parents also advocated for other aspects of traditional schooling. For example, they suggested that students should wear uniforms and the school should have single-grade classes. In terms of wearing uniforms, Mrs. Chan reasoned, "I would like them to wear uniforms actually because when we were in Hong Kong, we all had to wear uniforms. And I think it's for tidiness and for discipline. Now they're wearing sweatshirts, and whatever. I think they'll be more respectful for going to school."

All parents were against combined classes and had talked with the school about it, but this was never changed. Mrs. Chan and her husband, who along with the others did not support the idea when it started many years ago, expressed their disagreement with the school practice: "Actually we didn't agree with [putting] grade 1 and 2 together when it started many years ago. We didn't have children at that time. We found the idea very strange at that time. But now we have to accept it because [it's] the school system here, because we can't figure out why [and] how grade 1 can learn with grade 2. I know they are talking about grade 2 will be able to help grade 1. But I don't totally agree with the concept whether you agree or not."

In addition to supporting these perspectives, the parents interviewed also interpreted the different language experiences at school as "too much play." They thought that it was more relaxed for the children to learn through "play" in Canada, while in Hong Kong "it was formal: you go to school, you listen to the teacher," as Mrs. Chan said. Mrs. Chung worried that "some kids don't know whether it's play or study. Some end up not learning much." Similarly, Mr. Tang thought that "they draw too much at school" and "the teachers just want students to have more freedom to choose what they want to do." According to Mrs. Haines, several parents who recently came from Hong Kong went to her to express concern that their children were not learning adequate vocabulary and were not speaking English, and asked for more traditional ways of teaching beginning reading, that is, to teach systematically, from letters and sounds, to words, and then to sentences. Some even provided Mrs. Haines with a wordlist to prove that the children knew more words previously in Hong Kong than they did now in Canada. I was told that these concerns were the reasons why the parents chose to emphasize more academic aspects at home.

Mrs. Haines understood the parents' concerns, and pointed out to the parents that "the words were not related. They were not based on experience and meaning." She stated, "I'm not willing to compromise on what I see as objective learning, authentic, happy, healthy, and deep learning for the children. I'm not going to compromise to appease the parents." Instead, she decided to "try and show them that we are doing the things that help their children learn." However, Mrs. Haines did make some compromises—she incorporated phonics time in her instruction. For each phonics lesson, Mrs. Haines focused on one or two letters and the corresponding sounds. She first brainstormed words with the letters and sounds and recorded them on a Post-It. She explained to the students how to pronounce the sounds and the words, and then asked them to copy two words and make sentences with the words or draw pictures about the words in their phonics books. She told me during our second interview, "Because a lot of parents worry that their children aren't getting phonics, I make sure that that's obvious in the classroom and in the program, and they have this spelling book and spelling test."

However, Mrs. Haines did not support the parents' segmented phonics approach; nor did she want phonics to be the dominant literacy instruction. Similar to many progressive educators, she believed that "for children to become fluent readers, phonics and phonological awareness must be woven into language and instruction in a child-centered, meaningful context." In her opinion, this way of teaching phonics would enhance students' learning: "Last year when we were working on the /sh/ sound, one of the kids said 'chamish,' so they remembered it, and it sort of comes up. I guess the way I teach it, I don't teach in a unit and then we're done, it's more like weaving. The concepts, and the learning comes up again and again throughout the year. It's not just, OK, done that and we finished, and we move on—everything is on a continuum."

To educate the Chinese parents who pushed for traditional schools or traditional approaches to literacy instruction, Mrs. Haines posted several of her educational philosophies on her classroom door so that the parents could read them when they came to pick up their children. In one of the messages, she stressed her stance on education: "Effective learning in the classroom must be in sync with the learning experiences in the real world. Instructional plans will not work effectively if they are tight, contrived or artificial."

Many parents were also worried about math instruction. Mrs. Haines's math curriculum was integrated into different literacy activities, and this integration was very different from the Chinese practice of teaching Math separately and as one of the core subjects. Although Mrs. Haines did not follow a traditional curriculum, her instruction covered a wide range of areas such as subtraction, addition (including three-digit addition), and measurement. Many of her math activities were related to real-life problem solving. For example, to teach the children how to measure, Mrs. Haines planted an amaryllis in the classroom and the students' task was to measure its growth each day. The Chinese parents did not view this kind of "fun" math activity as serious instruction of math. They often compared math instruction with that in their home countries, and said that math education in Canada was two grades behind that in Hong Kong and China. Many parents chose to teach math at home using textbooks from their home countries, since most of them could manage to teach their children math at this level. Since both of Anthony Chan's parents worked full time, they sent him to a math school once a week. Later when Mrs. Haines advised them to drop the math class, Mr. Chan decided to teach Anthony math himself at home.

Ms. Dawson's Literacy Beliefs and Instruction
in Her Grade 4/5 Classroom

Ms. Dawson defined literacy as "the ability to use and understand language in all of its forms, written, oral, spoken, visual, and kinesthetic, and how one strand affects another." She also emphasized that "it is how we communicate, how literate we are in our understanding and in our ability to communicate what we know." Different from Mrs. Haines's language-experience approach, Ms. Dawson adopted a literature-based approach to literacy: "We have such a wealth of very good literature and children are really getting engaged in good stories, good books, good nonfiction. I think using that as the base for learning to read and learning more about the world [is] really important."

Ms. Dawson also believed in an "integrated process of learning." She suggested that when students were excited about reading, a teacher should really nurture that strength. The teacher should "make connections for [students] between what they're learning in terms of their reading and what they're learning in terms of expressing their ideas in written form or orally, or whether it's role-playing." She regarded reading as the most significant literacy activity, and believed that students should be challenged "to read and listen to stories and books that are perhaps a little bit higher reading level than where they're at, what their comfort level is." She strongly felt that in the past teachers had been inclined to pigeonhole children in terms of their reading ability and did not think students could read difficult books. In her opinion, challenging children "encourages them to challenge themselves and choose their own books to read." Ms. Dawson's literature-based approach was most evident in her read-aloud activity and the literature circle activity.

For their daily read-aloud activity after recess in the first semester, Ms. Dawson chose a novel about bats, *Silver Wing* (Oppel, 1999), to read to the class. She first asked the students to summarize what had happened in the story with a few sentences, following the cues or key words she wrote on the blackboard. After this reviewing activity, she read a chapter or several pages to the class and then asked the class comprehension questions about the reading. I observed that the students were attentive to the story during the reading, and were generally quiet during the discussion. They mostly tried to answer the questions initiated by Ms. Dawson. During our first interview, Ms. Dawson explained that the novel was challenging to the class as "there might have been two children in the class that would have been able to read that and really understand it." And as she read more to the class and became more involved in the discussion, she realized that "there were still lots of children who were not really fully understanding it." However, she believed that the students were able to understand at different levels: "Whether they were able to understand all the nuances of the story itself, there was something in that story that each individual could relate to in some way." After she finished reading the novel, she asked the class to design a cover and write their own reviews and endorsements for the book. The students were very enthusiastic about the project and produced excellent artwork. Their covers were later displayed on the walls of the classroom.

For the second semester, Ms. Dawson replaced the read-aloud activity with literature circles. She first took a week to explain and familiarize students with the six different roles (discussion director, connector, word hunter, artful illustrator, passage picker, and friend of the character) in the literature circle group. Then she divided the class into four groups that read four chapter books, *Amazing Grace* (Hoffman & Binch, 1991), *Stone Fox* (Gardiner & Sewall, 1980), *George's Marvelous Medicine* (Dahl & Blake, 1991), and *The Magic Finger* (Dahl & Blake, 1995). Students did their assigned readings and prepared their roles for homework, and discussed their readings in class. These novels also appeared to be above many students' reading level. Ms. Dawson rotated around the class to help each group with their discussion. However, as she noted, only one group might be "getting it" and the rest of the groups were "not as strong." I noted that many students did not complete their role descriptions in their homework books, and the discussion often revolved around who did not do their homework or bring their books. As a result, they were seldom on task and often drifted into arguing in Chinese. Ms. Dawson did not make many comments or suggestions on students' written work; many times she wrote, "Fill up the page" but did not provide students with any suggestions on how to expand their ideas.

For the second semester, Ms. Dawson also incorporated a writer's workshop in which she guided students through the seven steps of writing: topic search, prewriting, drafting, conferencing, editing (self, peer, and teacher editing), proofreading, and publishing. Students were asked to choose their topics. Once their topic was chosen, Ms. Dawson asked the students to use mapping skills to brainstorm ideas about the topic. Students would then proceed with writing their first draft. Ms. Dawson read the first draft and conferenced with each student about their writing. Students revised their first drafts and then typed their stories into the computer for publishing. This writing process, which allowed students to develop their own interests, was a very effective way to engage students in writing. Even some of the weak students could write much longer and better pieces.

Ms. Dawson's integrated process of literacy learning was also reflected in her instruction of math, social studies, and science content areas. For a unit on Canadian history in social studies, she first assigned readings on the Canadian fur trade, and then took students on a field trip to a fort that was a historic fur trading post. After the field trip, students wrote about their experiences and made connections between their field experiences and their readings. As Ms. Dawson noted, the students "read every day, they have silent reading every morning. And there is always some writing going on, whether it's within a language arts activity or whether it's in science or social studies." For these activities, Ms. Dawson appeared to see her role as a facilitator of learning: she seldom offered direct instruction; rather, she allowed students to work independently or in groups to construct their own literacy (J. Anderson & Gunderson, 1997).

Besides these reading and writing practices, Ms. Dawson had some routine spelling and vocabulary activities throughout the school year. She pretested the students at the beginning of the school year and found great variability among their spelling skills: "There are some students whose spelling is probably at grade 8 or grade 7 at least, and there are other children whose spelling is [at] grade 2 level." She devoted about one hour each morning to spelling, using the spelling program she had been using for the past several years. Each morning after math time or a math quiz was spelling time. Students worked in pairs to check each other's spelling using a master wordlist Ms. Dawson handed out. Ms. Dawson generated these wordlists from spelling programs at different grade levels and mixed them to accommodate students of different spelling skills. The wordlists, randomly grouped, were glued onto the front of the students' spelling books, and students worked with these master wordlists for the rest of the year. Based on the words they misspelled on the pretest, some children had many words on their spelling lists. The more advanced students did not have many words at all.

Ms. Dawson also gave the class four challenging words taken from math, science, or social studies. The students had to master these four words and copy them into their spelling workbooks. On Fridays they usually had a spelling quiz on these words, together with several words studied during the week. After the spelling time, students were given a worksheet to work on independently. These worksheets, taken from *Grade 5 Spelling Skills and Drills* (Ketchum, 1997), were about the spelling of different sounds related to certain general spelling rules, or phonetic groupings such as words with -or, -ar, and -er endings, the sound of the letter k, or prefixes and suffixes such as "-ness," or "-ly." The worksheets mostly required tasks such as filling in the blanks with the words provided.

Ms. Dawson did not offer any direct instruction for these activities either. She explained that "it's not in a direct instructional way, but

I hope that those who're having difficulty would seek some assistance." Many students asked for assistance during these activities, and many appeared to have difficulty understanding the instructions on the activity sheets. Several students told me that they "hated" studying the words and completing these worksheets. One student commented, "It's dumb."

Ms. Dawson firmly believed spelling was significant for children's studies in the higher grades and was looking into "making the program more individualized" to meet the needs of different students. "I think there's a concern about spelling in our society. I think it's very important." She further commented, "Usually the better spellers are generally the better writers. The more exposure you get to written words, the more familiar you become with how to spell those words." She explained that there was a huge misconception about whole language:

> Some teachers had this impression that they didn't have to teach spelling, that spelling was just going to happen, and that children would just learn how to spell. And then there are those parents, and people outside of the education system who looked at what was happening in classrooms and went, "Where is the spelling program? I don't see my child coming home with spelling words every week." Because it didn't look like it always looked before, they made an assumption that spelling wasn't deemed to be important. And by far the majority of people that I know who are teachers never threw spelling out of as being unimportant. I mean nobody thinks that. Really, it's just how you teach it in a meaningful way.

Although Ms. Dawson spent a lot of time on spelling, she also realized that there were many other important skills, such as "skills that go with reading and writing, and all the skills that go with math, all the understanding of social studies and science concepts." She understood that it was important to find "a balance, trying to keep all those balls in the air at the same time." However, she noted that teaching as a generalist at the elementary level can be difficult: "It's a juggling act and often the balls do end up on the floor because they just sometimes do."

Parent Perspectives

Although Ms. Dawson spent some time on vocabulary, which she thought was a weakness of the students, her effort went unnoticed by the parents. Several parents noted that there were only a couple of pages of spelling lists sent home. "It's not enough," Mrs. Ling told me. "The kids can't read and write." Because of the greater demands on reading and writing at this level, the parents were more concerned with grammar instruction. They realized that although their children might be able to speak fluent English, they could not read or write grammatically correct English, and they had to take the provincial Foundation Skills Assessment exams, which required strong reading and writing skills. Mrs. Ling told me that among all the subjects, English (in terms of grammar and writing) was her son's weakest subject: "They don't teach grammar at school."

The parents expressed concern over Ms. Dawson's literature-based approach because it did not have a standard textbook or offer explicit instruction to reading and writing. Mrs. Chung told me about her frustration with the indirect approach to reading instruction: "The teacher only gives [students] books to read. Let them do it themselves. But she doesn't explain the books to them in class. So my husband and I have to teach him one on one." The parents wanted more traditional whole-class instruction where the teachers use the same textbook with all students, and explain to students, line-by-line or paragraph-by-paragraph; the teacher should read to the class, ask the class to repeat after her, or ask a group to read together orally. Based on her experiences while learning English, Mrs. Lou, who was the most outspoken parent, also suggested that the school needed to establish language labs so that students could learn and enhance their English through tapes and video recordings.

Similarly, the parents criticized the school's indirect approach to writing. During our interview, Mrs. Lou expressed her anger about the school's approach to writing:

> I don't think they teach writing. They ask kids to write but they didn't teach writing. Asking the kids to write doesn't mean you teach them. They ask you to write several [paragraphs], but how to write, they didn't [teach]. This is the subject I; this is the verb, run, I run; this is the object, they didn't.

How to produce the things, no. How to express the things, how to express more, to put more adjectives in, to put more adverbs in, to make the sentences look more full, more fluent, no. They ask the kids to do that. They thought from reading the book themselves, I emphazise "themselves," they should know. But no, I don't think they should know. They know it because their family, their parents read with them. They know because the parents have a tutor for them.

Another concern among the parents was about the disjuncture between the primary grades and grade 4 in terms of correcting writing errors. Most of them believed that grammatical errors should be consistently corrected from early on, but they discovered that there was a gap in school practices. Mrs. Lou expressed this concern: "Generally in school in grades 1, 2, and 3 they don't correct students' errors in writing. The teachers said that it'll discourage their thinking. If you're not pointing out [errors], you're not punishing them for making these errors. But my son is in grade 4 now, and Ms. Dawson thought that he should have perfect English. He has to proofread his paragraph. One teacher does that in previous grades—now you want him to write perfect English, [and] proofread his own work?"

Besides these concerns, many parents also raised other instructional concerns that they perceived to have a negative impact on the students' learning, including the previously mentioned combined classes, group seating arrangements, and other issues such as a lack of student uniforms. Thus, the parents in Ms. Dawson's class also sent their children to various after-school classes to enhance their learning. They believed that these after-school studies were effective in complementing what was lacking or ineffective in the school.

In sum, Mrs. Haines and Ms. Dawson had respectively adopted a language-experience and a literature-based approach to literacy instruction. However, these methods were not well received by the Chinese parents, who favored more traditional approaches to literacy instruction. The Chinese parents therefore enrolled their children in different after-school tutoring classes to make up for what they considered to be missing in the public school. As the following section will demonstrate, the teachers who believed in a more holistic approach to learning considered these classes, together with some other aspects of the Chinese home literacy practices, as counterproductive to the children's learning.

Students' After-School Literacy Learning

Although Mrs. Haines and Ms. Dawson regarded Chinese parents as being supportive of their children's education and having extremely high expectations of their children, they did not agree with the approaches at home. Both teachers were aware that the Chinese parents wanted traditional literacy instruction and had enrolled their children in a variety of study activities such as attending math and English classes, Chinese school, and piano lessons. Ms. Dawson interpreted this as a supply-and-demand phenomenon: "There's a demand by Asian families, Chinese families . . . but they were not there to do it for them or with them, so good entrepreneurs and some companies can meet that demand." She did not see the phenomenon as the Chinese parents' distrust of the public schools; rather she regarded it as a safety net for the families to protect what they regarded as important since they moved from one country to another. She noted, "I don't think that they're saying that we don't value what's happening in school and that we don't trust that you're going to teach our children. [They're] just not quite sure what this [Canadian school] all looks like."

Mrs. Haines, who had more direct contact with the parents, did not share Ms. Dawson's optimism and saw it as parental distrust. A parent wrote to her that the parents' rationale for sending their children to the after-school classes was "to provide something that [is] missing in our existing public school system." Mrs. Haines was afraid that the school was going to lose out in this "invasion" of the Chinese parents' traditional school campaign, as many students took their after-school classes more seriously than their regular classes at school. She described one of the incidents she had with students:

> When we were learning about magnets, I sent home a sheet and kids were to go around their home and find out all the ways magnets were used in their home. And it didn't come back. I asked one of the little guys in my class, "Why didn't you do this?" He said, "I had to do my homework." I said, "This is your homework." He said, "No, I had to do my other homework." He was going to math classes and several classes after school, so he had homework from them so he couldn't do school homework. The other homework came first. He didn't do his school homework and it was not such

a big deal; but if he didn't do the other homework he'd be in trouble.

Ms. Dawson suspected that a traditional school would be set up in Richmond because of the well-concerted efforts of the Chinese parents and the powerful influence of the learning companies and private tutoring institutions. She realized that the Chinese parents expected schools to be a formal place of learning and Canadian schools did not fit into this mold of expectations; the Canadian model is more than mere formal learning. For example, the Chinese parents did not consider some field experiences, such as a student field trip to a pumpkin patch, as part of a formal education. She noted, "It's a whole different value. It's a juggle of the different values between what one culture values and what another culture values, and trying to come to some common grounds."

Mrs. Haines and Ms. Dawson believed that the Chinese students were deprived of natural running, jumping, and playing—just being children—because the families imposed so many academic activities outside of school on their children. Mrs. Haines thought that "a lot of them are really regimented." She commented, "This situation doesn't happen only with Chinese students. I think that out of school classes are important and beneficial for our children. My son attended Japanese language classes and played soccer during his school years. The important point that we as parents and educators have to be aware of is that if we overload our children with too many things the good results become lost."

Ms. Dawson expressed similar concerns about the Chinese children being overprogrammed at home. She understood that the parents looked at the public school practices as separate from their home practices, and they had very different expectations for the public schools. But she believed that that there should be a balance between children's academic pursuits and the development of social skills: "From my own cultural bias, I value play and recreational activities and time spent socializing with other children. In some families, they really feel that learning English and improving English is the most important thing, and they feel the way to do that is to study more, and I guess I'm philosophically not on that same page. At this age, I think that children learn language by being around other children who speak the language and doing the things that children do."

Mrs. Haines also strongly disagreed with the Chinese parents' narrow emphasis on academic activities at home, and believed that empowering children to participate in housework or family shared home activities was a crucial part of children's cognitive development: "My strong belief in education is that broader base of learning which includes the work of home and involvement in activities other than just sort of the rigid rote, traditional, mythical idea of this sitting, and studying, and working, being the one way of academic achievement. I see that as very limiting because . . . if you have been in that tight little box, you don't have the broad-based experience to relate to, on a literal level or even on a cognitive level, and problem solving level."

The two teachers also discovered that the children's home experiences seemed to have, in Ms. Dawson's words, a "lack of human interactions in many ways" and the students' home experiences included mostly going to the mall, to restaurants, and to different classes. In Mrs. Haines's words, their home life "is very sheltered, very protected, and very closed." Ms. Dawson explained, "I guess that's the difference in our value systems. It's not that I don't think children should be involved in recreation. I think it's great to have children learning other things besides what they learn at school. But I also know it's important to establish some relationships. It's just good to have those kinds of conversation with the parents. Whether they really take those conversations and those discussions and do anything with it, I don't know. But at least it's some kind of sharing."

Both teachers looked at the children's lack of involvement with housework or shared home activities as the parents' overindulgence of their children. They saw this as a contradiction of the parents' high academic expectations. Mrs. Haines pointed out that this contradiction might have resulted in the children's unwillingness to take risks in learning and often waiting to be helped rather than helping themselves:

> So it takes a lot of time and energy trying to get them to do things for themselves, [because] they have things done for them, like feeding, dressing, toileting—they get a lot more assistance than I think is typically the norm in the North American culture. . . . And oftentimes even at a very young age, they're very reluctant to try. It's really important to try but they tend to be almost fearful of making mistakes. I find that sometimes they almost freeze, they'll just go totally quiet and blank if you ask them questions. Sometimes I wonder if they're disciplined very harshly, so it's safer to say nothing than to say something to get them into more trouble. It's this

sort of feelings that I have about them. So I think on the one hand they have very high expectations academically and behaviorally. On the other hand, they're really, really indulged. So there is inconsistency there.

Both teachers believed that reading was an important family activity in which the parents could spend time with their children and model reading for them at home. They had sent books home for the parents to read with the children as homework, but found that it was difficult to get the parents to cooperate because they did not always understand the significance of it. Both teachers realized that the parents did not consider reading as homework and often did not read with their children at home. Mrs. Haines described one experience of trying to get a Chinese parent to read to her child at home:

I had one mother [who] came in one day. She was quite apologetic. She said she didn't have time to read the library book to her daughter. It's one picture book, and they can have it at home for a whole week, and she didn't have time to read that with her daughter. I said, "Well, that's your homework, it's to read at home." And I said that she really should have more practice with that sort of thing. And I said, "I know she goes to math school but her computational skill is really good. So it would actually be better for her to spend more time reading and drop the math." And her mother said to me, "She gets homework in that." And I said, "You mean she gets the work that she can do by herself?" and she said yes. So I'm aware of that sort of different way of defining homework and the different importance that's attached to it.

Another concern the teachers had about the Chinese home literacy practices was the amount of time they spent watching TV or playing video games at home. Both teachers believed that not only did the parents overindulge their children, they were also afraid to say no to them. Ms. Dawson suggested that parents needed to take a firm stance: "I don't hear what other options are given to the children. They need to be told no in some cases." She gave her perspective on the role that TV and the media played in the children's home life: "I think that's not just for the Asian kids, but probably more so in Asian families than non-Asian families, because I don't feel that the Asian community yet utilizes their community resources and recreational opportunities as much as they could be, considering the number of Asian families that we have. As a result, children have a lot of time in their own homes and they choose those activities that don't require anybody else."

My observations and interviews with the parents seemed to suggest that watching TV and playing video games was the children's pastime between studying and going to different tutoring sessions. In some families, TV watching or game playing may have been the children's only exposure to English after school. Some parents therefore did not object to the TV watching or game playing. Mr. Ma, for example, believed that some game playing (e.g., Asian Empire) was beneficial for his son to learn English and Asian history at the same time.

Parent Perspectives

Mrs. Haines and Ms. Dawson had both tried to persuade the parents to reduce the pressure on their children and to eliminate some of their after-school classes. As mentioned earlier, out of respect for the teachers, a few parents dropped the math classes, but started to teach math themselves at home. Mrs. Chan said that if they did not teach their son math at home, he would lose what he had learned in the classes, and they really wanted him to do well in that subject. She (and several other) parents insisted that "there's distinction between the performance of the kids who take extra classes and those who don't." Some told me that they had gone to school to request more homework but were disappointed. Mrs. Chung complained, "I told them that kids should be given homework to do at home every day. I told them that when my kid was in grade 1, grade 2, and grade 3. They said they would consider it, but they didn't." Realizing that there was resistance, Ms. Dawson commented, "I really don't have a right to tell them or to comment on whether their children should be going to [these classes]. I encourage them to get them involved in sports groups and in service groups, not so much math, piano and Chinese school, but whether they listen to me or not, it's their choice."

Mrs. Haines was very concerned with the Chinese children's heavy schedules at home. In order to communicate her concerns to the parents, Mrs. Haines joined a homework discussion group with the Chinese parents and communicated with some parents through e-mails. In an e-mail message to one parent, she expressed her concerns about out-of-school classes:

Some kindergarten and primary students attend many out of school classes which assign homework. I have had students taking as many as ten out of school activities per week. These include math, grammar, language, swimming, music, and martial arts classes, to list the most popular ones. The unhealthy combination of school work and other activities was addressed clearly under the Junior Secondary and Senior Secondary sections. Perhaps a statement regarding a healthy balanced lifestyle should be included for all of the age categories. A significant number of primary students also go to bed very late, some regularly as late as 11:00. From the stand point of development of habits and dispositions, perhaps a statement regarding the importance of adequate sleep and nutrition could be noted as part of the home responsibility (work). Part of homework expectations of primary students is to develop responsibility for remembering routines such as returning library books and home reading materials at the required time.

The parent wrote back and explained that "education in the eyes of Chinese people is of particular importance and we always want our kids to grow up as a well educated person." However, different parents have different definitions of what "well educated" is and their ways to achieve such goal are also very different. The parent continued:

I am a Chinese parent and I know many Chinese parents that send their kids to attend out of school classes. . . . Why do these Chinese parents want their kids to take all these out of school classes? Below are some of my findings:
  1. ESL students need to put in extra efforts in learning English in order to catch up with the regular students.
  2. Many Chinese parents do not want their kids to give up Chinese because as advised by the Canadian government, new immigrants should always keep their own mother language and traditions. Moreover, Chinese will in the future become a very popular language in the world.
  3. Math is a very important subject and many Chinese parents find the Math program now implementing in the

Public School system very insufficient and at least 2 grade levels behind the Asian students.

4. As for music and sports training, they are both very good and meaningful extra-curriculum activities which the Public School system for one or another reason cannot sufficiently provide to our students.

It is clear to me that the rationale of these parents is to provide something that are "missing" in our existing Public School system, of which I believe they do this out of simple love of their kids. I obviously agree the fact that "excessive" love can be harmful to their kids too. (personal communication, Feb. 15, 2000)

Mrs. Haines strongly disagreed with the parent's view and believed that more creative play and "down time" would be more beneficial to the development of the children. She wrote:

I'm beginning to think that perhaps there is too much emphasis being put on homework especially in the elementary years. Maybe we should be encouraging more down time, relaxation and just being kids. If the students' entire environment is being structured to accommodate homework, how on earth are they ever going to develop the self disciplines needed to become self motivated? Are we encroaching on their time to interact with family members, imagine and just be? I am having some uneasy feelings about the message that we may be inadvertently sending, particularly as mentioned above, with regard to elementary school years. I don't think that children today have enough time to play, to be immersed in unrestricted, imagination driven, unsupervised, unorganized free play. (personal communication, Feb. 17, 2000)

Mrs. Haines's suggestion for more "down time" was in direct conflict with Chinese parents' emphasis on discipline and effort in order to achieve high academic success (Chao, 1996; G. Li, 2002; Stevenson & Stigler, 1992). In response to Mrs. Haines's concern about encouraging more play, the parent wrote back:

Many parents tell me something exactly the opposite to what you think. Below is the summary of some of their opinions:

1. Students of KG–G2 have been spending too much time in playing and should work on Math and Writing on a more regular basis;
2. Students that do not have good basic skills in Math and English Writing usually will have problems in their school work when they are in G4 and above;
3. Students get addicted to TV in a very early age because they do not have homework to do in the junior grades; and it is extremely difficult for these students to cut off from TV when they are in G4, it is already a habit to these children;
4. One of the reasons why parents send their kids to after-school classes is to get more homework for their kids to do after school;
5. Parents believe that homework can develop self-discipline of a child;
6. Parents do not agree that homework will kill the imagination of a child;
7. Parents want their kids to learn sense of responsibility, conduct, manners and time-management skills as early as in G1 because these are very important elements of educated person;
8. Parents do not believe homework will zero-out time for them to interact with their children.

I think the diverse opinions about homework [are] on the volume of homework rather than homework itself. (personal communication, Feb. 18, 2000)

The parent's perspectives were typical among the Chinese parents. For example, many parents expressed their dissatisfaction with the reading homework. They did not feel that it was their responsibility to teach English reading or writing. Some parents did not know English themselves and saw teaching English as the responsibility of the teachers. Other parents, who could speak English, did not feel they could help their children due to their limited English proficiency, nor did they want their children to pick up their accents. Mrs. Lou, who had gone to the school several times to protest the reading homework, expressed her anger over the school's reading homework: "Every time they keep emphasizing, you parents are supposed to read with the kids every day. The other day I was really mad, and I said,

'Yes, what? Chinese or English?' English? I mean, your [the teacher's] English is good and my English is, well, maybe so so. For my kids to have good pronunciation or correct pronunciation, my English is not good. I rely on you guys to teach him English but instead you rely on me to teach my son English."

In order to let the parents know more about the school's practices, Ms. Dawson and Mrs. Haines both tried to invite the parents into their classrooms to be involved in the classroom literacy activities. These efforts, as the teachers' perspectives on parental involvement will demonstrate, were not very successful.

Parental Involvement in School

Both Mrs. Haines and Ms. Dawson believed that it was important to involve parents in the students' learning, and they agreed that it was difficult to get the Chinese parents involved. They had tried different ways of involving the parents in their classrooms, but none seemed to work.

For Mrs. Haines, the challenge was to deal with the contradiction between the parents' high academic expectations and their overindulgence of their children. She had invited the parents to her classroom to read to the children every morning and to listen to her read a story on Fridays so that they could learn how to read to their children at home and develop their own English, but the parents gradually stopped coming for these activities. She expressed her disappointment:

> But they wouldn't come in to be involved in [academic things]. . . . Like in the morning, there's an open invitation in the classroom for the parents to come in and read to the students during the book time and very few of them do. . . . Jenny's dad used to come in, but it's hard to get them in for that. And then what I tried last year was to invite in for that, and on Fridays they were invited to stay for a story while I read. My theory was that [if] they heard me reading, that would help them learn how to read to their children, and maybe even develop their own English, but a few of them stayed for a few times, but they just didn't come any more. And I tried to pick the old short stories that were really easy pieces, but it didn't work. It really fizzled out.

Instead, the parents often came to the classroom to help their children in ways that Mrs. Haines regarded as bad for the children's independence. For example, instead of helping the children read or learn academically, they often pampered the children by supervising all their movements: they would come and hang up the coats for the children in the morning, toilet the children at recess time, and then come to deliver hot lunches and spoon-feed them. Mrs. Haines tried to push these parents away and tried to get them to give the children a little more independence. She was particularly puzzled by the deep-seated Chinese belief that if these children did not have hot lunches they would become ill. She believed that "this is where the parents should start to accept the North American culture a little bit more." So finally about two years before the time of this study Mrs. Haines decided to take some action against it. She made it clear to the parents and grandparents that they were not allowed to come into the classroom. She explained:

> When the school first opened, a lot of parents would come in and sit with the children when they ate and we felt good because we felt that parents were comfortable enough to come into the school. But then it became a problem because they were doing too much for the kids, feeding them and it . . . wasn't good for the children's overall learning and independence. Some of them would come in and berate the children. One grandmother particularly yelled at this little guy. She brings this huge big serving of rice that was probably enough nutrition for two or three days' worth, and she wanted him to eat all of it before he went out to play and the kid would be choking his food down. There was a lot of pressure on them to eat. So it's becoming quite negative. So I ended up really putting a stop to it, and then feeling bad about it.

However, Mrs. Haines's action was interpreted by Chinese parents as discouraging their involvement in school settings and they retreated from what was experienced as intimidation and rejection (Winters, 1993; Chavkin, 1989). Mrs. Haines hoped that the parents would come into the classroom to help their children learn to read and write English, but the Chinese parents gradually stopped taking part in any school-related activities; they did not even try to talk with or say hello to the teachers—even when they came in every day to deliver lunches to their children. Mrs. Haines realized that it was more difficult to get through to Asian parents, but she was unwilling to change what she considered to be good for the children. She believed that the parents needed to learn to adapt to the new environment.

Differing from Mrs. Haines, Ms. Dawson did not try to get the parents into the classroom to read or learn how to read to the children. She did not believe in having parents as classroom helpers because some children felt uncomfortable about having their parents in the classroom. In the past, she had had negative experiences when parents were involved in the classroom for different reasons (for example, professional confidentiality issues). She stressed to the parents (who came to listen to children read or work with them on certain activities) that what happened in the classroom stayed in the classroom, but some parents were unable to see the importance of this policy and would go and talk about the reading proficiency (or lack of it) of some children. These experiences made Ms. Dawson cautious about inviting parents into the classroom to help. Instead, she preferred to have parents help supervise school activities such as field trips, and classroom activities in which parents were able to interact with children in a more relaxed and casual setting. For example, she had invited parents to come and speak about their careers. However, she admitted that this was unsuccessful because of the parents' language ability.

For Ms. Dawson, another challenge was communication with the parents. In her grade 4/5 class, the Chinese parents continued to deliver daily hot lunches to their children, but only a few of them would come into the classroom. Some would wait outside the classroom until the children finished eating. Like Mrs. Haines, Ms. Dawson also noted that many parents avoided talking to her or even saying hello when they delivered their children's lunch. She was not used to this kind of interaction and was quite puzzled by the parents' distant behavior. From a teacher's perspective, this made it hard for her to initiate communication with the parents because she was not sure what the parents were thinking or were comfortable with. She also noted that there were differences between the beliefs of mainstream parents (as child advocates) and the practice of the Chinese parents: "It's not easy. You can make [parental involvement] sound all wonderful, but when it comes right down to it . . . parents are their child's advocates. And if there's something happening that [the Chinese parents] don't agree with, they should feel totally within their rights to question it or at least have a discussion with the teachers. But that doesn't happen a lot directly with the classroom teacher. I don't know if it's the language difference or maybe the cultural barrier."

Ms. Dawson also noted that there was a socioeconomic barrier for the parents to be involved. She realized that many of the families were either functionally single families (the mothers lived in Canada taking care of the children while the fathers worked in Hong Kong or Taiwan), or dual-worker families and therefore it was difficult for the parents to find time to get involved in their children's education at school. Reflecting on this, she thought that as teachers they needed "to be a little more creative," and suggested grandparent involvement if the parents continued this working lifestyle.

During the tenure of this research study, I witnessed many parents who came to deliver lunches every day. Few actually came into the two classrooms to help during class time. Of the two field trips taken by the two classes, only one parent came to help. During several schoolwide initiatives to inform the parents of the school's philosophy and guiding principles such as parent nights, open houses, and discussion groups, low attendance was reported.

When I talked to parents about their involvement in school, they echoed concerns about the practicality of getting involved in the school activities. Most of the families were dual-worker families and the parents could not attend some of the parent meetings. For many, the best they could do was to deliver lunch every day. Several parents told me that they used to take part in all the school activities, but since they had to work or help with the family business, they did not have time to go to the school activities any more, not even to the parent meetings. Some just sent their older children who were in higher grades to those meetings. Even if they had time, many parents did not think they could be effectively involved in the school's literacy activities as they did not speak English or speak it well enough to help the children with English in the classroom. Mrs. Yep, who knew the community quite well, confirmed that language difficulties were the Asian parents' most formidable obstacle: "They don't feel quite comfortable to come to school because they don't have enough English." She also pointed out that parental involvement was a foreign concept for many Asian parents as "they don't have all this volunteer work in the school in Hong Kong, and so they're not so used to that." Some parents, as I observed, regarded parental involvement as cooperating and participating with school activities such as entering school raffles or signing papers that were sent home. Some parents were quite frustrated by the school's drive for parental involvement. Mrs. Lou, for example, interpreted the drive as an indication that the teachers could not help the children: "Because then [the teachers] don't have to work so much. And then their responsibility is less. [They think,] 'This is not my fault, but the parents'.' They didn't know that parents have to work; they give the money to them. The other thing is we are multicultural, and a lot of parents [don't] really speak fluent English. This is why the multicultural kids had difficulty in language, because they didn't receive proper training from school. [The teachers] rely on parents instead of relying on [themselves]. This is the big problem. . . . they force the parents to go out for tutors because [the parents] can't help the kids."

In sum, both teachers had tried different ways of involving the parents in classroom learning in the past, but these efforts had not been very rewarding. The parents were not active in the classroom due to their limited time, limited language proficiency, and their different understanding of parental involvement. The differences between the teachers' expectations and the parents' response to these expectations further fortified the tensions and dissensions between the two.

Conclusion

In this chapter, I have described the teachers' and the parents' perspectives on the sociocultural contexts in which they were situated, and their respective understandings of Chinese at school, English literacy instruction, literacy instruction and learning at home, and parental involvement at school. The two teachers' perspectives reveal that cultural tensions and educational dissentions were manifested in the two teachers' interactions with the Chinese parents, who held fundamentally different cultural and pedagogical beliefs. The different layers of tensions and dissensions reflected the conflicting ideologies between the teachers and the parents, and further widened the distance between school and home for the Chinese English-language learners. These cultural conflicts between the teachers and the parents played a key role in shaping the educational experiences of minority children. Unless effective measures were taken to resolve these conflicts, the mismatch between school and home would remain a formidable barrier for the students to overcome in order to achieve academic success, and the cultural differences might become risk factors in the education of the Chinese English-language learners.

The nature of the home-school mismatch, however, represented a new problem space in minority education. So often, research has explored the cultural distance between middle-class teachers and English-language learners from low-income families. The cultural conflicts between the teachers and the parents embodied an atypical power relationship in minority education. The middle-class parents actually voiced educational concerns that minority groups often do not articulate as they feel less empowered. In addition, these parents' financial capital afforded them resources to pursue their educational aspirations for their children.

Another problem space that the different perspectives embodied was the different conceptions of the quality of instruction and the best way to raise achievement through instruction. Progressive student-centered teaching has been considered by many researchers and practitioners (such as the two teachers) as beneficial to minority students' learning. The parents, however, did not welcome this kind of educational innovation and preferred the traditional teacher-centered education. This school-home divide on literacy instruction, as the children's lived experiences will demonstrate, may have an adverse effect on the children's learning in and out of school.

In the next chapter I describe the literacy experiences of four focal children in Mrs. Haines's grade 1/2 class; in chapter 5, I describe the literacy experiences of the four focal children in Ms. Dawson's grade 4/5 class. As the children's experiences in and out of school will demonstrate, the battles over literacy and culture between school and home had significant consequences on their learning and development.

CHAPTER FOUR

Beginning Forays in the Battles

Sandy, Anthony, Kevin, and Alana

In this chapter, I bring you into the worlds of four first and second graders who have just been caught in the battles between school and home literacy practices. I will look more closely now at how the conflicting ideologies are reflected in the children's everyday learning in school and at home. I will trace some important aspects of the battles enacted in the children's lives. These aspects include clashes between Mrs. Haines's learner-centered, language-experience approach to literacy instruction (in which she emphasized play, drawing, and a flexible view of development and learning) and the parents' preference for more traditional teacher-led instruction, parental expectations of the school and their involvement at home, and children's language use in and out of classrooms.

The four learners featured in this chapter were recommended to me by Mrs. Haines. In the case of Sandy Chung, Mrs. Haines wanted to understand why a young girl could be so negative. She described Sandy as "a sour little girl," and speculated that it might be the result of pampering and indulgence by her family.

Mrs. Haines was very concerned about Anthony, whom she had taught since he was in first grade, because of his overprogramming and the pressure put on him by his parents. She had many long sessions with his parents and school counselors, who were also involved trying to get his parents to relax the pressure on him because "they were so uptight and had such high, high expectations."

Mrs. Haines recommended Kevin because of his idiosyncratic behavior in the classroom. Kevin often appeared to be nervous,

101

walked like a "robot," to use Mrs. Haines's word, and often mur-
mured unintelligible words. Mrs. Haines wondered whether Kevin's
family, like Anthony's, exerted too much pressure on him.

Alana Tang became one of the focal children because of her slow
progress in English. She had been in the school for over one year, but
had not achieved the expected level of proficiency. One reason was
that she had been traveling back and forth between China and
Canada. At the onset of the study, she had also failed to submit complete home reading records, despite the fact that Mrs. Haines had sent
notes home to request the parents' help to fill in and sign the record
forms. Mrs. Haines wondered whether her parents were at all
involved in Alana's learning at home.

As I became familiar with the children in and out of school, I
came to realize that the different barriers experienced by these children were not simply the result of family practices, but a combination
of school, home, and social factors. Within the complexities of their
lives, the different cultural beliefs of the teachers and the parents
about language and literacy instruction as well as the misunderstandings of these differences seemed to play a major role in shaping these
children's school and home experiences.

Sandy: A Serious First Grader

Sandy was a six-year-old first grader in Mrs. Haines's combined first
and second grade class. When I first met her, I noticed one thing that
was very unusual for a six-year-old child—she appeared to be very
serious and displeased with things around her as she always looked at
others with disapproving eyes. I wanted to find out more about her
and to try to understand her unique attitude in and out of the school.

Sandy's Literacy Practices at School

At the beginning of the term in September 2000, Sandy was pulled out
from her regular class for four 40-minute periods per week to work
with an ESL/resource teacher, Mrs. Vincent, in a small ESL language
group. In this small group, she participated in activities related to
Christmas, families, animals, and winter in order to develop her
vocabulary and to practice speaking, reading, and writing skills. These
small group studies had helped her learn English. At the beginning of
February 2001, she attended the small-group ESL study for one 40-

minute period per week, and she started to join the larger class group for chapter-book literature studies using the *Blueland Dragon* series. By March 2001, Sandy was able to identify almost all of the sounds that letters represent and was able to read an increasing number of words.

Sandy told me that she did not like the stories she read at school: "It's not fun." I speculated that she did not fully understand the stories because of her limited vocabulary. I noticed that during large-group readings or literacy activities, Sandy seldom raised her hand or spoke up, and she often sat quietly and looked timid. Although she was beginning to read picture books on her own, she was not fond of reading, especially stories. I seldom saw her read in school. Even when she read, she always claimed that she did not like the books. One time I saw her reading Dr. Seuss's *Green Eggs and Ham* with her friend Melissa. Melissa pointed to a picture and said, "Look at this! It's funny!" Sandy flipped the book closed and said unhappily, "I don't like *Green Eggs*. I played this on a computer."

Sandy liked drawing, particularly coloring her drawings. In one of her journal entries, she wrote, "I like paiting Wha I gow up I will be a ats." [I like painting. When I grow up, I will be an artist.] Her favorite color was pink, so she always used pink colors to paint herself. She gave me many of her paintings of hearts and friends as presents.

Although Sandy could complete her written work with support, she passively resisted independently completing the writing tasks such as phonics or journal writing. For phonics, she had to write down the letters that were taught as well as words beginning with those letters. Sometimes she had to draw pictures about the words and make sentences with them. For journal writing, she had to write about stories that were read in class. She was able to finish the drawing part; however, when it came to printing and writing, Sandy often waited at her desk for help or refused to do it, even if the words were provided for her on the blackboard. One day after the class finished reading a story about Hanukkah, another teacher was asked to come to class to do a Hanukkah dance for them. After the teacher's visit, Mrs. Haines asked the class to write a thank-you letter to the teacher and to wish her a happy Hanukkah. Sandy finished the letter following the model on the blackboard:

Dear Mrs. Bullock, I like your dance. Thank you. Sandy

Then she waited at her desk, seeming not to know what to do next. I went over and checked on her work,

Guofang: You finished the letter already? Good job!
Sandy: Yeah.
Guofang: Would you like to wish Mrs. Bullock a happy Hanukkah?
Sandy: No, I don't know how to write it.
Guofang: The words are on the blackboard.
Sandy (unhappily): I don't want to.

Mrs. Haines was well aware of Sandy's resistance to writing tasks. She realized that Sandy might have taken her words literally in phrases such as "would you like." Instead of giving her options, it was better to give Sandy direct instructions, such as "Okay, it's time to write out 'Happy Hanukkah.'"

Sandy demonstrated the same resistance when learning math. She always waited for help before trying anything on her own. For example, she was presented with the addition problem, 18+2. I knew from her work that she could figure it out on her own, but instead she asked me for help. I encouraged her to use the strategies she had learned in class to figure it out, but she would not do it. "I don't want to do it," she said.

Sandy also appeared to be afraid in front of the class. For example, as a "morning calendar" helper, she could accomplish some roles of the job such as pointing out the date, yet was often afraid to speak up. As a result, she occasionally relied on the class's help to finish her task. Sometimes, when called on to answer questions in front of the class, she appeared very timid. During one of the math sessions, she was asked to do addition with her fingers. She put out her hands, but was apprehensive. She then lowered her head, staring down, unable to speak up although she was able to count on her own. Mrs. Haines commented that "she was afraid to take any risks" because she was afraid to make mistakes, which was very common among Chinese children whose families emphasized "getting everything, every word right."

Sandy: The Classroom Rule Maintainer

Sandy's unwillingness to undertake any new tasks might have to do with her critical attitude toward things around her. She was too serious about classroom rules and others' behaviors, and therefore she did

not want to take any risks. Sandy was known among the children as
the classroom rule maintainer, and therefore had very few friends.

Sandy was very particular about Mrs. Haines's English-only rule
in the classroom. Many times, I observed that she reminded the students who spoke Chinese that they should follow the rule. This happened one day when a group of students were discussing what the
word "地" (di) meant in English:

Alana: zhe ge kan shang qu xiang nu zi. [This looks like a
    Chinese character "女"]
Andrew: This is a Chinese word "地" (di).
Anthony: It means floor.
Lucy: Ground.
Andrew: It's not floor, it's ground.
Anthony: Floor means ground.
Sandy: I don't want you to speak Chinese because it's Eng-
    lish here.
Josh: Alana doesn't even speak English.

Many times when I explained some of the class activities to Alana
Tang in Chinese, Sandy would frown and come over to remind us that
we should not speak Chinese in the classroom. Sandy maintained not
only the English-only rule, but also several other rules. Several times
she came to complain to me about students who did not follow the
rules. For example: "Miss Li, Amy has secrets. Mrs. Haines said that
we're not supposed to have secrets here."

Sandy was also eager to correct other students' errors in speaking
English. For example, during one class, Alana was called on to spell a
difficult word, "xylophone." Kara was going to help her, but other students in the class suggested Alana do it on her own. Their use of the
third person singular pronoun was apparently influenced by their first
language as in Chinese, "him" and "her" have the same pronunciation, and Chinese learners usually mix up the two:

Other students: Kara, don't help him [Alana]. Don't help
    him. He can do it.
Sandy: Not him, her. Don't help her.

Sandy's consciousness of the English-only rule gradually diminished as two new Chinese-speaking students, Kara and Alicia, joined

the class. These two students relied heavily on Alana and other Chinese students' translation to understand the classroom activities. Their constant use of Chinese among themselves in the classroom virtually shattered the English-only environment. Beginning in January 2001, I noticed that Sandy started to use Chinese, mostly Cantonese, during the free playtime when she played with her friend Amy. One time, after observing her speaking in Chinese, I asked her in Chinese what they were playing. She looked a little surprised at the question, but answered quickly using both English and Chinese, "玩 (wan) [play] center."

Sandy's use of Chinese seemed to have a positive effect on her attitude toward others in class. She was able to concentrate on tasks and even play activities in which she was engaged, and she was able to express herself more in free-play situations. She appeared to be happier than before and started to have a smile on her face. Mrs. Haines also noticed that "she started to loosen up a little bit." I observed that Sandy also used Chinese with Amy in many imaginative play situations during their play center time.

One time, Sandy and Amy pretended to be a family driving to Disneyland. Sandy played the mother and child, and Amy played "Popo" [Grandma]:

> Sandy: You take the baby. nngo dik heoi dik si nei. [We'll go to Disneyland.]
> Amy: Disneyland! Oh, wo men de dai chi de. [We've got to take some food.] You know where it is?
> Sandy: Oh, I'd better bring a map! Map? wo de hua ye ge. [I have to draw a map.]
> Amy: Ask Miss Li to draw us a map.
> Sandy (Gets a piece of paper and a pencil): "Miss Li, could you draw a map for me? nngo dik hoi ce heoi Disneyland. [We're driving to Disneyland.]

Another time, based on their recent visits to a doctor's office, they did an imaginative play about a doctor seeing a patient. Sandy played a doctor, and Amy, holding a baby bear, was a mother with a sick baby:

> Sandy: What can I do for you?
> Amy: My baby is sick.
> Sandy (examining the baby bear on the desk): Let's see. He needs some medicine. (She goes and pours some water

Fig. 4.1. *Sandy's writing about her and Amy's experiences at the doctor's office.*

into a bowl and puts it on the examination table). You need to give him the medicine. nei ng zi dik joek gei gwai. [You don't know how expensive this medicine is.]

Amy (patting the bear): Ok, ok . . . ngo dik wai taa. [I'll feed him.] (She takes a spoon and pretends to feed the baby bear.]

Later during their journal writing time, Sandy wrote about the experience and she and Amy told Kara, who sat at their desk, about their play at the play center. In her journal she wrote about her experience with the doctor (see figure 4.1).

Sandy not only started to use Chinese during unstructured class time, she also started to code-switch during this time. For example, in March 2001, when they finished reading two versions of the story *Pinocchio* and watched a play about it, they were asked to write a letter to the actors or actresses about how they felt about the play. Sandy decided to write to the actress who played Pinocchio, but she was stumped on the actress's name:

Sandy (frowning): Taa go ming hai? [What's her name]? Christine, Kristin, or Christy?

Amy: Bu she la. [Not that.]
Sandy: Ng hai laa? [Which one?]
Amy: Ngo ng zi. [I don't know.]
Sandy: Maybe Mrs. Haines will tell us.

Sandy's attitude change had a positive impact on her in many ways. Mrs. Haines commented that she was "gradually gaining confidence at school." I noticed that she started to read more during in-class free time. One day I saw her read a book, *Jack and Jill*, (Cousins, 1989) by herself, and went over and joined her. I asked her to read with me; she was able to read it with fluency although she had a problem reading a few words such as "that," "time," "those," and "why." When Amy came over to join us, Sandy decided to play teacher; she held the book open and asked Amy to read with her: "Ok, Amy, it's your turn." As Amy was reading alone, Sandy helped her with a few words. When it was time for the class's chapter-book reading, Sandy said to me, "Miss Li, we didn't finish the book. Can we put a bookmark in there?" Then she turned to Amy and said, "We'll finish it later."

Sandy at Home

Sandy's negative attitude may have come in part from her home literacy experiences. Many times Sandy told Mrs. Haines or me that she did not like weekends at home. On Mondays when the class was asked about their weekends, Sandy always had similar stories about her home life: "My mom wouldn't let me play unless I finish my homework," or "My mom didn't want me to watch TV because she said it was a waste of time," or "I can't play because I didn't finish my homework." After many informal chats with Sandy and a formal interview with her mother, I learned more about Sandy's home life.

Everyday after school, Sandy and her brother would take a half-hour break to eat some snacks or watch TV. After the break, her brother Billy practiced piano while Sandy worked on her homework from her Chinese school, math homework assigned by her parents, or reading homework from school. Unlike her brother, Sandy refused to take swimming and piano lessons as she did not want others to watch her. Mrs. Chung explained that Sandy was very shy and was always conscious of how other people thought of her, especially in public or outside of their home setting. Mrs. Chung did not know why Sandy was so sensitive about how others viewed her and what shaped her personality. She speculated that maybe she was too lenient or indulgent with her when she was a baby, or she did not educate her properly early on. Whatever it was, Mrs. Chung hoped that Sandy would loosen up and become more confident in participating and interacting with others.

Since Sandy did not take any piano or swimming lessons, Mrs. Chung asked her to put the time into her studies: "She has a lot more time to study than her brother." She enrolled Sandy in a math tutoring school for a while as she found that many other kids in the school took extra classes and performed better in math. But later she withdrew Sandy from the math school because of her protest. Sandy told me during a lesson on counting that she had learned counting in the math school: "My mom sent me to that school. But I don't go there anymore." Mrs. Chung understood Sandy's protest to be the result of school's emphasis on individual freedom: "The school gave them too much freedom and it's hard for me to make them study hard at home."

At home, Sandy liked to play with Barbie dolls and her Hello Kitty toys and watch cartoons. Like many young girls, she liked to act like the mommy of her dolls and change the dolls' clothes. She did not like the fact that her mother asked her to study all the time. "Study is boring," she said. Mrs. Chung always insisted that Sandy do her homework first before playing, which always made Sandy very unhappy. Mrs. Chung told me of her frustration: "I always have to get mad at her if I want her to study!"

Consistent with her attitude at school, Sandy disliked reading at home. Mrs. Chung seldom read stories to Sandy; most of the time Mrs. Chung asked her to read by herself. The best way to learn to read, according to Mrs. Chung, was to learn to pronounce and spell words and then make sentences using the words. So when Mrs. Chung asked Sandy to read the storybooks sent home by Mrs. Haines, Mrs. Chung always felt that Sandy did not master the books: "I asked her to read the books sent from school, and she picked them up and flipped through them and told me she could read them, and she didn't like to read those storybooks. . . . I have to fight with her about her study all the time. It's always such a headache."

In Sandy's reading record (see figure 4.2) submitted to school, I noticed that many of the books Sandy read were recorded on several consecutive days or for quite a few times at different dates. This may indicate that Sandy was asked to read and recite these books over and

Sandy 's Reading Record		
DATE/ BOOK TITLE/ INITIALS		**DATE/ BOOK TITLE/ INITIALS**
Mar-9, 2001 Anthology	14	Mar-17, 2001 dragon
Mar-9, 2001 Winnie the -Pooh's Colors	15	Mar-23, 2001 The Tale Of Tom Kitten
Mar-11, 2001 Winnie the -Pooh's Colors	16	Mar-25, 2001 Grove's Day at the Beach
Mar-12, 2001 Winnie the -Pooh's Colors	17	Mar-25, 2001 Sasquaech
Mar-15, 2001 The Tale of Tom Kitten	18	Mar-25, 2001 Skinnamarinky
Mar-16, The Tale of Tom Kitten	19	Mar-25, 2001 What Can We Do
Mar-16 Toron-to-to ☆☆☆☆☆☆☆☆	20	Mar-25, 2001 Down Down
Mar-17, 2001 Elmer dragon	21	Mar-25, 2001 Toron to to
Mar-17, 2001 Elmer dragon 2	22	Mar-27, 2001 antholog/
Mar-17, 2001 Elmer dragon 3	23	Mea-28, 2001 colours
Mar-17, 2001 Elmer dragon 4	24	Mar-28, 2001 colours
Mar-17, 2001 Elmer dragon 5	25	Mar-28, 2001 Antholog y
Mar-17, 2001 Elmer dragon 6		CONGRATULATIONS !!!

Fig. 4.2. *Sandy's home reading record.*

Fig. 4.3. *Sandy's picture about writing.*

over by Mrs. Chung, as is the custom in Chinese education of learning through repetition and rote memorization.

Mrs. Chung had already noticed Sandy's resistance to learning. From her experience with her son, Billy, who had also resisted learning since he was in first grade, Mrs. Chung thought it might be better not to be as rigid with her as with her brother: "I think she is a little shy. I think maybe by giving her more freedom or being less strict with her she'll have a better personality than her brother."

Despite her dislike of reading at home, Sandy did express a like for writing better at home. When Mrs. Haines asked her to draw about writing, she drew a picture of herself playing and writing at home. She wrote, "I like to write" (figure 4.3). Sandy was becoming trilingual and she code-switched between three languages at home, especially when visiting her grandparents' house. Every weekend she went to study Chinese in a Chinese school for three hours, along with visiting her grandparents. She would speak Mandarin with her grandparents and Cantonese with her parents. She also watched Chinese TV and read Chinese books. But she often conversed with her brother in English when they talked about school events.

Anthony: A Second Grader with Great Expectations

Seven-year-old Anthony was the largest child in Mrs. Haines's grade 1/2 class. In talking with Mrs. Chan and Mrs. Haines, and in observing Anthony in school, I discovered that Anthony had very different personalities at school and at home. At school, he was shy around teachers, but was independent and a leader among his friends. At home, he was talkative and dependent on his parents. Although he was only in the second grade, his parents had already set a goal for him—to become a professional such as a medical doctor or an engineer (preferably a doctor).

Anthony at School

At school, Anthony usually sat and worked, and played together with two other Chinese boys, Andrew and Josh. He was actually the leader among them. He set the tone for what to play and how to play it. Mostly he enjoyed playing with Legos with them. Sometimes Anthony invented games, such as imitating a cat jumping or running away. Mrs. Haines commented, "He has come a long way and is much more relaxed this year." The classroom assistant, Mrs. Yep, told me that in the previous year Anthony was quite nervous and rigid. Mrs. Haines shared the same opinion: "He was very uptight. He'll draw these little tiny, tiny pictures and he'll press really hard with the pencils, and tear this big [hole]. There was a lot of encouragement for him to open up and use the whole paper and to work more quickly because he seemed to be very afraid of making mistakes."

Anthony had made dramatic progress this year in his drawing and writing. His pictures were mostly very small, but his writing was big and typical (see figure 4.4). He actually enjoyed drawing and writing. He seldom made spelling errors in his writing and demonstrated a good command of writing mechanisms such as capitalization, sentence structure, and spelling. Mrs. Yep also noticed that Anthony had made great improvement this year: "Last year he was really really tense. Now this year he's more relaxed and he's really comfortable now. I think in a way among the boys, he seems to be the leader of them. You can see that the boys follow him and they listen to him too. Now he's really not too slow in his work, because he builds up his confidence, and his confidence has built up. Last year he was afraid to make mistakes. That's why he was so tense. Whenever he had to write something, he had to make sure that he did everything correct. Now he's more relaxed and he learns that it's okay to make mistakes."

Although Anthony had opened up quite a bit during the time of the research study, I found that there was something about him that was hard to capture. For example, he was very cautious about speaking up and participating whenever there was a teacher or other adult around. He would do the work as required but he would not go beyond what was required. When he was asked to do some task that he did not like, he would not complain, but neither would he do it. Sometimes, it took him a long time to finish a task, though Mrs. Haines knew that he could finish it faster. She could not quite describe his behavior in words, but had a feeling that he had developed a tacit way of avoiding learning: "He behaves in a very quiet way, and he doesn't act out behaviorally. But he is, it's hard to explain, almost like, resisting passively." Because of his passive resistance, Anthony sometimes went unnoticed during group or class literacy activities. He seemed to have developed an awareness of when he could get away with not working. For example, when a group of students were sitting at a table working on writing or drawing activities, he would sit there playing until a teacher or teacher assistant walked over to check on everyone's work. He then would quietly but slowly get started on his work.

Because of his passive resistance, Anthony was not doing the best he could, and his writings were generally descriptions of events, very matter-of-fact without much detail or creativity. Mrs. Haines commented, "He's not very spontaneous, and you don't feel a lot of creative ideas in his writing. He stays in a very safe zone. He doesn't step out [of his safe zone], and you have to push him out." Here are some examples of Anthony's writing (see also figure 4.4):

"We learned a song called trust your feelings. Responsible is part of star."

"When I went to the doctor I got a shot. I think I was five years old when I took that shot."

"The Gingerbread Man is running away from the grandma."

Fig. 4.4. *A sample of Anthony's writing.*

Some of Anthony's tendency to stay in his safe zone was also reflected in his writing during phonics and spelling activities. In these activities, Anthony could spell a lot of the words correctly, but sometimes the sentences he made did not connect or make sense. He seemed to pay more attention to making grammatically correct sentences rather than making sentences that were personally meaningful. For example, after a phonics lesson on *fl*, he copied down three words that started with *fl*—"flashlight," "flute," and "fly," and he made a sentence with these words: "A fly used a small flashlight to look into a small flute." Here are some other examples:

"Someone is saying whee in a car. The car has a white wheel."

"On Friday French people who live in France eat french fries."

"The French painter Monet is an impressionist. We painted suflowers on Wednesday. Flea jump on animles."

"Jonathan whent into a jet to eat jello!"

Maybe because Anthony liked to stay safe, he seldom spoke up or volunteered an answer in reading or writing activities unless he was called on. For example, he liked reading the words and sentences in the salutations for the class's morning routine, but he seldom raised his hand to volunteer reading. He usually did very well with reading words and sentences aloud and felt really proud of it when he did well. Anthony was more of a risk taker while reading silently at school. Every morning during the sustained silent reading time, he usually read with his "reading buddies" from the sixth and seventh grades or with his two best friends, Andrew and Josh. He was able to read books with some advanced vocabulary such as *The Day of the Dinosaur* (Berenstain and Berenstain, 1987). He enjoyed the literature study of the chapter book series *Elmer and the Dragon* (Gannett, 1987). Mrs. Haines noted that although he was able to remember the details from the stories and was able to respond to them, his response was usually brief. Figure 4.5 is an example of Anthony's response to the literature study.

Anthony also enjoyed the daily math problem solving which was also part of the class routine, and he was more active in volunteering his answers during this class activity. He was able to quickly and accurately compute addition and subtraction equations which required regrouping, borrowing, and carrying. Mrs. Haines noted that he was very enthusiastic when participating in some of the math games. He was even able to figure out some multiplication problems. For example, one of the units was about the school's Hundred Day activity (Mrs. Haines used one hundred as the content of their math instruction). One of the activities was about counting to 100, and they played different games to practice different ways to count to 100. One of the tasks in the morning routine was to count how many total fingers class members had:

Mrs. Haines: Boys and girls, can you count how many fingers we have in our class? (Anthony raises his hand after some computing in his mind.)
Mrs. Haines: Anthony?

The dragon is hiding behind the rock.

Fig. 4.5. *Anthony's response to the literature study of* Elmer and the Dragon.

Anthony: 200!

Mrs. Haines: Wonderful! How did you get this number?

Anthony: Everybody has 10 fingers. Then we just count how many people in the class. If we count 10 people, then we have 100 fingers. Then we count another 10 people, then we have another 100.

Mrs. Haines: That's a very clever way to count. Thank you, Anthony!

Anthony took pride in his math ability. He told me that he used to go to a math school and now his father was teaching him math at home. He also talked about going to a Chinese school with his

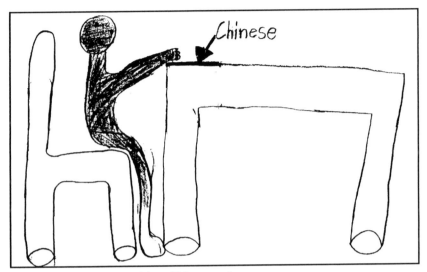

Fig. 4.6. *Anthony is writing Chinese at home.*

friends Andrew and Josh. "I'm in level 1 Chinese. I go once a week. We have class for about two hours. We have a lot of homework, writing Chinese." He drew a picture of himself writing Chinese at home (figure 4.6).

However, I seldom heard Anthony speak Chinese in school. When I asked him about his Chinese, he said, "I don't know how. I'm supposed to know, but I don't know. My mom and dad always speak to me in English at home."

Anthony at Home

After school, Anthony went to a daycare center and stayed there until his father came to pick him up after work. Anthony was one of two children in Mrs. Haines's class who went to daycare because both of his parents worked late. He liked it there as he could play freely and could do whatever he wanted, such as play sports, watch TV, or draw.

Every day Anthony's mother, Mrs. Chan, started working at 9:15 a.m. at the children's hospital and got off work late in the afternoon. When Anthony's grandmother was alive, Mrs. Chan went to see her after work before going home, so she usually came home later than Anthony and Mr. Chan. After she came home, she made dinner for the family while Anthony played with toys or watched TV. Although Anthony was very independent at school, he was demanding at home. During every meal at home, he still needed his parents to feed him. Mrs. Chan told me that his supper time usually took about an hour and a half to three hours. Anthony was a slow eater and he did other things while eating, like playing with his Game Boy at the dinner table or watching TV. Otherwise he would not eat.

Due to the longevity of his eating habits, Mrs. Chan asked Anthony to practice the piano for a while before going to bed if they did not have any other lessons to attend. She admitted that they "don't have much time to read." Occasionally when they had more time after supper, she or her husband would read with Anthony. Anthony preferred to read with his mother because he could ask her to read to him while his father would ask Anthony to read to himself. Mrs. Chan told me that "his daddy doesn't accept when [Anthony] does not read." Also, when Anthony wanted to read the same books he read before or his favorite *Franklin Book* series, Mr. Chan would not allow him to do so, while Mrs. Chan would normally let him read those books. Anthony obtained many secondhand books from his aunt's children, who lived in another western Canadian city. His reading records suggested that he had read about 100 books at home since grade 1.

Mrs. Chan tried to take him to the public library to borrow books a couple of times, but their experiences at the library were very stressful so they stopped going. The problem was the differences between their choices of books. Mrs. Chan explained: "I didn't like the experience because when I picked out books for him, he didn't want this, he didn't want that. He picked the ones that were not suitable for him, so I would rather pick the books myself, because some of the words were too hard for him. He likes the pictures. They were not appropriate for reading. He picked the ones he liked the cover, but it was too hard for him. When I went, I would like to pick the more educational ones, like table manners, telephone manners, things like that, or talking about the moon, anything. But he would pick different ones, and he would say, 'Oh, don't pick this. I don't want to read this one.' So I didn't enjoy going with him."

Although Anthony no longer went to the library, he went to quite a few other places to take different lessons. His after-school life resembled the life of many white middle-class children. He was a busy child, especially on weekends—he took lessons in six different subjects:

1. Swimming lessons once or twice a week
2. Kickboxing lessons once a week on Tuesday (to learn self-defense and self-discipline)
3. Piano lessons once a week on Sunday and practice nearly every day
4. Chinese lessons two hours per week on Saturday
5. Soccer games and practice once a week on Saturday
6. Math school several times a week (this was dropped later at Mrs. Haines's suggestion, but continued at home by his father).

Mr. and Mrs. Chan enrolled Anthony in these different classes because they liked the approach in Hong Kong where children had a lot of homework to do (according to Mrs. Chan, many children do homework until 10 p.m. or 1 a.m.), and they were more academically focused. In contrast, they liked the fact that there was more free time for children in Canada, so as to give Anthony an opportunity to do other things. Mrs. Haines believed that Anthony was "overprogrammed" after school and suggested parental counseling for Mr. and Mrs. Chan to improve their parenting skills. Mrs. Chan was apparently embarrassed about the parental counseling sessions and was reluctant to talk about them during our interview. Mrs. Haines also recommended that Anthony drop the math classes. The Chans did not want to sign Anthony out of the class, but complied out of their respect for Mrs. Haines. Instead, Mr. Chan started to teach Anthony math using grade 2 and 3 math books three times a week at home so that Anthony could continue with what was taught in the math school. From listening to the Chinese radio broadcast in Richmond, they were aware that the math curriculum the children were learning in Canadian schools was not challenging enough and was two to three grades behind their Hong Kong peers. Mrs. Chan's own observation of Anthony's math in school seemed to confirm what they heard. She explained why they did not really want to give up the math classes for Anthony:

I find when he went [to math school], he was able to do more of the addition and subtraction just the beginning of the school year when he was in grade 1. He was able to subtract three digits, but now at school, they're still learning two digits. It's almost a year and a half later! Because we stopped him from going to math classes now, he probably has forgot

what was taught. But I think we just have to [drop it]. We
have much respect for Mrs. Haines and she is his teacher, and
we respect what she asks us to do. We live in Canada. We
have to respect what the education system is; and we leave it
to the system to teach him, especially as we don't have time
to do so many things with him.

Anthony did not like the math classes. He found them hard and
boring and was happy to drop them. Among all his after-school
classes, he liked soccer the best. One of the pictures he drew about
himself included three of his favorite things to do at home: soccer, his
Game Boy, and his scooter (see figure 4.7).

Anthony did not like Chinese classes either. However, both Mrs.
Haines and his parents believed that it was important for him to learn
his first language. They all wanted him to know both languages.
Although the Chans did not expect him to be able to write as it was
difficult to write Chinese, they expected him to know how to speak
and to learn basics in the language (for example, writing his name).
Mrs. Chan commented, "I think it's important to have both languages.
Even if one is proficient in English, I don't think that's enough. People
will look at you as Chinese and they expect you to know Chinese."
Mrs. Chan considered Anthony's English to be better than his Chinese. She noticed that Anthony sometimes used "Chinglish," that is,
he spoke English sentences "in Hong Kong style." Mrs. Chan was not
happy about this as she did not want him to pick up a Hong Kong
accent: "I want him to learn real English."

Mr. and Mrs. Chan noticed Anthony's resistance to learning Chinese. Even if they spoke Chinese to Anthony, he would reply in English.
Sometimes when they insisted, and Anthony wanted something des-
perately, he would reply in Chinese. Otherwise he refused to use Chinese even though he knew how. The Chans tried to force him to speak
Chinese on weekends, but the plan was not followed through because
of Anthony's reluctance to comply. Gradually, Mr. and Mrs. Chan had
to use English to communicate with him. Mrs. Chan could not figure
out why he started to reject Chinese as she recalled that in preschool
Anthony actually preferred Chinese to English. Her narrative suggested
some answers to Anthony's change in his choice of language use:

I don't know why. When he was in preschool in Richmond,
there were a lot of Chinese, and most of them, a lot of them
moved from Hong Kong recently. Sometimes [they] don't

Fig. 4.7. *Anthony's favorite things to do at home.*

speak English at all. When they came to preschool, they all liked to play with him because he speaks English and Chinese. We had a Filipino nanny, so he spoke with her in English even when he was very little. So he knows both. By the time he was 3 he went to preschool. I didn't like it when they

all spoke Chinese at preschool. My husband actually talked to
the teacher, and she said, "There's nothing I can do because I
don't understand what they're talking about." And the same
thing [happened] when he went to kindergarten. But since he
was in grade 1, the first few months, he spoke some Chinese
but then I think the children learned to speak in English
already, so he refused to speak in Chinese anymore.

Despite the fact that Anthony did not like to use Chinese, he still
dutifully went to Chinese school every Saturday and did his Chinese
homework. Mrs. Chan told me that the Chinese homework was
almost all the writing Anthony did at home. She shared with me one
anecdote about a note that Anthony wrote in English to Mr. Chan
about six months before the interview, which said, "Daddy, if you
don't buy something for me, then you are a dummy." They did not
think it was the right thing for Anthony to write, but they thought the
writing was funny and it was innovative for Anthony to think of writing as a means of communicating what he wanted, so they just
laughed at it.

Although the Chans had been in Canada for over 14 years, they
still did not feel that they knew much about the education system in
Canada. Mrs. Chan had attended parent conferences and some parenting counseling sessions with the teachers, but she did not feel that
she knew much about the school. She relied on some of her friends,
who were also from Hong Kong, to find out information about Canadian schools. She heard that there was not much homework in Canadian schools until grade 4 and there was "a lot of freedom." She
already started to worry about Anthony's adaptation to the sudden
increase of homework in the fourth grade, and proposed that the
school should establish a daycare or work with daycare centers to
help students like Anthony make the transition: "I think the school
would help with the transition and then at the daycare. I think daycare is experienced . . . and they know that kids spend some time
doing their homework at daycare. . . . I was thinking that everyone
has to do something. Like schools have to help them with transition.
Daycare has to assign sometimes what he has to do. And as the
parent, I have to spend some time with him when he comes home.
But I wouldn't expect to do it, like, one party to do everything. I think
it's a shared responsibility."

Mrs. Chan said that she had not yet felt the pressure other parents
had felt at the moment because Anthony was still young. She was not

sure whether it would change once Anthony got to grade 4. She agreed that she rarely saw homework from school but she was not worried because "Anthony was busy enough with other stuff."

Kevin: An Idiosyncratic, Struggling Writer

Mrs. Haines recommended Kevin as one of my focal children because of his idiosyncratic behavior in the classroom (for example, walking like a robot and murmuring). Sometimes he was so nervous that he would sit down for a minute and then get up again. Also he often broke into tears when he could not write a word or do an assignment. Mrs. Haines speculated that his idiosyncratic behavior might be a result of pressure from a home that did not encourage risk taking: "He couldn't find his math book yesterday, and tears were running down the face. I said, 'If you have a problem, then come and tell me.' So there seems to be that fear of making mistakes. Last Friday after our little spelling test, he was in tears. I said, 'What's the matter?' He said it was because his hands were sore. His hands were very dry, and there was a crack cut, and so I think it may be part of that. But part of that is he didn't get all the words right. There's this pressure, pressure, pressure to be correct, so I think they there might be some pressures that have not been obvious before."

Despite his idiosyncratic behavior, Kevin was a proficient reader. He was already able to read and comprehend many books at his age level when he entered first grade. By the end of the academic year, he was already reading at a level well above that expected of a student of his age. Because of his high reading ability, he did not receive any ESL support although his report cards indicated that he received "in class ESL support through ESL/resource teachers which included oral language practice and reading and writing skills." Kevin read a variety of books in class during silent reading time every morning, but his favorite subjects were informational books about science, plants, planets, and animals. During a morning reading session, he read to me a story from a textbook titled *A Dino-Mite Discovery*. It is a story about a boy named David who discovers a dinosaur egg on a field trip with his family. The two-page story involved guessing words from picture clues and used many difficult words such as "fossil," "remind," "scientist," "paleontologist," "million," and "dynamite." Kevin was able to sound out all the words except for the big words like "paleontologist," and was able to understand the content of the story.

Kevin not only liked to read books from the classroom bookshelf, but he also liked to bring his favorite books from home. One day, he brought his new book, *Youth World Encyclopedia*, and proudly showed it to Mrs. Haines and me: "My mom bought it for me from the library. I don't have to borrow it." Mrs. Haines showed the book to the class and read a chapter from it about paper and pencil making.

Because Kevin read widely, he was able to contribute to class discussions about their readings. He was able to answer questions many other students could not. For example, at one class discussion about different provinces, Mrs. Haines asked the class "What is sweet that comes from the trees in Ontario? " Kevin replied, "Maple syrup."

Although Kevin was a good reader, he was struggling with writing, particularly printing and spelling. He seemed to lack fine-motor skills. At the beginning of the school year, his printing was unreadable. Over the course of the school year, his printing had improved a little, but he had difficulty spelling. He was unable to spell many simple words even if he could read them and recognize them while reading. For example, he was able to read the words "like," "was," and "Richmond" but he was not able to spell them. He was often frustrated with spelling. Unlike many other children who made use of their knowledge of phonics and invented spelling, Kevin would not do so. When he was unable to spell the words he wanted to write, he often stopped writing or started crying. Mrs. Haines worked hard during the term to encourage him to try to write unfamiliar words even if he was not sure of the correct spelling. Toward the end of the school year, he was much more relaxed with unknown words and his writing had improved—he was able to try to spell words on his own. For example, he wrote "schol" for "school", "colrl" for "color," and "ice crerm" for "ice cream." In a letter he wrote for a teacher, he said, "Dear Mrs. Bullock, Thank you for your belttfao daofing" [beautiful dancing].

Similar to his writing, his drawings were also very hard to read. He liked to use pencils and crayons to scribble, but after sitting down with him and talking with him, I discovered that most of his scribbles were stories he made up. For example, in figure 4.8, the scribbles are about a person (himself) doing homework. Some of his drawings were more reader friendly, for example, when he drew about how the class was learning how to read at school. One drawing of people with a big bubble indicated a teacher talking. Facing the teacher were some students who were sitting at their tables. Some of his drawings

Fig. 4.8. *Kevin's drawing of a person doing homework.*

showed very original and profound thoughts about his reading. For example, after listening to the story *Smoky Night* (Bunting, 1994) about violence and racism, he drew a picture of arrows (figure 4.9). Although he could not write, he told me what he drew: "Racism makes me think about shooting arrows."

Although he could draw, Kevin did not like drawing. Often when the class was asked to draw or write their responses after reading a storybook, Kevin became very unhappy and was unwilling to draw. However, with some guidance, he was able to focus on a task. For example, after reading the *Gingerbread Man* story and making a real gingerbread man with the class, Mrs. Haines and her assistant asked the class to draw a plan or a trap to catch the gingerbread boy or girl if they tried to run away. Kevin, who was in a bad mood, sat at his desk and muttered to himself, "I don't want a plan. I don't want a plan." He walked over to the aide who was handing out paper, grabbed a piece of paper from her without even looking at her, walked to the pencil station and grabbed a pencil, and slowly walked back to his

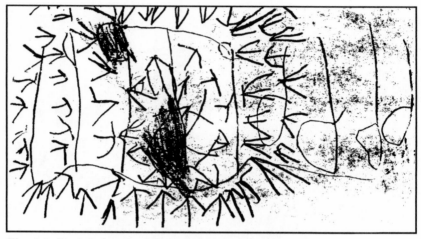

Fig. 4.9. *Kevin's drawing about racism and shooting arrows.*

desk, still muttering, "I don't want a plan." I noticed that he was sitting all by himself and went over to join him:

> Guofang: Kevin, how are you? Are you ok?
>
> Kevin: I don't know what to do.
>
> Guofang: Do you think the Gingerbread boy and girl will run away?
>
> Kevin: No! Sneezed!
>
> Guofang: What?
>
> Kevin: Sneezed.
>
> Guofang: The Gingerbread man sneezed?
>
> Kevin: No, I sneezed!
>
> Guofang (jokingly): I thought you said the Gingerbread man sneezed.
>
> Kevin (laughs and is now in a much better mood.)
>
> Guofang: You don't think the Gingerbread man will run away?
>
> Kevin: Maybe.
>
> Guofang: What will you do if he's trying to run away?
>
> Kevin: Stand in their way.
>
> Guofang: Maybe you can draw you standing in the way of the Gingerbread man.
>
> Kevin: But they'll run away underground.

Guofang: Wonderful! Maybe you can draw that too.

Kevin (not very happy): How can I draw two plans at the same time?

Guofang (folding the paper): You can fold the paper, and draw plan #1 on one side and plan #2 on the other side. How's that?

Kevin: Maybe I should just chop the legs and arms off the Gingerbread man. (He draws a Gingerbread man without legs and arms.)

Guofang: Do you think the Gingerbread man will like it?

Kevin: No! (He continues drawing his plans.)

Kevin became very excited about his plans, and started drawing right away. After he finished, he went over to talk to his friend Evan about his clever plans: "Look, this is the Gingerbread man. Stage one he's in an egg! And stage 2 he's in a tunnel, rolling!"

Although he did not like drawing and writing, Kevin enjoyed the daily math activities that were part of the class routine. He demonstrated a good understanding of math concepts and was able to quickly and accurately compute addition and subtraction equations. He was often one of the first in class to figure out the math problems presented during the routine every morning, even though he may not have been able to articulate how he arrived at the answers. For example, one morning, they were counting to 100.

Mrs. Haines: How many groups would you need to make it 100 if you count by 25?

Kevin (raising his hand): Four

Mrs. Haines: Why?

Kevin: I don't know.

Contrary to his active participation during class activities, Kevin was not active in small groups or during free-play time. Even if he sat with others at the desk, he did not seem to engage in conversation with them. Sometimes during pair work, he did not seem to understand how to work with a partner. For example, during one pair work activity with Sandy, they were asked to research what frogs eat. One would read the text while the other took notes. Kevin picked up the book and read on as if he was working alone. "I can read this!" he said after he finished reading and he left Sandy sitting at the desk not knowing what to do.

During the academic year, I rarely saw him play with other children except for his friend Evan, whom he occasionally played with after school. Mrs. Yep commented, "He talks with Evan but not with other kids." With Evan, he was able to talk about a variety of topics such as movies or videos he saw, things he did for Chinese New Year, and the games he played with his brother. One time when he and Evan were talking about a video they had watched, *Indiana Jones*, I pretended that I did not know about the movie and asked who Indiana Jones was. Kevin and Evan were very keen on explaining the movie to me:

> Kevin: He's a guy in a tape. He went to a treasure hunt, then the bad guy came, and then when he poured the water from the cup, the bad guy turned into some kind of bones. Then his father was in danger, and Indiana Jones saved his father with the cup. There are five stories of Indiana Jones and one is boring, doesn't have a lot of fighting.
>
> Evan: Did you know a new Superstore? You can buy Indiana Jones in that store. A new big one! My dad and my mom and my sister go there together.

During their free-play time, Kevin and Evan always played with Lego blocks. They often built high structures and imagined they were different buildings or volcanoes. Here is one of their typical conversations during play:

> Kevin: Yes, I felt it.
> Evan: It's weak, just shaking, no cracks.
> Kevin: If there's a crack, then you fall down.
> Evan: You'll turn into lava.
> Kevin: There'll be a volcano.
> Evan (laughing): You'll be cooked.
> Kevin: No, you melt, not cooked.
> Evan: Cooked.
> Kevin: Melt. Everything melts, dead.
> Evan: Ok.

At school, Kevin never spoke Chinese. He told me that he could not speak Chinese. Only on one occasion, I captured Kevin and Evan talking in Chinese about going to the mall:

Evan: In the mall, I keep up with my dad and my sister keeps
 up with my mother.
Kevin: I go home, play, and eat and watch TV.
Evan: I do that too.
Kevin: Do you talk in Chinese?
Evan: I learned Chinese before I went to school. I learned
 Chinese at home because I'm 中国人 (zhong guo ren)
 [Chinese].
Kevin: I can write Chinese. I go to Chinese school.
Evan: I can too. . . .

Kevin at Home

Kevin demonstrated the same kind of nervousness at home—the same
walk and the same way of talking. When I asked his father, Mr. Ma,
whether Kevin was nervous, he denied it at first and observed that
Kevin had been like this since he was a toddler. Later, he acknowledged that Kevin did not know how to communicate with others and
this caused his nervousness. Mr. Ma noted that Kevin was more serious than other children of his age. When he did not understand something or when he saw people not following the rules, he would be
very unhappy: "Our former neighbor used to tease him and Kevin got
very nervous and serious whenever he did that. He is just like this. At
school when I pick him up, sometimes he would say to me, 'Dad, why
didn't [the other students] line up?' And he was very upset about
it. . . . I told him to loosen up and smile more, and I want him to play
more with other kids."

Mr. Ma also thought that Kevin was mature for his age. Kevin
liked to play with kids older than himself. He had his own ideas and
principles and his own requests of others, and these ideas and principles made him more serious than other kids. Mr. Ma believed that
more extracurricular activities at school would help him relax, but he
was disappointed that the school had cut all its after-school activities.

Kevin also spoke English to his parents and brother at home,
although they all spoke Cantonese to him. He went to Saturday Chinese school for two and a half hours every week. Although Kevin
rarely talked about it, Mr. Ma told me that it was hard for Kevin to
learn to read and write Chinese because of the limited time he put into
studying the language. Mr. Ma also believed that Kevin could speak

Cantonese, but just did not want to. He also told me that Kevin disliked going to the Chinese school: "He seldom watches Chinese TV programs. He likes to watch English ones, and he has got used to it and English has become his language. He dislikes speaking Chinese and he seldom speaks. I know why he dislikes the Chinese school, for the Chinese school is not like his school where he can play a lot. In Chinese school, he has to sit there for two and a half hours. He once asked me why there was no playground in the Chinese school."

Kevin also went to a Beaver's (Boy Scouts') group every Monday where he could learn to play with other children and learn discipline. Mr. Ma told me that Kevin really enjoyed the activities of the group. Mr. Ma was also going to enroll Kevin in piano, swimming, and tae kwon do lessons, but Kevin was not interested so Mr. Ma decided not to pursue those lessons for the time being: "He just was not interested in it. If he didn't want it, I'll just drop it." Mr. Ma said.

Kevin did not attend a math school either. Mr. Ma considered it "not necessary now since he's still young." Mr. Ma sometimes taught Kevin math at home and asked him to recite challenging addition and multiplication formulas following Chinese math-teaching traditions. Though he thought that it was important to learn the basics, Mr. Ma admitted that Kevin did not enjoy it and sometimes refused to recite the formulas: "For example, the pithy multiplication formula, it's really simple, and it will help children figure out many math problems. If the school doesn't require the kid to learn it, then it would be difficult for the child in the beginning."

Kevin took math homework very seriously. Whenever a math problem (for example, counting money) was assigned, he would come home to prepare for it, try to figure out the formulas himself, and then recite the formula every night. Gradually, he was able to do more complicated addition and multiplication problems such as adding by 10s or 20s.

Kevin was an avid reader at home. He read every day before going to bed. He read not only information books but also short stories his parents borrowed for him from the public library and bought for him at bookstores. He usually read by himself and constantly asked his parents questions about the readings. "Sometimes, he asks too many questions when he reads," Mr. Ma noted. For example, he asked many questions about the sun and the stars when reading about the solar system in his favorite book, *Youth World Encyclopedia*. His parents were unable to answer many of his questions. Over the course of the research, his home reading record suggested that he had read

The following text appears within the drawing:

stars

Astronauts

can and UP

down

Moon

orbit

solar

system

SUN

Fig. 4.10. *Kevin's drawing of astronauts in orbit in the solar system.*

over 100 books and many of them were collections of stories or chapter books such as *50 Favorite Stories, 50 Bedtime Stories, Volcano,* and *Haunted House.*

Kevin not only read books, he also drew pictures or wrote about what he read. For example he read about the solar system, and he drew and wrote about astronauts in space: (figure 4.10) "Astronauts can and up and down orbit solar system." [Astronauts can go up and down the orbit in the solar system].

Mr. Ma was aware that Kevin's penmanship was problematic. He was, however, not overly worried. Mr. Ma believed that different children had different developmental stages and as Kevin grew older, he would have better fine-motor skills, and therefore his printing would improve. After all, he just started school as a first grader.

Mr. Ma was more concerned about Kevin's expressive writing. He noted that although Kevin could read and comprehend what he read, he could not express his understanding through writing. In order to foster Kevin's writing, Mr. Ma encouraged Kevin to write e-mails in English to his grandparents in Hong Kong. Although it was very simple, Mr. Ma believed that it would be a good way to practice writing at home. Mr. Ma hoped that Kevin would not have problems similar to his brother Rob's. Rob was in ninth grade and was struggling with reading and writing, relying on tutors and extra classes so that he would be able to get into one of the universities in the city when he graduated. If Kevin couldn't improve his writing, they would have to send him for tutoring as well.

Besides reading and writing, Kevin often spent time at home watching TV and playing video or computer games. He watched a variety of cartoons such as Pokemon and Digimon on several kids' channels such as YTV and KTV. Mr. Ma also took Kevin to the library once a week to borrow CD games. Some of these games were for learning English or general knowledge. He believed that it was useful to play these games while learning. For example, with games such as *Roman Empire* and *Asian Empire,* Kevin had learned a lot about Western and Eastern history, including the Roman Empire and ancient Egypt.

Alana: Adjusting to the New Environment

Alana's parents' uncertainty about whether to stay in Canada or not had an impact on how they perceived their children's education. Mr. and Mrs. Tang wanted Alana to become literate in both English and

Chinese so that she would be prepared for living in both countries. At the time this study began, Alana had been at Taylor Elementary for a year and a half, and had not yet developed proficiency in speaking English. She was a beginning ESL student, and was pulled out of class every day to work with two ESL teachers in small language groups for 40-minute periods. However, she was able to name all the letters and almost all of the associated sounds, and read some simple words. Mrs. Haines observed that Alana could complete her journal writing with support and was beginning to spell some words on her own. Mrs. Haines told me that in the previous year Alana was frequently absent from class because she went back to China several times and this discontinuity resulted in her slow progress in English.

Alana formed an instant bond with me when I started the research study because she found out that I could speak Mandarin. She told me that she missed her kindergarten in China: "I like China a lot. My teacher liked me the best. She always asked me to do things. But it's not like that here."

Alana at School

Alana loved reading at school. I noted during the 15-minute morning reading time that she often appeared glued to her book—she looked intently and closely at the book as if the world around her did not exist. She looked mostly at the pictures, as she could not yet sound out many of the words. Mrs. Haines told me a story about the day when she first started to read the letters: "Alana was reading *Ten Apples Up On Top*. And all of a sudden one day she made that connection between the print on the page and the words we were saying out loud. It was a formal reading process that started for her, and she was so excited about that. She came to read the book to me, and then to Mrs. Gambell [the principal]. It was a real transition for her. I photocopied the page and put it in her file."

Although Alana began to make sense of the words on the page, she was struggling with listening and speaking. Her lack of ability in these two skills prevented her from fully participating in classroom activities. Mrs. Haines told me that most of the assessment on Alana had been focused on her understanding English, and it was hard to assess her other curriculum areas. During the whole-class reading time, she often appeared quiet and confused and often looked at other students to try to understand what was going on. Sometimes she looked around the classroom and appeared to have lost interest in the activities. For example, when the class was listening to the story *Happy Yo Yo* on tape, or listening to songs like *Junk Food Blues* and *Canada in My Pocket*, Alana often appeared lost and was unable to follow the activities. And often during these activities, she was unable to ask Mrs. Haines's aide or me for assistance, so she just sat there and watched the students around her.

Alana also appeared to have trouble understanding some of the writing activities. During their Christmas unit, one of the tasks was to write a letter to Santa about their wishes for Christmas presents. Mrs. Haines wrote the letter format on the blackboard and asked students to write their own wishes following the letter format:

Dear Santa,
Please may I have ___
I wish_____
I hope you_____
    From_____

Alana took a piece of paper and sat down at her desk, but she did not know what to do. Mrs. Yep went over to help her and asked, "Alana, do you know what to do?" Alana answered, pointing to the blackboard, "No." Mrs. Yep explained in English what the task was. But Alana turned to tell me in Chinese, "I don't know what I was supposed to do." I explained to her in Chinese and she understood.

I speculated that her confusion about the task might be related to the concept of Santa rather than simply language. She did not appear to understand who Santa was and why she had to write a letter to him to ask for things. In a subsequent conversation with Mrs. Haines, Alana spoke about her wishes for her mom, which differed from other children who expressed wishes for themselves:

Mrs. Haines: What do you wish for?
Alana (thinking for a couple of seconds): My mom.
Mrs. Haines: What do you wish for you mom?
Alana: ABC book.
Mrs. Haines: You want one ABC book, for you or for your mommy?
Alana: For Mommy.
Mrs. Haines: Why?
Alana: No why.

Mrs. Haines: You want your mom to learn English?
Alana: Yes.

Alana came over to me and asked me to write for her in her notebook, "My gift Mom, one ABC book."

Alana appeared to dislike drawing in school. She often complained that her drawings were ugly and did not want to show them to classmates or teachers. One of their activities was to observe the school environment and write about what they saw. Alana drew a picture of herself playing on the playground. She drew it and erased it and drew it again. She told me in Chinese, "I feel that my drawing is really ugly." I encouraged her in Chinese, "No, it's not ugly. It's quite nice!" Hearing this, she felt good and wrote about what she drew: "I went to the playground to play slide and swing."

On another occasion, when Alana came back from the class's field trip around the neighborhood, she was supposed to draw and write about their trip. She sat at her desk and did not appear to be working on her drawing and writing. I went over and spoke to her.

Alana: I can't draw. It's not that I don't want to.
Guofang: Of course you can. What did you see today?
Alana: Oh, I know now. Guess what it is?
Guofang: I don't know.
Alana: Something long and small.
Guofang: A snake?
Alana: Correct!

After she finished, she came to me and said in Chinese, "I finished, now what should I do?" I told her to show her drawing to Mrs. Haines. She replied, "I don't know how to say it to her." I taught her how to say "snake" and she went to Mrs. Haines. Mrs. Haines praised her work, which made her very happy.

Although Alana was critical about her drawings, she did draw quite a bit. Her drawings demonstrated her comprehension of the stories she read or listened to. Afterward, Mrs. Haines or Mrs. Yep would normally sit down with her to talk about her drawing, and to write down her stories for her. For example, in January 2001, after the unit about the Gingerbread Boy, she was able to describe in her picture the details of the story, and instead of drawing a picture about a gingerbread boy, she decide to draw a story about a gingerbread girl (figure 4.11). Her writing was not just about school readings, but also about

Fig. 4.11. *Alana's story of the gingerbread girl.*

her home life. She even used Chinese characters in her writing. She wrote the following about her Chinese New Year dinner and added traditional Chinese "Dui Lian"—antithetical couplets posted on Chinese doors during the Chinese New Year (figure 4.12).

Alana expressed her home experiences not only in her writing, but in other ways as well. She was always very excited when she could recognize Chinese characters. For example, when Mrs. Haines read the New Year's card I sent to the class, Alana was quite excited and said in Chinese, "I know that word! Happiness!" In January 2001, she brought her math book from home to show me. The math book was for grade one students in China and was brought over by her parents to teach her math at home. Another day she brought in her per-

Fig. 4.12. *Alana's writing about her Chinese New Year dinner.*

sonal phonebook and wrote down our telephone numbers. Other times, she liked to teach me different things she learned from home. One day she played the role of a teacher with me:

Alana: Do you know how to draw a rabbit?
Guofang: I don't know.
Alana: I'll teach you how. (She takes a pencil and draws a rabbit step by step)
Alana: This way, then this way.
Guofang: Wow! Who taught you this?
Alana: My cousin.
Guofang: What's your cousin's name?

> Alana: I won't tell you. Now you draw. Remember don't
> draw it the wrong way.
> Guofang: Ok (I start to draw a rabbit following her example.)
> Alana: This way. Ok. You forgot to draw the carrot. . . . Try to
> do it better . . . this way. (She takes over the pencil and
> shows me how to improve my drawing.)

Although Alana was a cheerful child, I found that she was not socially content in the classroom. In September 2000, Alana first befriended Shivani, an East Indian girl with autism. Since it was hard for Alana to understand Shivani's speech, Alana did not play with her that much. As Mrs. Yep had observed, Alana did not make many friends in school. Many times Alana told me that she had no friends and nobody to play with. I often found her alone during recess:

> Guofang: Are you going out to play?
> Alana: I don't want to go out and play.
> Guofang: Why not?
> Alana: I don't have friends to play with.

Alana often expressed that she missed her friends in China. In December 2000, when Mrs. Haines was doing the Christmas unit, Alana came to ask me to read *Rudolph the Red Nosed Reindeer* to her in Chinese because it had too many words in it. I started to translate the story from English into Chinese for her. When I got to the part where no other reindeers would play with Rudolf because he had a red nose and he was small, and he felt lonely and sad, Alana started to relate the story to her own feelings: "I have nobody to play with because I can't speak English. I used to have a friend to play with me, but she doesn't play with me anymore. But I have other friends in Liu Zhou [her hometown in China]."

To make a change, I continued reading the book in English, and Alana appeared to have lost interest in the book, "Oh, too many words." She took the book, closed it, and put it back on the shelf.

When I informed Mrs. Haines of Alana's expression of loneliness at school, Mrs. Haines speculated that it was a combination of her family who did not like their children to be out of their supervision, and Alana's lack of socializing with other kids: "The kids in that neighborhood rarely have out of school playtime so any friendships they form are just the school friendships. . . . I don't think she has a lot of out of school play time away from the family, and there is very little after-school socialization amongst the children that I'm aware of. The families do a lot of going out in the evenings to restaurants and that sort of thing, but it's with the family, not with other children, so that might make friendships difficult."

In early January 2001, Alana befriended a Cantonese-speaking girl, Melinda, who was much better at English than she was, and this friendship greatly helped Alana. During one of the sessions about the *Gingerbread Man*, for example, they were required to write their understanding of the story in their notebook, and they copied some of the big words such as "gingerbread" from the blackboard. Alana was not sure she was copying correctly. Melinda explained to her in Cantonese, "This letter should be capitalized. Look, you can see it on the blackboard."

Alana's constant use of Chinese was, however, against the unofficial English-only rule. Although most of the students understood that Alana had a minimal English vocabulary, a couple of students (for example, Sandy) protested her constant use of Chinese. One time when Melinda, Sandy, and Alana sat at a table coloring, Alana was talking to Melinda in Mandarin and English, and again Sandy protested:

Alana (in Chinese): I finished!
Melinda (in Chinese): I haven't yet.
Alana (pointing to Melinda's pattern): This is not right.
Melinda: Right. I need more color here.
Sandy: Alana, no Chinese, you know the rule.

Regardless of Sandy's protest, Alana continued to code-switch between Chinese and English with Melinda. Her status in the classroom changed dramatically when in mid January 2001 a new student, Kara, joined the class from China. Kara could speak Mandarin and Cantonese, but could not speak any English, and Alana immediately took the role of assisting Kara and translating for her. When I walked into the classroom on Kara's first day, I saw Alana and Kara sitting on the floor with a book open in front of them, and Alana was translating some words for Kara. Other students who also saw the change in Alana came to report to me, "Alana is helping Kara!" I went over and praised her: "What a good girl, Alana!"

Alana became more active in class activities and was always eager to make Kara understand what was going on around her. For example, if there was a drawing and writing activity, Alana would explain to Kara what to do in Cantonese: "You draw a picture, and then you write a sentence. If you don't know how to spell the words, they're on the blackboard. See there." Alana also took up a teacher's role during their play station time. The following conversation took place in Mandarin:

> Alana: Let me teach you. How much is eight minus one?
> Kara: Seven.
> Alana: Let's do another one. This one is very hard! How much is eight plus one plus two?
> Kara: Ten?
> Alana: Wrong!
> Kara: Eleven!
> Alana: Correct! But how much is eight minus one plus two?
> Kara: I know, I know. Nine!

During free play time, Alana and Melinda fully embraced Kara into their group, and they code-switched between Mandarin, Cantonese, and English. They worked together to make necklaces from colorful beads and played different games together such as hand string games. When making necklaces, they had the following conversation:

> Alana (in Cantonese): Kara, you can pick the colors you like.
> Kara (in Cantonese): I like red and orange.
> Melinda (in Cantonese): I like red too.
> Alana (in Mandarin): I like purple.
> Kara (in Mandarin): I don't like purple.
> Melinda (in English): Is this ok? Ew, it's ugly!
> Alana (in English): You make one more.

At the end of April 2001, another new student, Alicia, from China, joined the class. Alana also took her into their group. She enjoyed her new friends and wrote about learning different things at school with these friends. Mrs. Haines commented that it had been fruitful for Alana to have some new students come into the class: "She is really acting as a translator for them, which is good because she has to understand English. . . . She's very happy and relaxed in school and she's probably socializing less with the whole group now that Kara and Alicia have come in. She's gravitated towards them, and she's the leader in that group now because she had more experience than they do."

Alana's Home Literacy Practices

Alana's home was a distinctly different world from school although it was located across the street from the school. Every day, Alana's father, Mr. Tang, came to pick her up from school at around 3:00 p.m. when he finished his lunch and some on-line business. At home, Alana would generally watch TV for a few hours until supper time. She usually watched English cartoons such as *Sailor Moon, Digimon, Pokemon,* and *Power Ranger.* These were the only few hours that Alana had contact with English at home. Mr. Tang was not happy that Alana spent so many hours in front of the TV (it was bad for her eyes, he said), so sometimes he took her to play in nearby parks, or he asked her to play outside the house for a change. Occasionally, Alana played video games on the computer and watched Chinese TV. On weekends, Mr. Tang took her along to go shopping and to get together with some Chinese friends they had made in Canada. He also drove Alana to her weekly piano lessons.

Since Mr. and Mrs. Tang could not speak English and were not sure they wanted to stay in Canada long-term, they were very serious about Alana's Chinese development. They taught her Chinese reading and writing at home and required her to speak Chinese at all times. Although they understood that there were cultural differences between school and home, they expected their children to "act in Canadian ways at school and follow Chinese ways at home." Mr. Tang felt strongly about the importance of keeping the Chinese language and culture: "As a Chinese, she has to learn her mother tongue to maintain Chinese culture and tradition. I ask them that if we go back to China 10 years later and they can't speak any Chinese and can't communicate with their grandparents, what will they do then?"

He also believed that it was important for his children to learn English as well: "Since we came to Canada, they have to learn both English and Chinese. Some Chinese cultures and traditions are really good and we have to keep them. We also need to learn the good aspects of Canadian culture." Mr. Tang perceived that his role as a parent was to "teach them Chinese at home." He did not think he could do much to teach his children English: "They have to learn English themselves, because our English is poor. They have to depend on themselves to learn it."

Every evening after supper, Mr. or Mrs. Tang would teach Alana Chinese characters using textbooks they brought over from China. Mr. Tang told me that Alana was already studying at a second grade level in Chinese and could read many words. They followed the textbook instructions and other Chinese literacy instruction methods they were familiar with such as copying. Mr. Tang explained, "We're not as strict with her as we were in China. We used to ask her to copy a lot, but now we're here in Canada, and we still require her to finish all the assignments, and learn more new words, and that's ok. But we're not as demanding as we were in China, strictly monitoring her progress every day."

In March 2001, Alana told me that her mom had changed her schedule so that she could come home from work at around 4:00 p.m. to teach her Chinese characters. "I have Chinese homework. I also have to practice the piano. Chinese is hard."

They also brought many Chinese children's storybooks from China. Alana had read many of them with Mrs. Tang at home (figure 4.13). Mr. Tang believed that Alana's skills in Chinese would help her in learning English. However, Alana's extensive Chinese reading at home was not communicated to Mrs. Haines, who thought that Alana did not read at all at home. Mrs. Haines asked me to talk to Alana's brother twice and later once with Mr. Tang about the home reading records. After my conversations with Alana's brother and parents, I realized that they did not know they were supposed to record Alana's readings in Chinese or English on a reading record form, sign it, and return it to Mrs. Haines. Once they understood this requirement, Alana began to bring these records to class regularly on time. These readings demonstrated that Alana was a sophisticated and avid reader in Chinese. Alana drew a picture of herself reading in her bed and told me that she enjoyed reading stories at home.

Mr. and Mrs. Tang taught Alana not only Chinese at home but also math. Like many new Chinese immigrants, they quickly learned from their son's seventh grade experience that math in Canadian schools was three years behind schools in China. Mr. Tang commented, "What is taught in eighth grade math is the fifth-grade level in China." And like many parents from China, they already used Chinese textbooks to teach Alana math, and she had already finished working on the first-grade math textbook.

Although Mr. and Mrs. Tang could not understand much English, they tried their best to watch Alana's progress by listening to her talk about school. They noticed that Alana's English had improved and they were pleased that she was making progress. Since they were new to the country, they relied on their new Chinese friends to understand the differences between Canadian schools and Chinese schools. They

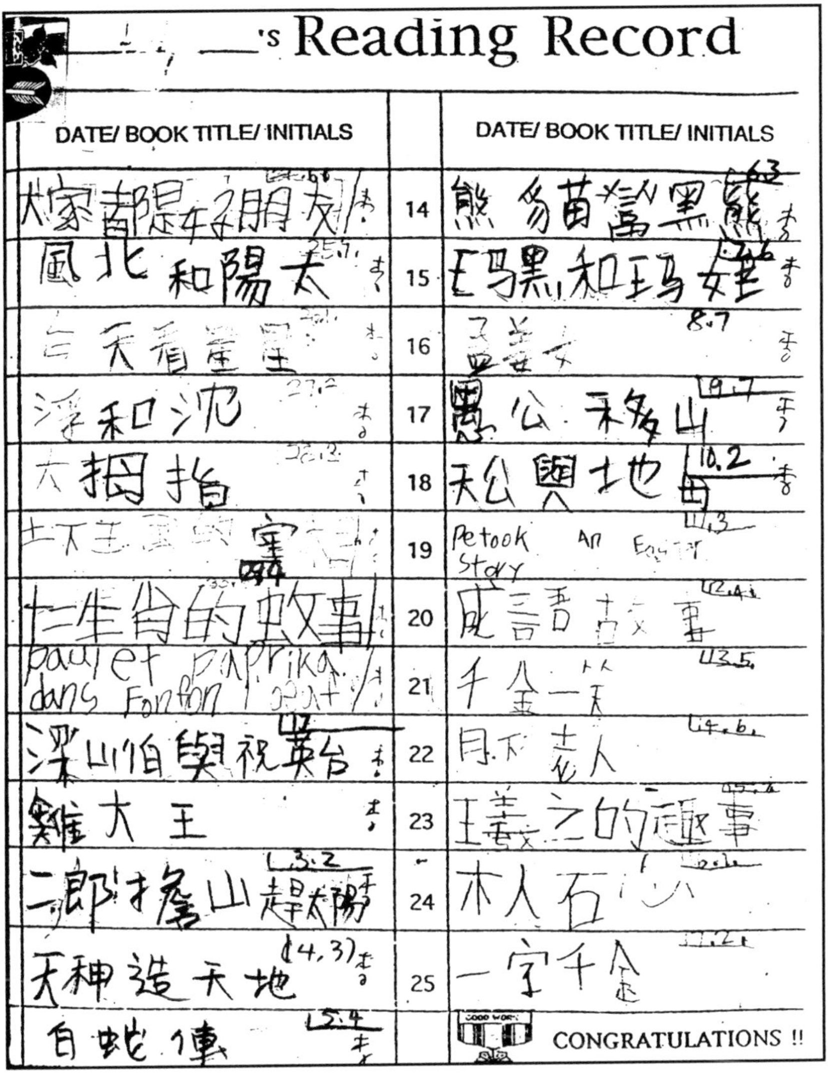

Fig. 4.13. *Alana's home reading record.*

had asked many of these friends about Alana's slow progress in English. Mr. Tang recounted, "One year ago when I was worried about my daughter's progress in English, one of my friends told me that I didn't need to worry and that my daughter would catch up in a couple of years. I've asked many friends, not just one, and they all had this experience. So with Alana, if her teacher didn't say she wasn't doing well, I would just pay some attention to her report card. If one area is really bad or not meeting the standards, I'll be very worried. I feel that she's doing ok, and she's also slowly making progress, as my friends have predicted."

Mr. Tang felt that as long as his children were performing well in school without failing any subjects, he did not need to communicate with the teachers. For example, although he did not like the fact that the school emphasized drawing, he chose to make adjustments at home rather than talking to the teacher about it: "They do draw too much at school, so at home we emphasize more academic aspects. I think the teachers just want the students to have more freedom to choose what they want to do." Mr. Tang reiterated that he was not worried about Alana's studies so far as she was still young.

Conclusion

In this chapter, I have described school and home literacy experiences of the four grade 1/2 learners: Sandy, Anthony, Kevin, and Alana. Although each child had their distinct experiences at home and at school, they were all caught in the school-home conflicts and miscommunications. These forays, which had become part of their daily literacy and living, have had a significant impact on their learning experiences.

It was encouraging to see Sandy smile more often over the course of this research study. Although Sandy had made some progress in her negative attitude in the classroom, she still had a long way to go. Her negativity was not a result of parents' pampering and indulging, but a result of the school's English-only policy and pressure from home. With her brother Billy's failure in a higher grade (see chapter 5), Sandy was faced with more pressure to do better in school and not to follow suit after her brother. This pressure will continue to have an impact on her academic learning in and out of school as she moves up to higher grades. As Mrs. Haines commented, "It would be interesting to see how she's developed [over time]."

Mrs. Haines had not had much contact with Anthony's parents since he dropped the math class. She thought that "they must have given up [putting pressure on Anthony] because any advice that we gave them was picked up." Anthony was indeed overprogrammed given his busy schedule every week. However, Mrs. Haines was not aware that he was overprogrammed not only with academic studies (math), but also with other extracurricular activities such as swimming, kickboxing, piano, and soccer practices. He soon had a new item on his busy schedule: learning how to use a computer—a skill his parents considered critical to becoming a professional in the future. Like Sandy's parents, Anthony's parents' overprogramming was a response to their perception that school practices lacked rigor and their constant reference to schooling in Hong Kong.

Over the course of the research study, Kevin's idiosyncratic behavior did not seem to change much. Mrs. Haines and her assistant continued to work hard to help with his nervousness and were trying to communicate this aspect to his parents. However, his school and home experiences seemed to suggest that his condition was not a result of family pressure as Mrs. Haines had assumed; rather, it was his personality and part of who he was. Understanding this would encourage his teacher to find ways to help Kevin open up and learn to effectively express himself through writing.

Similar to Alana's ESL teacher, it was a joy for me to watch her develop her English language skills as she made more friends at school. Alana continued to be pulled out for ESL support. Her ESL teacher said, "With a continued effort and support from home and school she should continue to develop her English language skills." Alana made progress in her reading, writing, speaking, and listening in English. She became much better at understanding instructions for class activities. Toward the end of my data collection, she was able to read a few picture books to me. I also noted that she started to use English when speaking to me.

The four children's experiences in and out of school show that the parents were actively involved in their children's learning at home, and their ways of involvement were shaped by their cultural beliefs that they brought from their home country, their understanding of Canadian schooling, and their perception of their own status in Canada. The children's differential experiences at home and in school not only reflected the different educational philosophies discussed in the preceding chapter, but also revealed serious misconceptions and misunderstandings between the teachers and the parents regarding the students' learning and development. The parents, out of their deference to the teachers, showed a "pattern of relatively passive cooperation" with school even though they were unsatisfied with school practices (Harry, 1992, p. 427). However, unlike other low-income parents documented in other studies who felt hopeless, these Chinese parents had financial capital to invest in after-school classes as well as human capital to teach their children at home. Inevitably, these investments brought more pressure on the children and further reinforced the teachers' conception of the parents' overprogramming of the children. The children's experiences suggest that the battles between teachers' and parents' educational beliefs can have an impact on these learners as early as the beginning grades.

However, the statement "They're still young" expressed the common optimism that the parents held regarding their children's school performance in the early grades. Will this optimism last for parents whose children entered fourth grade and faced their first Foundation Skills Assessment tests? In the next chapter, I present the experiences of four focal children who were at the critical grades, grades 4 and 5. Their stories will demonstrate a greater school-home dichotomy that had become a hindrance to their academic achievement.

CHAPTER FIVE

Living through the Battles

Billy, Andy, Jake, and Tina

The four learners featured in this chapter were from Ms. Dawson's grade 4/5 combined class. They volunteered to participate in the study with the consent of their parents. Round-faced Billy Chung was 10 years old. Like his sister Sandy, he took everything very seriously, and was under tremendous pressure to achieve and do well because he had not seemed to be able to improve his English language proficiency much since he had entered the fourth grade.

Andy Lou, age 10, Billy's best friend in school, was the opposite of Billy. He was sociable and easygoing. He lived in the shadow of his older sister's school failure and also experienced tremendous difficulty in school, especially in English reading and writing. Frustrated at the school's failure to teach Andy English, his parents withdrew him from the ESL list and considered moving to another school district.

Eleven-year-old Jake Wong was in grade 5 and was very verbal, outgoing, active, and well liked by his classmates. He was a leader among his small group of friends. Judging from his interaction with other students, it was hard to believe that Jake would soon be referred for psychoeducational testing due to his lack of academic progress since grade 1.

Twelve-year-old Tina Wei was tall and thin. She was shy, quiet, and timid looking. Being the only Mandarin speaker who had recently come from Mainland China, Tina had a hard time making friends at school. Although she was struggling with writing and math, Tina had a strong desire to learn English and to fit in. She soon began to develop a negative attitude toward the Chinese language and culture.

147

Starting in grade 4, all children in British Columbia were required to take part in the provincial Foundation Skills Assessment tests. The tests, though not counted toward students' grades on their report cards, created much anxiety among the Chinese families. In addition, departing from the emphasis on learning through play in the primary grades, the curriculum in the intermediate grades increased in both scope and depth, also causing great concern to the parents. When the children did not perform well in school, the parents held the school practices accountable. The parents not only critiqued the school's literacy instructional approaches, but also its assessment and placement practices. To compensate for what they perceived as lacking in the school program, they also employed their own financial resources to seek more teacher-centered, traditional instruction after school.

As the children's school and home experiences will demonstrate, the children were socialized into culturally different literacy practices and were subjected to a cultural mismatch that was detrimental to their academic success. In order to highlight these cultural mismatches, in the descriptions of each child's school and home experiences, I include separate sections on the teachers' and the parents' perspectives of the children's struggles with schooling. Since I did not interview Tina's parents or visit their home, I do not provide the home experiences or parent perspectives of Tina's learning in and out of school.

Experiencing the "Fourth-Grade Slump": Billy's Story

At the end of May 2000, Billy finished third grade with Level 3 (intermediate) ESL skills. However, since he had started the fourth grade his literacy performance had not improved: in May 2001, he was still classified as a low Level 3 ESL student (with Level 3 in oral and writing skills, and Level 2 in reading). He was, however, at or above levels expected of his age group in math, fine arts, music, and physical education, and he took pride in his accomplishments in these areas.

Billy was a serious fourth grader, conscious of other students' comments about him. He was sometimes defensive and abrupt in his interactions with others. After observing him for a few months, I discovered that he was a child of paradoxes and contradictions. He expressed high interest in learning. He wrote during one of our focus group interviews, "Leaning is fun because you can learn more about Science, spelling, and lots of other stuff." But he often resisted learning and doing home and schoolwork; he often appeared "lost" (as Mrs. Smith described it), and sat in his seat staring blankly and doing nothing when he was assigned independent tasks in class. Yet he was talkative and active among his friends and during some group work. These contradictions enticed me to want to know more about him.

Billy's Literacy Practices at School

At school Billy constantly spoke in Cantonese, despite Ms. Dawson's frequent oral and written reminders that he must speak English at school and that it was rude to carry on a conversation in another language when non-Cantonese speakers were present. He conversed during recess, lunch time, and even class time with his friends in Cantonese. He used Cantonese for a variety of purposes: to exchange information about video games they played and movies they saw; to talk about their weekends, Chinese school, and homework; and to help each other with academic work they were doing. He only spoke English to teachers and classmates who were not Cantonese speakers. Both Ms. Dawson and Mrs. Smith commented that he was not developing oral English skills as steadily as he should, and he needed to practice speaking grammatically correct English. During one of the interviews, Billy expressed his feeling that speaking English, especially "speaking science," was difficult because of the new words.

Vocabulary, a causal determinant of reading comprehension ability (Beck, Perfetti, & McKeown, 1982), was also a problem for Billy when he read. When I read along with him during silent reading time, I found that he would often become stuck when he ran into a new word; he could sound out some words, but often failed to guess the meaning from the context. Billy worked really hard on his vocabulary. He recited all the words on Ms. Dawson's word lists, and usually did well during the spelling activities. However, he did not seem to be able to retain these words and many times he could not recognize some of the words when he read, nor spell them when he wrote. Billy's difficulty with spelling indicated that he lacked some of the knowledge in sound-to-spelling mapping that is significant for independent decoding ability (Perfetti, 1984). This lack of phonological decoding skills is considered by some to be the most important predictor of why children have difficulty with reading acquisition (Snow, Burns, & Griffin, 1998; Stanovich, 1986). Billy realized his weakness and wrote that he needed to "learn how to spell hard work [word]." I observed that whenever he ran into words or passages he did not understand, he would not continue. He did not appear to use any strategies such as predicting from the context to make sense of the unknown words. One time when he was working on a grammar worksheet on suffixes, I went over to help him. He pointed to the page and told me, "I don't get this!" He told me that he could not understand the word "parentheses" in the instructions that said, "Look at the suffixes in the parentheses below. How are they spelled? Use a dictionary to write the meaning of each suffix." The word "parentheses" prevented him from understanding the whole sentence.

Billy's low reading ability affected his comprehension in the other core subjects of science, social studies, and math. Ms. Dawson also noticed that he needed to improve his fluency and expression in reading, and to pay more attention to punctuation. In terms of reading for comprehension, Billy might have been considered a "field-dependent" learner (Irvine & York, 1995). Ms. Dawson noted that when he talked to somebody about what he was reading or when worked with others in a group, he was more successful; when he was given a reading exercise to do by himself, he was not able to comprehend as much. I noticed many times that when independent reading or writing tasks were assigned, he often stared at something, motionless in his seat, as if he was lost in some deep thought.

Billy's difficulty with comprehension was reflected in his reading for his literature circle tasks. He was able to complete tasks such as "Word Hunter," for which he just copied the definitions of the words from the dictionary without understanding them in contexts, or "Passage Picker," for which he copied some passages or some conversations on a page without any explanation of his choices. However, he had more difficulty completing the other more challenging tasks such as "Connector" (connecting what happened in the book with his own experiences) and "Friend of the Character" (writing about the characters). For example, after reading *George's Marvelous Medicine* he wrote for his "Friend of the Character" role: "The character is George and his grandmas. George's grandma went crazy and told George to not grow." Although he was able to identify main ideas, he was unable to make inferences about relationships between events and characters or draw reasonable conclusions from the readings. These reading skills are, however, significant according to the provincial Foundation Skills Assessment test. During the literature circle discussions, Billy was more concerned with discipline or behavior issues (such as who did or did not do the homework or bring their books) rather than the discussion of the content and comprehension, especially when he was the discussion director. Several times, when students in his group did not do their homework, he would get very upset and would not be able to continue the discussion. Since his group members were all Cantonese speakers, many times their discussion and arguments ended up in Cantonese. He wrote the following about writing and literature circle: "I like writing because it is good for you. Sometimes I just dont want to write because I have too much homework to do. I like writing because sometimes I can learn more stuff and I can print better. Writing is importend because when I am in high school I will have to write a lot. I like writing sometimes because it is fun and sometimes it is not fun. It is fun because you can learn more things and sometimes it is not fun because you have to write about boring stuff. Literature circle is not fun because my group are all not doing their homework."

Like many poor readers, Billy suffered from the "poor-get-poorer" Mathew effects: his limited vocabulary and low reading comprehension prevented him from reading more; and reading less in turn inhibited his further growth in reading ability (Juel, 1988; Stanovich, 1986), even though he wanted to become a good reader. At the beginning of the school year, Billy set a goal for his reading by saying that he wanted to "read more books at school." Along with this goal, he drew himself reading four *Harry Potter* books. However, he was unable to read *Harry Potter*. As the year progressed, he often sat in his seat with a book open on his desk, his eyes wandering around the classroom. Even if he decided to read, he often chose short, simple books during silent reading time. For example, he often chose short readings such as poems from *Nelson Language Arts*. When I asked him whether he had a favorite story from the book, he said, "No, I don't like any of the stories." I asked him why he chose the book. He answered, "I don't know." Billy wrote about his feelings toward reading as follows, "But sometime I hate reading because it is boring. I like reading because sometime it is interesting and it has lot of detail, when I am in highschool or secondary school I will have to read a lot so now I will have to read a lot."

Making Sense of Billy's Struggles: Teachers' Perspectives

In order to understand Billy's literacy performance, I interviewed Ms. Dawson and Mrs. Smith about their perspectives. They suggested two factors that might have contributed to Billy's struggles in learning:

(1) Billy's serious personality, and (2) his extensive first language use at school.

Ms. Dawson observed that Billy was a very somber, serious, and sensitive child who sometimes could be quite negative to other children in class and quite defensive, although he had cheered up a little during the school year. Ms. Dawson explained that his serious personality affected his school learning: "He'll hold a grudge. He will let some comment or some disagreement really influence him for the rest of working time. If there's somebody that has said something to him that annoys him, he can't just let it go. I think he has a little thundercloud over his head a lot of the time."

Ms. Dawson also noted that although he could generally get along with his friends, he did not have a real sense of how to cooperate because of his unforgiving personality. This personality also affected his learning during group work. Ms. Dawson pointed out, "He is one of those children that really benefits from group kinds of work. But his personality is his biggest problem in being successful in those situations. He really does benefit from having a discussion or hearing other people's ideas or working on something together. But he doesn't have the cooperative, collaborative skills that make that easy for him."

Billy's lack of progress in English literacy was also attributed to his frequent use of Cantonese at school. Although Ms. Dawson felt strongly that it was important for children to learn their first language and that they needed to feel comfortable speaking their first language, she thought that it was important for them to try to speak English at school in order to improve. Mrs. Smith, who marked Billy's annual reading test noted: "He speaks so much Chinese. He won't have made any progress. He never pays attention. He's always joking around, and so he might be a little bit attention-deficit too."

Mrs. Smith predicted that Billy might be designated as a special needs student because he might have a learning disability or cognitive problem and would soon need a modified program.

Billy's Literacy Practices at Home

Billy's home literacy practices were similar to many Asian (Chinese) children in North America (Peng & Wright, 1994): his parents actively supervised his learning activities by assigning him additional homework tasks and willingly investing in his educational needs, including buying him a computer and sending him to private lessons.

Billy had a very busy schedule after school. On a typical day, when he came back from school at around 3:30 p.m. he had a snack, played with his sister or watched TV for half an hour, and would then practice the piano for an hour. After his piano practice, at around 5:00 p.m. he headed over to his tutor's (a family friend who agreed to help them out) house to study math, English, and French. The tutor sometimes gave Billy some math homework to do; sometimes he helped Billy read storybooks. After supper Billy would review some of the lessons taught by his tutor and continue to do the math homework assigned by his mother or his tutor and do Chinese homework from the Chinese school. He took swimming lessons two evenings a week. When he had some free time, he liked to watch cartoons such as *Pokemon* and *Digimon*, and to play video games on his computer.

Billy's parents, especially his mother, spent a lot of time with him to improve his learning. Mrs. Chung believed that the best way to learn how to read and write was to "pronounce and spell the words and make a better sentence using the words." She (as well as her husband) not only supervised his reading assignments for the literature circle, and other storybooks, but also helped him prepare for his spelling quizzes. Whenever Billy read, Mrs. Chung asked him to check the dictionary to find the meaning of new words. Billy would tell her that there were too many new words and would refuse to check the dictionary. He just read and told Mrs. Chung that he could understand all of it. But when she checked his comprehension and spelling of the words, Billy did not know them. She was very upset and regarded him as lazy and rebellious, and not eager to learn more to improve himself. During our interview, Mrs. Chung expressed frustration over his behavior: "The more pressure I give him, the lazier he gets." Besides the reading he had to do for school, Billy told me that he liked to read *Pokemon* and *Digimon* books because "they're cool." But he told me that sometimes he did not have time to read because he had "too much homework."

At home Billy code-switched between Cantonese, Mandarin, and English. Most of the time, he spoke Cantonese with his family. Sometimes he conversed with his sister in English when they talked about school. When he visited his grandparents every week, he had to speak Mandarin. Like his parents, he believed that it was important to learn Chinese, although he did not think it was easy to learn the language, especially writing the characters, and he often talked about his Chinese homework and tests. He explained to me, "My mom teaches me other languages. Because if I grow up and go to another country and work or something, I have to speak another language." He also told me that he learned more at home than in school. He said, "I learn more things at home than school, because my mom and dad teach us. Because my mom and dad teach me more things—Chinese homework, I learn how to speak Chinese more, and I learn how to speak [Mandarin] . . . in school, [the teachers] don't know what you like."

Making Sense of Billy's Struggles: Parental Perspectives

Billy's reading and writing in English greatly concerned his parents. Mrs. Chung considered the school practices, Billy's own attitude toward learning, and peer influences to be the causes of Billy's struggles in school.

Mrs. Chung believed that Billy's grade 1–3 education was problematic, and it did not prepare him for grade 4 standards: "From grade 1 to grade 3, the teachers thought that he was fine and always praised him for his good work. When he got to grade 4, all of a sudden his teacher said that he wasn't meeting the standards. Since they didn't prepare him well for the first 3 years, how can he cope with the exams in grade 4? Of course he won't be able to do well."

Mrs. Chung thought that because Billy was weak in academic studies, the school should teach more academic content and give the students more homework, even very easy homework. But to her disappointment, the school did not give any homework. She had asked the school to give more homework since Billy was in the first grade, but the school did not respond to her request, so she had to seek outside assistance to help improve Billy's learning: "I think what's taught at school isn't enough for him. And I also feel what he's learning at school is not deep enough. Each child should be given some homework to do. Even some simple exercises would be ok. But there's no homework for them from school. The children have very little practice after school. And sometimes the teachers feel that they can't understand the lessons. Because they can't understand the content, the teachers should give them more practice—even some simple practice is better than nothing."

Mrs. Chung also thought that Billy's teacher did not provide sufficient instruction for the students in math as well as in reading: "The teacher only gives him books to read. She doesn't explain the concepts to them. She only assigns them books and lets them read by themselves. But sometimes Billy can't understand, so sometime my husband and I have to teach him one on one."

Another factor that Mrs. Chung thought was not advantageous to Billy's (and other children's) learning was the combined class: she preferred single-grade classes like the ones in Hong Kong. She believed that combined classes were too distracting for students. Also, the school gave children too much freedom and was not strict enough, which made it hard for her as a parent to discipline Billy at home, especially when it came to changing his attitude toward learning.

Billy's resistance to studying was considered detrimental to his progress. Mrs. Chung characterized Billy as a lazy student, not interested or proactive in studying and completing homework, and she sometimes had to put more pressure on him and force him to work harder: "In fact, I think his performance could be better, but he doesn't work hard. He won't make it better. He just wants to be so-so. . . . Sometimes when he reads the book chapters from school, he'll flip through several pages and that's it, without much understanding and he won't tell me the truth, saying that he understood it."

Similar to his teachers' perspectives, Mrs. Chung also discovered that Billy often did not pay enough attention to his studies and often thought about playing with his friends or video games. She deemed Billy to have acquired this passive attitude toward learning from his friends (that is, Jake) at school who also disliked studying: "He always plays with those kids in school, and he was influenced by them. . . . The older he gets, the less obedient he becomes."

Resisting the ESL Label: Andy's Story

In conversations with Andy, I found him to be a talkative, outgoing, and sweet boy who was extremely interested in video games. He liked to walk around the classroom to talk to classmates, and sometimes was willing to offer help to new students in the class. He particularly liked to chat about video games he played with several of his good friends, such as Billy and Wilson, whenever he got a chance.

Andy excelled at math, but performed below his age and peer-group level in English reading, writing, listening, and speaking, and all other core curriculum subjects such as science and social studies. He was a Level 2 ESL student when he finished third grade. According to

Mrs. Smith, he was also diagnosed with Attention Deficit Disorder. At the beginning of fourth grade, his mother came to the school to request that his name be taken off the ESL list. Since Andy was the only student in the school whose parents did not want ESL support for him, I was curious to learn more about Andy and his family.

Andy's School Literacy Practices

At school, Andy was a pleasant boy and was well liked in class. He was eager to learn everything: "At school we learn handwriting, spelling, animals, social studies, or something like that. And we learn science; we usually figure out things." He wanted to learn English and French well, and he understood the importance of knowing Canada's two official languages. To him, "Learning is like when people are talking to you, and you can speak to them in English or French, and you learn more." He wrote the following about learning: "Learning is fun because we can learn more stuffs. We can learn at home and school. I sometimes don't like to learn." He realized that learning is important because "you can learn more so you can go to university or make more money on work."

Andy's desire to learn English was exemplified by his work for the literature circle assignments. Unlike the other focal students, he was able to complete his tasks. His responses to the different roles, though very short, suggested that he understood much of what he read. As Ms. Dawson commented, "If he pays attention, he can do more." His discussion of these tasks with others in his groups, however, was more problematic. He and a couple of peers were often off task during these discussions, and spoke in Cantonese about funny TV commercials and video games. For example, one time, instead of discussing the story they had read, Andy got up from his seat and demonstrated to his friends how he had played video games with both his hands and feet that weekend.

Whenever he had a chance Andy would converse in Cantonese with his classmates. As Mrs. Lou noted, Andy seldom spoke English at school. I noticed that he spoke English only when Ms. Dawson was explaining the lessons or instructions or when he interacted with a couple of the English-speaking students. He used Cantonese during unstructured class time (for example, during activities such as folding cubes and other hands-on activities with different shapes) or when he wanted to get away from schoolwork to talk about Pokemon games, TV shows, and movies, to ask questions about the work, or simply to explain something he knew to some of his classmates. He regarded the Chinese language as very important and took pride in his ability to speak Cantonese. He dreamed of visiting Hong Kong to play with his cousin Victor, who had a lot of video games and knew how to play basketball. He stressed the importance of knowing how to speak Chinese: "When you go to Hong Kong if you don't know how to [speak Cantonese], if I go to Hong Kong, and they see that you are Chinese, they will start calling me an idiot!" He told me that he wanted to go to a Chinese school to learn Chinese, but his parents would not let him because they wanted him to focus on English.

Andy liked reading in English. He wrote about his feelings about reading, "I like to read books that has pictures in it like pokemon. We can learn things. I like to read many chapter books. I do not like to read [text] books. I think reading is fun and cool." During his class's routine silent-reading time, he enjoyed picking out books from the classroom library. Andy enjoyed picture books that he could understand (for example, picture books about animals such as dinosaurs), but he often chose books that were beyond his reading ability. Ms. Dawson commented that "he might not understand the nuances of some of the reading, but he liked to read, which was a good thing for him." When I read with him some mornings, I noted that he read with some fluency, but like many poor readers, he was unable to pronounce unfamiliar words, and often could not continue to read if there were new words. He would wait for me to sound out the words for him. These unfamiliar words often prohibited him from understanding the stories. This reading block also occurred when he read long textbook instructions in math and other subjects. For example, one time he called me for help because he could not understand a question in math. The question read, "Sue is 14 years old. Irwin is 17 years old. What is the sum of their ages? What is the product of their ages?"

Guofang: What does the word "sum" mean?
Andy: Something you add. You add one to the other.
Guofang: Ok, now, what does the word "product" mean?
Andy: I don't know.
Guofang: Product means—[I show him the meaning of "product" in the textbook.]
Andy: Oh product means you multiply: 14x17!

As research has demonstrated, poor readers are often poor writers (Snow et al., 1998). Andy was also a struggling writer, and he stated that he did not like writing. He wrote: "I hate writing because I always get tired of it. You can write anything storeys, notes anything." As he wrote this, he thought about math, a subject that he liked, so he continued, "You can write so much and learn so much." Most of his writings lacked coherence among ideas and were less than a page long except for two pieces, which were based on movies or TV series he had seen. In one piece, he retold the movie *Spy Kids*; his other piece was entitled *The Alien* and was based on the *Star Wars* movies and the *Star Trek* series.

His writing demonstrated his struggles with vocabulary, tense agreement, paragraphing, and basic grammar. Here is a sample of his writing about his cousin Victor:

> Victor is my cuson. Lives in Hong Kong. It is crowded. He likeshis dog. The dog is called Rocky. He is a good basketball player. His friends is a good basketball player too. He likes his family. He likes to play with me, learn Taikwondo with me, play computer games with me, watch funny shows with me. Me and him don't like to shop that much. Rocky, stinks. That's why the house is stinky. Goes to Kuman with me. I like his video games like Crash Bash . . .

Andy apparently enjoyed the weekly spelling time as he often received a perfect grade for wordlist quizzes. He told me his secret for getting all the spelling right: "My mom already tested me twice at home. My sister even tested me twice!" He was, however, very sensitive about his math quizzes, and was very eager to get 100%. Whenever he did not get 100%, he became very upset. One time, he scored 22 out of 24 on a math quiz and he was very unhappy. With his head down, he told me, "It's not good enough. I should do better."

In sum, Andy struggled with reading and writing at school. His struggle may have been further complicated by his preference to use Chinese most of the time. Ms. Dawson noted that although he continued to move around a lot in the classroom, he could sit and read for a period of time, which "was a huge leap for him." She saw an increased effort in him to complete his work and noted that the support from home had really helped him in math, a subject in which he took great pride.

Making Sense of Andy's Struggle: Teacher Perspectives

Because Andy's parents demanded that Andy be removed from the ESL list, both Ms. Dawson and Mrs. Smith were cautious about their comments on Andy. Both teachers agreed that Andy was not reading or writing at a grade 4 level. In trying to understand Andy's difficulty with literacy, they suggested three problems: (1) speaking too much Chinese, (2) his immaturity; and (3) lack of ESL support.

As mentioned earlier, Andy played mostly with Cantonese-speaking children in school and used Cantonese extensively in and out of class. Both Ms. Dawson and Mrs. Smith believed that like Billy, Andy's constant use of Cantonese in school hindered his English development. In addition to his lack of practice in English, Ms. Dawson believed that the main reason for Andy's lack of progress was his immaturity in comparison with other students: "[At the] beginning of the year, he was out of his desk constantly, and didn't get anything done, was wandering, was playing with toys in his desk . . . [he] was this really very young young child, unable to focus for any period of time."

Because Andy was a very "young fourth grader," Ms. Dawson concluded "he's one of those kids that throughout the rest of elementary school teachers will have to keep an eye on him, and make sure that he is not kind of sliding off the edge there." For example, although he could benefit from an exploratory kind of learning, without structure, Ms. Dawson believed that he could "spend his whole day exploring."

Since Andy was off the official ESL list, he was not eligible to receive pullout ESL support as in previous years. Mrs. Lou wanted Ms. Dawson "be really on him in class," but with so many other ESL students in the class, it was hard for Ms. Dawson to do so. Mrs. Smith believed that this was a disadvantage to Andy: "As far as his language development . . . he hasn't been out for any small groups or anything. So if I'm in there, or there's an educational assistant, he might get a little bit of help or something. But otherwise, he's pretty much on his own, but his mom requested that."

Since Andy could get little ESL support from school, Ms. Dawson believed that he needed more support and encouragement at home. During the interview I told Ms. Dawson about Andy's home support. Ms. Dawson was "thrilled" to hear that the parents were taking an active role at home. Although she believed that Andy had made some progress at school, she cautioned that he needed the right kind of help from home: "I think that if he continues to get the kinds of support that he gets at home—but what I don't want for Andy is his parents end up doing all of his work for him, sort of misguided help. Andy needs to do the work himself, he needs a lot of encouragement, a lot of refocusing at home. But at school, I think he's done well."

Andy's Home Experiences

Andy was the second child in the family. His sister, facing graduation and the provincial tests, was struggling very hard to get by in school (especially in English writing and math). Compared to other class-mates who came from Hong Kong, her academic skills were far behind those who had had educational experience in Hong Kong. Andy's sister's academic failure had made Andy's parents lose their confidence in the public school system. They realized that the public school system had failed to educate their daughter, especially in Eng-lish and math. Andy's parents were very worried about her future, and were trying to do the right thing for Andy so that he would not follow the same path as his sister.

One thing Mrs. Lou decided to do to help Andy's English was to speak more English to Andy at home. When I first met Andy, he told me that he was born in Canada, but he could speak Chinese: "When I grow up, my mom keeps on speaking Chinese, Chinese. Now I really learn more about Chinese." Mrs. Lou realized that Andy's English was already a problem: "You can tell Andy, he's not speaking really fluent English. [He] sounds like, pronouncing like, a kid immigrant from other country like Hong Kong." They also realized that Andy had problems with Chinese as well: "But if you talk to him in Can-tonese, [he] didn't really understand completely. Some of them he understands; some of them he doesn't know what it is. He's in-between the gap." However, realizing that learning English was more important for Andy, they decided that they would not send Andy to a Chinese school to learn Mandarin because they wanted him to con-centrate on one language first before he went on to learn another. In order for Andy to have more exposure to English, his parents actually thought of moving out of the area to live in a predominantly English-speaking community.

In order for Andy to receive more exposure to English in school, Mrs. Lou asked the school to take him off the official ESL student list so that he wouldn't be pulled out of regular classes. Mrs. Lou thought that the school was putting him in a level lower than his ability. This placement may have blocked his learning because he was not challenged. She explained: "Because if they put him in the much much lower grade, that means he won't improve himself. They pull him out from the regular class and he loses the exposure of regular learning. This is why I pull him out. One thing true is his lack of concentration and that makes the problems more serious. They thought maybe because he is ESL, he cannot understand English. But they didn't realize he doesn't really understand Cantonese too."

Mrs. Lou agreed with the school that Andy had Attention Deficit Disorder. However, she never used the term "attention deficit" during our interview. Instead, she said he had a "lack of concentration." She didn't interpret Andy's problem as biological, but more of an effort issue. She disagreed with and refused to comply with the school's recommendation to use medication to solve Andy's problem. She commented, "I ask them, how can you improve him? They say only medication. I say, no, medication only worsens the case." Instead, she sent Andy to piano schools and swimming lessons once a week to improve his concentration skills. She believed that playing the piano, for example, would coordinate his body and mind as he had to read, think, and play at the same time.

In order to improve his math skills, Mrs. Lou sent him to a private tutoring school, Kuman Math School, twice a week. The Kuman Math School, which originated in Japan, was very popular in Richmond. The school accepted children who were at different levels in math. At each lesson, the instructors would hand out math worksheets and the students would finish the work at the school and submit it for correction. If a student had a problem or question, the teacher would provide individual help. At each lesson Andy would pick up a folder that contained his work for the day. He finished his work by himself and turned it in to the teacher, and then he could leave. Mrs. Lou said that this kind of training gave Andy more initiative.

According to Mrs. Lou, Andy liked to play games on the computer and watch his favorite cartoon shows *Pokemon* and *Digimon*. But he would always do his homework or practice the piano after half an hour's break.

Mrs. Lou bought Andy different kinds of storybooks from different stores such as the Superstore, Costco's, and Chapters. She even bought the popular *Harry Potter* books for Andy at his request, although she knew that he could not read them. In the summer, Mr.

and Mrs. Lou also took him to the community library where he borrowed many books. For example, the summer before this research study, he finished all the detective stories that the library owned.

Mrs. Lou required Andy to read aloud in English every day and encouraged him to write on the computer. Sometimes when they were not busy, Andy's parents would read with him. If Mrs. Lou had too much homework to do herself, she asked Andy to record his reading aloud on a tape recorder so that she could check it later. This method was very effective for checking Andy's pronunciation, but she admitted that Andy often lost interest in recording his reading because she often pointed out his pronunciation mistakes. Mrs. Lou and her daughter would occasionally help Andy with his weekly spelling quizzes. Sometimes, they pretested him several times before quizzes.

In sum, Andy had a variety of literacy experiences outside of school, between his homework, reading, games, TV shows, and swimming and piano lessons. He said that he learned more at home than at school, and described his home as a school: "Sometimes when you're at home, you can learn. My mom actually thinks my house is a school. So she taught me everything—15 minutes' recess, and then an hour of studying, then recess, then another 45 minutes, and then recess."

Parental Perspectives on Andy's Struggle

Mrs. Lou considered that the main reasons Andy was behind in English literacy were insufficient teaching and instruction from school, a classroom environment that did not suit the needs of the students, and Andy's late introduction to after-school tutoring.

Insufficient Teaching and Instruction from School. Although Mrs. Lou was doing her best to help Andy learn, she felt she was under heavy pressure to "get it right." She felt that the school was not doing its job; instead much of the job of educating children was dumped on the parents, who were not proficient in English. She became very frustrated with the responsibility that the school placed on immigrant parents like her: "Most of the time, 90% or 80% it depend on your parents. . . . And the book reading, every time, you get a book and then you sign it. And the parents, you have to listen to your kids to read or you have to read to your kids. As I said, how can he learn English? Even though he goes to school, learn nothing except playing,

playing, playing . . . I rely on the school to teach him English instead of me to teach my son English."

For reading, Mrs. Lou seemed to think that a good reader is a reader with correct pronunciation. Coming from this understanding of what reading is, she questioned the school's methods and practices. She commented that the instruction did not have enough reading aloud or choral reading. She said that the students never read aloud; they only did silent reading. She added, "So [the teachers tell] the parents you have to listen to your kids to read or you have to read to your kids." She suggested, "The teacher should have some reading aloud at school to make sure all the kids pronounce correctly. They don't have [that]. They should have a language lab to make sure every kid pronounces the same." Again, she stressed that it was not a good idea to ask parents like her to read to their children: "If I pronounce it wrong, [he] pick up the wrong thing."

Similarly, Mrs. Lou felt that the teachers did not teach the children how to write in proper English: "The other thing is grammar. The didn't teach grammar in school. Not much, but they ask much. They ask a lot, 'Hey, this is past tense.' The other day, I said [to the teacher], 'Do you think they know what is the past tense?' [The teacher said,] 'They should know. They should know because the book they read is past tense.' I said, 'You're telling me that because they have to read so much in order to pick up [what a past tense is] instead of you teach them what is the past tense."

Mrs. Lou also questioned the inconsistency between first, second, and third grade teachers, as well as the fourth grade teacher's approaches to students' writing. She learned from talking to Andy's primary-grade teachers that they did not correct students' errors in writing because they didn't want to "discourage their thinking." However, she noted that when Andy advanced to fourth grade, the teacher's expectations of students' writing were much different:

Ms. Dawson thought he's in grade 4 and he should have perfect English. [Se said,] "Andy, you have to proofread your paragraph." I say, my god, the teachers previously [were] so slackoff, and now you want him to be perfect, he can write perfect English, proofread his own work? [Or, if she] asks us parents to proofread for them instead she do the work. I found out teachers in here in Canada tend to do this—give the work to the parents.

Classroom Organization. Mrs. Lou told me that she sometimes thought it was not Andy's fault that he did not do well: "It's the class, the environment." In her opinion, two elements of class environment were detrimental. One was the group-seating arrangement, and the other was the combined class. In terms of group seating, she believed that the arrangement distracted students from concentrating, especially for students like her son who had difficulty with concentration. She told me that she discussed this with Ms. Dawson and asked her to change her group seating to rows. She was pleased that Ms. Dawson later made the change although she did not know whether it was because of her request. She told me about her discussion with Ms. Dawson,

> I said, it's because the way that you put the kids together. Instead of facing you and having them concentrate onto the blackboard the kids are talking to each other. I said, you're in a teaching classroom, this is not a group discussion. You want the kids to concentrate and listen to you, then they have to face you. I said, especially [Andy] has to be put in the front. I think [seating in groups] is not a good situation; they are not in a kindergarten, story time, fun talks. Now they have to study. They have to learn. You have to get a good way for them, a good situation for them, provide a good environment for them to learn. Of course, the kids, they're so hard to put them in order, to make them concentrate. Of course, each other facing each other, they just chat, chat, chat. Who want to concentrate, right?

Another classroom arrangement issue was about the combined class. Like many other Chinese parents, Mrs. Lou strongly believed that a combined class was not favorable to the children's learning. She wanted a single-grade class where "everybody in a class [is] reading the same book, and then the teacher can read the book to the kids. Then they can learn at the same level, the same pace, the same pronunciation. . . ." She further commented,

> I don't think this system [combined class] work well. I was fighting for the kids to have separate class, like, grade 4 is grade 4; grade 5 is grade 5, not a mix. Because once a mix, they depend on other tutor to teach the kids instead of teachers teaching the kids. Because the teacher have only half the

time to teach the class, that's why they need so much so-called assistants. Assistants [say] "Oh, I don't have time because there are so many kids. I can only help one at a time." That means the kids [are] going to the school wasting their time. They don't learn anything. One thing is if you put him in the higher level, it's hard for them to concentrate because they are nosy and it's hard to them to understand. Next year if you put him into a lower class, that means he heard [the materials] already, nothing new to him, no initiatives, no incentives for him to learn, to concentrate in the class.

Insufficient Private Tutoring after School. Mrs. Lou told me that on average the students in the school had at least two private tutors: one in English and one in other subjects such as math. According to Mrs. Lou, the Chinese parents "have to spend CAD24–CAD30 per hour to get their children to learn English from outside school." In addition to math and English tutoring, many children also went to Chinese classes. She believed that because many Chinese parents invested so much money and effort in after-school tutoring, the progress of many students who do well in school may not be the result of teachers' teaching, but of pervasive private tutoring: "It's not that the teachers' teaching that contributes to the students' academic achievement in school, they overlooked private tutors that most of the kids have." She believed that "if [the other children] didn't have the other alternative sources of education, their level would be the same as or maybe not too far away from Andy."

Mrs. Lou believed that Andy lagged behind other children because he did not receive private tutoring as early as other children: "He always thought he isn't as good as the others. He didn't know the others have so [much] help." Mrs. Lou told me that she did not know about private tutoring until a year ago when she talked to other parents who told them to find tutors for Andy and his sister because everyone else in the neighborhood had them. Many had had tutors for years already. She suddenly realized that it was too naive to believe in and rely on the school, and her children were far behind the game: "If I don't find him a tutor, he probably will fail." So she and her husband acted on this immediately, and sent Andy to Kuman Math School and his sister to A+ Mathematics (another private math school). At the time of the interview, they were also looking for an English-speaking science tutor for their daughter. Mrs. Lou was very disappointed and frustrated that she had to seek outside help instead of relying on the school to teach her children. She commented, "But how about the other kids like Andy who didn't have this kind of facility? This is why I say the system, the school system, ruins the kids. And then they make the kids think, 'Oh, I'm not as good as Owen.' Actually maybe he is more talented than Owen because his mom didn't provide him the tutor. That's why he's behind. This is the point I want to tell everybody in Taylor Elementary but people thought I was accusing them. I say, no, because you didn't treat every kid the same. The kids didn't have the same exposure. Yeah, if you can find a good tutor, that's good for you."

In sum, Mrs. Lou attributed Andy's low English ability to ineffective schooling. She wanted a traditional school where students sit in rows facing the teacher, with teacher-led instruction and a reading-aloud method, more instruction in writing and grammar, and a language lab.

Andy continued fourth grade without any ESL support. Although he had made some progress in his classroom behavior, he continued to struggle with his reading and writing. As Ms. Dawson noted, "It has been a difficult year for him."

The Road to Special Education: Jake's Story

Similar to Billy and Andy, eleven-year-old Jake entered fifth grade with below-grade-level performance in all subjects except physical education, and finished the year without much progress in these subjects. He was classified as a low Level 3 (intermediate) ESL student and was pulled out of class twice a week for ESL instruction with Mrs. Smith. In Mrs. Smith's small-group ESL instruction, Jake studied grammar such as the use of the present and past tense, word order, sentence fragments and run-on sentences, reading strategies such as predicting events in a story, reading for detail, and vocabulary. Mrs. Smith commented that his reading and writing appeared to be "a six-year-old child's Level 3" performance, and he would need a modified program soon. During the school's Special Needs Committee meeting in April 2001, it was decided that Jake would be tested for his learning problems.

When I first met Jake, I did not think that he was a low-level ESL student who should be classified as a special needs student. He had a pleasant personality, was respectful and polite to teachers and adults, and was cooperative in Ms. Dawson's class activities. Over the course of my observation, I found that during class time he always assumed a different personality and was generally quiet. He seldom raised his hand to volunteer an answer unless he was called on, asked questions, or asked for clarification. Although he never complained about his work or studies, he never went beyond the minimum requirements either. For example, if he was asked to write at least five sentences, he would write exactly five sentences, no more and no less. Jake's attitude toward learning was seen in both his school and home literacy practices.

Jake's Literacy Practices at School

Jake was never late for school. In fact he was always the first one to get to school. Sometimes he arrived even before Ms. Dawson. Since he was at school before other students arrived every morning, Ms. Dawson offered to help him with reading, writing, or math one morning a week.

At school, Jake was a leader among some of the "Chinese people" like Billy. Despite Ms. Dawson's constant reminder that he must speak English at school at all times, he preferred to speak Cantonese during lunch, recess, or less structured class time, and he did not play with the "English people" whose native language was not Chinese. Jake said that it was easier for him to use Chinese, and students should use Chinese if they were not yet good at English. During our interview, he told me, "Some students in English school don't know English well yet, but they know Chinese, so they should speak Chinese. . . . Sometimes you can explain the meaning of [an English] word in Chinese." Indeed, during class time he often consulted other Cantonese-speaking classmates about the meaning of words. For example, one time when he was working on a suffix worksheet, he did not know the word "elbow" and asked his friend Kyle what it meant in Cantonese. Kyle explained the word to him in Cantonese, pointing to his elbow.

Both Ms. Dawson and Mrs. Smith thought that Jake had no problem with oral English, and they agreed that Jake's main problem was with his reading and writing. He was unable to read over an extended period of time. During silent reading time every morning, he often chose books that were too difficult for him. For example, he wanted to read *Harry Potter* like his friend Kyle, but he could not understand many of the words. He often ended up flipping through the pages and did not actually get into the reading. Jake seemed to have conflicting feelings about his reading ability and his desire to be a better reader. He wanted to read difficult books as his friends did, but he could not, and he did not want to read easy books such as picture books, which he could actually read. I noted that for several of their library times, he did not sign out any books to read at home. He wrote why he did not like reading: "I don't like reading because at home I read so much at home. Sometimes I like reading because I read that book and it [is] good. But most of time I hate reading because I don't like books. When I was little I like the picture. But when I grow up I hate reading because I just don't like the pictures any more."

His attitude toward reading was also reflected in his reading and writing for the class's literature circle books *George's Marvelous Medicine* and *Stone Fox*. His writing did not demonstrate that he read and understood the content of the books because he left his homework pages blank. It was also unclear whether he understood the instructions for each role (for example, "Discussion Director" or "Friend of the Character") in the discussions, although he took very careful notes on the specifications for the roles in his notebook. For example, he did not seem to understand that he was supposed to write about the characters as if he were the character's friend. Instead, he wrote these lines about George in *George's Marvelous Medicine*: "I think the friend of the character is evil because he look evil. I think Grouge is kind of obad because He trying to kill his grandma."

Jake had the same problem with words and vocabulary as Billy did: he could not pronounce difficult words such as "distraction" and "extensive," and he did not master the "sound-spelling mappings" as he could not spell many simple words such as "travel" (which he spelled as "travil"), "tired" ("tierd"), and "quickly" ("quiekly"). Furthermore, he appeared to have more problems with verb tenses and gerunds: he had a poor mastery of past tense or irregular verbs. For example, he made these errors with verbs in writing: builded [built], try [tried], shaked [shook]. These difficulties were also evident when he read aloud. He often omitted verb endings such as -s, -es, and -ed.

Jake admitted that difficult words in science and math were problematic for him in understanding the concepts in school. He often could not understand the instructions in his math book because of the vocabulary. For example, he often got stuck on questions such as "Revise each of these estimates. Then divide," Or "Estimate by rounding to the nearest 100" because he could not understand the word "estimate." Often in this situation, he remained quiet in his seat and seldom asked for clarification from Ms. Dawson or Mrs. Smith. Occasionally, he would turn to his friend Kyle for help in Cantonese. However, Jake did not seem to be interested in his work or doing a better job. For example, when Ms. Dawson sometimes asked him to review his work, he did not seem to be willing to do it. Sometimes, when she asked him to go back and check his answers, he just passively complied without really checking his work.

Unlike Billy and Andy, Jake appeared less concerned about his vocabulary and was less enthusiastic about spelling exercises and grammar practice such as with suffixes and prefixes. He commented several times, "I hate studying these words. It's dumb." He seemed to enjoy other kinds of word games which he called "writing": "I think writeing is fun because you can learn. Also I like writing about is you can play with writing. Like crossword, scramble and the game is fun."

Making Sense of Jake's Struggles: His Teachers' Perspectives

Jake's situation was different from Billy's (who only experienced difficulty in reading and writing since he had entered fourth grade), because Jake had been experiencing difficulties with literacy since grade 1. In addition to the fact that Jake was exposed to so many Cantonese speakers and spoke too much Chinese, Ms. Dawson and Mrs. Smith suggested three additional factors that might have contributed to his learning difficulties: a possible learning disability, his attitude toward learning, and a lack of parental involvement.

According to Mrs. Smith, Jake's name in fact had come up every year at the special needs committee to be tested for a learning disability. It was not clear whether he had been seriously tested for special needs during the past five years. Both Ms. Dawson and Mrs. Smith had a real concern about his performance and both came to the conclusion that he might have a learning disability. Ms. Dawson learned from her Tuesday morning tutoring sessions with Jake that he could not retain what he learned. She explained, "For example, he'll be struggling with some concept and we'll work on it. He appears that he's got it. But then when you return to that same kind of question a week later, he really hasn't understood. . . . So he was one of the children who were identified as needing additional, not English, not ESL, but learning disability support."

Ms. Dawson believed that Jake would have the same language problem in Chinese: "Language is one of his difficulties whether it's

Chinese or English. . . . I think it's a global language difficulty." She also noted that Jake was very good at avoiding situations where his inabilities were evident. Similar to my observation, Ms. Dawson discovered, "He doesn't speak up when he doesn't understand something, because that would be identifying that he's got a problem understanding. So he never asks for clarification or for help. He chooses to be quiet and almost withdrawn from activities in the classroom."

Although Ms. Dawson had little information about Jake's home life, his failure to complete the tasks for literature circle and other readings made her realize that Jake did not read at home. She was puzzled that Jake's parents were not actively involved with his homework to make sure it was done because she understood that Asian parents wanted more homework for their children. She realized that there were probably differences in expectations between home and school. In her opinion, one important aspect of homework for young children was parental involvement, but Jake's parents did not seem to be involved at all in his homework: "The parents see what the homework is, see what their child is doing, and ensure that it's completed, whether or not they can help them with it, talk to them about it. But I get a sense that a lot of parents don't have that kind of involvement with their children and their homework. There's no follow-up, 'Have you got your homework?' 'Let me see what's in your bag' that kind of thing."

Ms. Dawson was trying to communicate this message to Jake's parents. She wrote on his report card that Jake needed to read daily at home, out loud, and discuss his reading with someone, and should be reading and rereading his literature circle selected pages, and preparing for his role in group discussions in class.

Jake's Literacy Practices at Home

According to Jake's mother, she did ask about his homework every day and required him to finish his homework before he went to play or watch TV. Mrs. Wong and her husband did not know enough English to help him with homework, but she could make sure that he finished it every day. Sometimes she asked her eldest daughter, who was in senior high school, to supervise his homework when she was at work in their family restaurant. Mrs. Wong asked her daughter to see whether Jake had completed his homework, but not to correct the errors for him, so that his teacher in school would know what his weaknesses were. Since she could not read English and did not know whether Jake read the words correctly, she sometimes asked her eldest daughter to read with him.

But often Mrs. Wong found that Jake did not have enough homework from school because he finished it in less than half an hour every day. Her daughter reported that sometimes Jake finished his homework within 10 minutes. Then Jake spent some time on his Chinese homework, which he characterized as "a lot," from his three-hour lessons in a Chinese school every Sunday. The Chinese homework involved copying and writing several pages of new words, reciting and memorizing several paragraphs of texts, or short compositions. He also had to prepare for tests at the Chinese school. The remainder of the time, he played with other kids in the neighborhood and spent a lot of time playing video games and watching his favorite TV shows, *Pokemon* and *Digimon.*

Jake often played on the computer and considered his time on the computer a significant part of his after-school learning. He learned not only how to type, but also how to search for information on the Internet. He wrote: "I can learn alot in computer because you can do anything. You can go on internet and I.C.Q. [stands for "I Seek You," an Internet chat room function]. And it fun to go on internet. It is important to learn in internet because you might need the internet."

Jake's after-school life was therefore much less structured than Billy's. On weekends, besides going to the Chinese school, Jake attended many family gatherings with his grandparents and relatives, and spent time doing different things with his family such as going to the public library, shopping, and skating. Like Billy, he spoke mostly Cantonese at home, although occasionally he spoke English with his sisters. Both Jake and Mrs. Wong considered it extremely important to learn Chinese and to speak Chinese at home, although she agreed that Jake should speak English at school. However, she did not think Ms. Dawson's recommendation that he speak English at home was fair: "Sometimes his teacher asks him to speak English at home. I tell her I can't. I'd rather that he doesn't do well in English than force him to speak English at home. It'll be unfair to both him and me."

Four months before Ms. Dawson offered to help Jake one morning a week, Mrs. Wong hired a local Canadian tutor, a Caucasian with a doctoral degree in education, to help Jake with reading and math for approximately two hours a week. The tutor not only gave Jake several pages of reading to do, but also taught him to read word by word, to recognize each word and understand the words he was reading. Mrs.

Wong would sit in on these lessons, listening to Jake read aloud. Jake made some progress, but it became too expensive for the family to afford the tutor. Since Ms. Dawson offered to help, Mrs. Wong decided to stop Jake's lessons with the tutor.

Jake seemed to do very little writing at home. He wrote journals occasionally but generally did not like to do work at home. He confided in me his feelings about writing at home: "I hate writing in my house because it is hard to write at home. Mostly I like writing at school. It [is] hard to write at home because I'm not used to writing at home."

Making Sense of Jake's Struggles: Parental Perspectives

Jake's mother did not attend the first parent conference with Ms. Dawson because she would have had to ask someone to translate for her. Instead, she sent her oldest daughter to meet with Ms. Dawson. Her daughter reported to her that Jake was at a grade 3 performance level and might have a learning disability. Mrs. Wong thought that although Jake may not be a very smart student, she did not see him as a learning disabled child. Similar to many Chinese parents' perspectives (Stevenson & Stigler, 1992), she described him as "a slow learner." In her opinion, he was slower to comprehend than many other children because he translated English into Chinese, and tried to understand it in Chinese. Mrs. Wong agreed that Jake had a hard time remembering what he read even if he was asked to read something a hundred times. She believed that the most important thing was that "his teacher should think of a way to help him remember what he studied." But to her disappointment, the school had not provided enough help in the past few years for Jake, and she realized that his problem had accumulated for several years and it was becoming even more difficult to resolve. She pointed out that many pedagogical factors, such as the school's combined classes, nonlinear instruction, and not enough homework, may have contributed to Jake's difficulty in school.

Mrs. Wong preferred traditional teaching methods and actually thought about moving to another district that had a traditional school. She strongly believed that the instruction in the combined grade 4/5 class confused slow learners like Jake. Using math instruction as an example, she explained that the combined classes were detrimental to him: "They combine the two classes, and confuse him. Sometimes when he's learning division, his homework is on addition. . . . You know, when children are led on forward they'll advance step by step. But now, he's being drawn backward instead of forward."

Mrs. Wong suggested that systematic and linear instruction would not only help Jake master the knowledge at his own pace, but also help her understand Jake's weaknesses: "They should teach them in proper sequences. For example, this term he learns multiplication, and next term he'll learn calculation. If he doesn't master the knowledge at one stage, I'll know at once when he comes home, and I'll help him with this stage. But now, I don't know at which aspect he is weak, so I don't know how to help him catch up."

For reading, Mrs. Wong believed that his teachers should teach him to read word by word and sentence by sentence. Furthermore, she thought that the teachers should ask some questions on the meaning of each sentence. No matter how many lines he read at one time, the teachers should find out what he did not understand. She also wished that his teachers could give Jake more homework so that he could improve. Although Mrs. Wong checked Jake's homework every day, she did not seem to be aware of his reading homework (for example, literature circle assignments). She noted, "Every day when my son comes back from school, I ask him whether he has some homework to do. He'll answer, 'No, I have finished it in school.' I say, 'Jake, do your homework after you have dinner.' He answers, 'Yeah.' But he'll only spend 5 or 10 minutes doing it, telling me he has finished it. . . . If the teacher can assign him one or two pages for him to do at home, and require him to hand it in the next morning, thus he can have a task, he won't watch TV instead, for he'll feel urgent to finish his homework before he watches TV."

Trying to Fit In: Tina's Story

Tina, a fifth grader, came to Canada with her parents in 1999 from Beijing. Neither of her parents was proficient in English. According to Ms. Dawson, Tina used her Chinese name when she first came to school, but later changed her name to Tina because she wanted to emulate a classmate by the same name who excelled in school. I did not have a chance to interview her parents in person, but was able to have a brief conversation with them on the phone. What I learned about Tina mostly came from our informal conversations during my classroom visits.

I was interested in understanding Tina's experiences because when I started the research study, she was the only Mandarin speaker in Ms. Dawson's grade 4/5 combined class who came from Mainland China. She not only had to juxtapose her position with other Chinese-speaking children from different regional, political, and socioeconomic backgrounds (such as those from Hong Kong and Taiwan), but she also had to negotiate her identity with other non-Chinese peers (McKay & Wong, 1996). As Tina's school experiences will demonstrate, negotiating between these multiple discourses and identities was not an easy task for her.

At the time of the study, Tina was designated as a Level 2 ESL student and was pulled out of class twice a week for ESL instruction with Mrs. Smith. She did not receive letter grades in core curriculum areas due to her limited English ability. Unlike many of her classmates' parents, Tina's parents were struggling financially. Her father worked in a Chinese restaurant, and her mother studied English in a college ESL program. According to Tina, her father worked long hours with heavy and tough duties and often hurt himself. Her mother was also very busy trying to cope with school and family. Tina once delivered newspapers for a couple of months and earned about CAD100. Like many working-class families, Tina's parents wanted her to learn English as soon as she could and to do well in school.

At the onset of the study, she was anxious to talk to me in Mandarin, and ask me about different things in Chinese. But gradually she chose not to speak Chinese because her mother forbade her to speak Chinese in school. Even when other students spoke Mandarin around her or with her and she understood what they were saying, she would just ignore them and not join in on the conversation. "My mom would be mad at me if I speak Chinese," she explained to me several times. Over the course of this research, I noticed that Tina gradually developed a negative attitude toward Chinese culture and her family, especially after her grandparents' visit. Not only did she refuse to speak Chinese, she also expressed a dislike of China, of the Chinese values of her grandparents who were visiting at the time, and of Chinese food.

Tina's Literacy Practices at School

Tina appeared quiet and nervous in the classroom. After observing her for a period of time, I realized that her uneasiness came from her lack of confidence in her English and her feelings about her family's situation, which differed from other Chinese children in the class. She always criticized herself: "I'm not very good at this" or "I don't like my pictures." She wanted to speak English like other students, engage in a variety of other activities such as swimming and skating like other children, and become successful in math and science like some of the students. Her inability to succeed in these areas significantly diminished her self-esteem.

Tina really wanted to learn English well, and was highly motivated. She kept a pocket Chinese-English dictionary in her drawer to check out the words she did not understand. But it became harder for her to use the dictionary because she did not understand some of the Chinese words in the dictionary either. Although she had some fluency in speaking English, at times her effort to translate her thoughts from Chinese into English were apparent. She also used this translating strategy in reading and other content areas such as science and social studies. This method, however, produced very slow and frustrating reading. Often she ran into many new words and vocabulary, and could not understand the instructions. During spelling and grammar exercises, she often got stuck on new words. For example, when she was working on a grammar sheet "The Sound of 'O'," she did not understand the words "sorrow" and "hollow." These new words often prevented her from completing the work sheets. However, Tina worked very hard on her vocabulary. She usually did well on her weekly spelling test, and she told me that every week she "practiced and practiced for it." Sometimes when she misspelled one or two words she would become upset.

Tina's comprehension of English relied heavily on her Chinese comprehension. She appeared not to be able to grasp some of the concepts in English and had to translate them into Chinese to understand them. She often consulted her dictionary, hidden in her desk drawer. Her small dictionary appeared to be very limited when it came to some special terms, for example, "equator" or "prime meridian." When I was available in the classroom, she often used me as a resource and asked me to explain some of the words in Chinese.

Although Tina worked hard reciting words on the vocabulary lists, she struggled with grammar exercises that required her to fill in the blanks to complete sentences. She had trouble understanding some of the words in the word boxes and some of the instructions, and she had more difficulty completing tasks that required more understanding of the context. For example, she often told me, "I don't know what to do" when she was trying to read the instructions, such as "Write the words with double consonants" or "What does this mean?" when she was trying to complete a fill-in the blanks task, for example,

If I____Ruff a bar of _____, he runs away and hides.

The Tolls had to____when the airline checked the____of their luggage.

She often was very frustrated with these worksheets. Whenever she reviewed the wrong answers, she would become very distressed. One time when she found out that some of the answers she had prepared at home were wrong, she felt hopeless. Pointing to the wrong answers, she told me, "I can never get those right. My uncle helped me with those blanks. See, my uncle told me those and they're wrong! Stupid! I'll never let him touch my homework again!" Another time, she decided to quit and left her worksheet blank. She confided in me, "I like to do all the wordlists, but I hate to do the exercise sheet."

Despite her dislike of the worksheets, Tina liked to read and spend time in the school library. She often chose readings that were too hard for her level. In November 2000, she started reading *Upchuck and Rotten Willy Running Wild* (by Bill Wallace) during silent reading time in the mornings. When I asked her what the book was about, she answered:

Tina: I don't know yet, I haven't finished yet.
Guofang: Who is Upchuck?
Tina: Don't know.
Guofang: Who're the characters in the book?
Tina: A dog and a cat, maybe.
Guofang: The dog's name is . . .
Tina: Willy.
Guofang: What's the cat's name? Is it Upchuck?
Tina: Maybe.

The next book she chose to read was the popular *Harry Potter*, which several other classmates were also reading. Although I predicted that she would have great difficulty understanding the book, she told me that she really liked it, and wrote about her experiences reading the book (see figure 5.1).

Fig. 5.1. *Tina's drawing about her reading experiences.*

Tina's limited vocabulary severely affected her performance and understanding of many new concepts in other subjects such as math. In some of the math questions, she often ran into many new words, such as "round trip," "puppet show," and "adults." She also appeared to have problems with some math concepts (for example, rounding and decimals) and instructions (write even or odd for each number or write the largest multiple of each number up to 83). Tina was very nervous during some of the math classes and frequently raised her hand to ask for clarification, "I don't understand this one." Her frequent demands for clarification demonstrated her desire to do better. She told me that she was good in math and normally scored 100% in math in China, but now she barely scored 85% on some of the quizzes. Whenever she got her quiz results, she was very unhappy with herself. Apparently she had pressure from home: "My mom, when she was in school, she always get 100 and she expect me to get 100 all the time." One time when she was graded 21/30 for her quiz, she became very distressed: "I never get 100 anymore. What I'm going to do? When I was in China, the lowest I got was 95. Now I always make a lot of mistake. 21 out of 30! Oh, my God! My mom is going to be so mad at me. Last Wednesday I practiced and practiced for this quiz, and I still get 9 wrong."

I tried to comfort her and pointed out that she had just come from China not long ago and it took time to learn math and English. She responded, "I don't think it has anything to do with my English. Look at this. I also got this one wrong. I don't know why I'm so bad." I asked her to tell her mother that she would do better next time. She sighed and said, "I've already told her that many times. Now I don't want to do it anymore. I'm tired of saying it. She's going to be so disappointed. Now my grandma and grandpa are here and they're going to know that I'm not as good as before, and they're going to tell other people."

At the end of the school year, Tina did get 100% on one of the math quizzes, but she just brushed it off—"Just first time."

Tina was able to complete her literature circle assignments and other reader response homework. She was able to write longer passages; however, her writing demonstrated insufficient understanding of the content as well as the instructions. For example, when she responded to the class reading book, *Voyager*, she was supposed to write a paragraph from a character's point of view. But she mixed up the characters and did not seem to understand what "point of view" meant. Here is a sample of her writing about the Voyager: "Voyager was very brave because they had travels long time and they also can't see their mom when they are traveling. They are so cheerful like dancing, play instrument, singing. They were very friendly to each other they never fight. They all speak French very well. They have to sleep on the ground."

Although Tina had made significant progress, she was still struggling with vocabulary, especially with spelling, and sentence structures. Most of her writing was stories that she made up for writing's sake and were not related to her real life. She wrote a long piece about her imaginary cat that her grandma bought her for her birthday. But making up facts was hard for her and she wrote that writing was "hard and boaring" for her and she hated it. In figure 5.2, she told me more about her frustration with writing.

Tina appeared to be lonely in school most of the time. Her low self-esteem often limited her participation in class discussions and interaction with other students. At the beginning of the semester, she tried to get attention by constantly requesting to go to the bathroom, sometimes at the most inopportune time. Later, she frequently asked for clarification during class, which I think, in turn, affected her perception of how others viewed her. She was generally quiet during group discussions such as literature circle. Often her group members

Fig. 5.2. *Tina's drawing about her frustration with writing.*

were not on task and joked about things rather than discussing the content. Tina sometimes protested but normally was not heard. She became so frustrated that she complained to me after one session, "This is completely boring, because they don't care at all! They always make fun!"

Tina tried to make friends and tried to fit in. Since most of her classmates had piano or swimming lessons after school, Tina sometimes made up stories about going swimming or skating so that she would have some common experiences to share with her classmates. These stories often backfired because she often gave inaccurate information about these activities. For example, she told her peers in a group discussion that she took swimming lessons for an hour and a half every weekend, came out of the pool to read for an hour and half, and then went in the pool again to swim for a while. The other students who took swimming lessons every week quickly debunked her story, which made Tina very embarrassed and she had even more difficulty fitting in. Tina also made up similar stories in her writing about her family life. These stories "seemed to be based on fact. But when you really start talking about what she is writing, there is a little bit of fact, but mostly fiction," Ms. Dawson said. "She has this fantasy kind of life or she likes to think of herself in a more positive situation."

Tina had very few friends, but had made progress in befriending some of the girls in the class. The year before, she befriended Sally, a girl from a Hong Kong Chinese family, but for some reason, the family did not want them to play together. This incident hurt her deeply. This year she was trying to build a friendship with Sharon, a Caucasian girl. Many times, she begged Sharon to visit her after school, but Sharon always declined.

After school, Tina would watch half an hour of TV in English. She said that at home, she was not allowed to watch Chinese TV because her mother wanted her to be immersed in English all the time. To improve her English, her mother even tried to converse with her in English at home. Every day after school, she would study for three hours by herself at home. When her father came home from work, he would teach her to read and write Chinese using a very thick Chinese anthology, and some tongue twisters—resources they had brought over from China. The family also had an uncle living with them who occasionally helped her with math and spelling homework. She told me that she read in English every night: "I read an hour and a half at least."

Making Sense of Tina's Struggle: Teacher Perspectives

Despite her constant struggle with reading and writing, and interaction with others in class, Tina had made much progress since she had come to the school a year and a half ago. Although Ms. Dawson was positive about Tina's progress, she cautioned that several factors such as her low self-esteem and her attitude toward learning, might have affected Tina's learning at school.

Although Tina wanted to excel, Ms. Dawson thought that her desire to achieve quickly might have some negative impact on Tina's perception of herself as a beginning English language learner. For example, she secretly competed with another top student in fifth grade, Cheryl, who was also a Mandarin-speaking student. Ms. Dawson observed that like Cheryl, Tina did not try to speak Mandarin, and always tried to speak English. Ms. Dawson noted that even when new Chinese students (who could only speak Chinese) initiated the conversation in Chinese, she obviously understood what they were talking about, but she never joined in the conversation. However, in terms of academic subjects, Cheryl was much beyond Tina's level. Ms. Dawson thought that her competition with Cheryl was "self-defeating." She observed that Tina sometimes was reluctant to try harder because of a feeling of failure due to comparing herself with Cheryl.

Tina's "self-defeating" attitude resulted in her passive approach toward learning. Ms. Dawson observed that in the beginning of the school year, Tina always made the assumption that she would not understand the instructions, so "she didn't really engage in listening, actively listening." Although she had made much progress in listening and was able to ask for assistance when not understanding, her passive attitude toward learning was still a barrier for her to overcome. Ms. Dawson noticed that she sometimes resisted working on tasks with which she had difficulty. Sometimes she could get the work done, but not always to the best of her ability. Ms. Dawson worried that if she continued to keep this attitude, it "will wear her pretty thin." For example, Tina did not even try to exert the most effort in math, a subject she cared deeply about: "I think because math is considered to be very important in her culture, and I don't think she sees herself as being as capable as other people she knows in math. So her work is often sloppy or she doesn't do it, but it's not that she doesn't understand how to do it. She doesn't seem to put that same amount of care into it as other children would."

Despite these barriers, Ms. Dawson and Mrs. Smith both were positive about Tina's ability to catch up with English. They agreed that she had demonstrated her commitment to learning English by consistently using it and by seeking out help when she did not understand something. Her determination would benefit her not only in her spoken English, but also in her understanding of English, her self-esteem, and her ways of interacting with others in class.

Conclusion

In this chapter, I have described the home and school literacy experiences of the four grade 4/5 learners in addition to the teachers' and parents' perspectives of the students' struggles. These children's worlds of literacy and the different perspectives between the parents and the teachers mirrored the existing tensions and discords between the school's cultural values and those of the Chinese families. Cultural conflicts (especially over literacy instructional approaches) between school and home permeated their everyday living in and out of the classroom. These two competing discourses of language and education had imposed a heavy burden on the students—they had one regular English school and another school (English and math tutoring, Chinese, music, extracurricular activities) at home. Living in two worlds, the students were often burdened with the consequences of the cultural clashes and experienced great discontinuity in and out of school. They were sites of struggle between school and parents, between two cultures, and hence, were placed in a dangerous position of school failure.

These children's worlds of literacy learning are a critical source of information on what literacy is and what it means in a new socioeconomic and sociocultural context. In the next chapter, the meaning of the literacy experiences of these four English learners as well as the four learners in the grade 1/2 class is explored.

CHAPTER SIX

———————————————

Understanding the Battles
of Literacy and Culture

Conflicts and Complexities

Culture now became a terrain inhabited by lived struggles
and conflicting levels of determinacy.
— Henry Giroux, *Theory and Resistance in Education:*
A Pedagogy for the Opposition

In the preceding chapters, I have presented multilayered hetereo-glossic voices—the teachers' and the parents' different perspectives, different understandings, and different instructional approaches as well as the children's different home and school experiences. All these different voices contribute to our understanding of the "battles" between the Canadian school and the Chinese families. In the description of the teachers' and parents' perspectives, I examined their different understandings of the social context, Chinese and English literacy education, and parental involvement at home and in school. With respect to the experiences of the four grade 1/2 students, I noted that the barriers to their learning were the result of school, home, and social factors, especially the different cultural beliefs between teachers and parents and misunderstanding of these differences. In the description of the grade 4/5 students' experiences, I revealed that the children were subject to a greater cultural mismatch between school and home, and the cultural clashes were detrimental to their academic success. Thus, the battles not only shaped the teachers' instructional practices at school and the parents' practices at home, but also the interactions with and perceptions of each other's practices. These different practices in turn resulted in the children's distinct social realities at home and in school as early as first grade. In this sense, cultural conflicts had divided the home and the school into separate spheres and erected powerful barriers between them, with the parents and teachers hewing to their separate roles with only minimum contact with each other across the family-school boundary (Ryan & Adams, 1995).

However, cultural conflicts were not the only battle between school and home. The teachers, parents, and students' perspectives and experiences were also complicated by the "multivocal, multiaccented nature of human subjectivity and the genuinely polysemic nature of minority/majority relations in education and society" (McCarthy, 1993, p. 337). That is, the battles between the teachers' and parents' different perspectives and their consequences were not only cultural, but also sociopolitical. As Walsh (1991a) points out, "perspectives of and approaches to literacy are shaped by theoretical and ideological concerns which extend beyond the classroom walls. These concerns are related to beliefs and assumptions about the nature of knowledge, of people (i.e., teachers and students), and of experience and to the relations of power and of social and cultural control which these beliefs and assumptions both construct and incorporate" (p. 9).

In this sense, the school and home had become "contradictory agencies engaged in specific forms of moral and political regulation" in which students were offered "selected representations, skills, social relations, and values that presuppose particular histories and ways of being in the world" (Giroux, 1991, p. xiii).

In addition to the cultural and political differences, the battles between the Canadian teachers and the Chinese parents were also complicated by several social and linguistic factors. For the Chinese parents, these factors included the contexts of reception, their own proficiencies in English literacy, and their own immigrant status. For the teachers, these factors included dealing with a large number of students (and parents) with limited English language proficiency from one ethnic background.

In this chapter, the meaning of these cultural conflicts and complexities is examined. I discuss the nature of different cultural values concerning literacy education, the underlying political nature of these cultural differences, social class and parental involvement, and the consequences of these differences and battles on the children's school achievement.

Cultural Differences and Literacy Education:
Understanding the Battles between the School and the Parents

As described in chapter 2, literacy is a sociocultural discourse. Because it is culturally laden, people of different cultures have different conceptions of what literacy is and how it should be taught. Looking at literacy as having this embedded and social nature, B. Street (1995) suggests that Western notions of literacy or school are just one form of literacy among many. As described in previous chapters, the two Euro-Canadian teachers' notions of literacy and its instruction were fundamentally different from those of the Chinese parents, and underlying these differences, there were inherent power struggles between the two divergent cultural practices.

Literacy and Literacy Instruction

An analysis of the differences between the two teachers' notions of literacy and its instruction and those of the Chinese parents revealed an interesting paradox: the teachers believed in progressive instructional approaches that are considered beneficial to the education of white, middle-class children (Reyes, 1992; Shannon, 1990). From the same progressive view, they saw literacy acquisition as developmentally appropriate to each individual child—therefore, some children are not as developmentally ready as others. The Chinese parents, however, had high expectations for their children, but believed that their children would achieve success in literacy through a traditional, teacher-centered instructional approach that is considered by some to be stifling to the education of minority and working-class children (Anyon, 1981; Finn, 1999). The teachers and the parents are therefore "traveling on parallel tracks" in terms of how literacy should be taught (Ran, 2001).

The two teachers, Mrs. Haines and Ms. Dawson, believed that literacy is the ability to read, write, and communicate with others. They further held that schooling is more than academic learning and good grades; rather, it is about learning how to become an ideal citizen and a well-rounded human being. In Mrs. Haines's class, for example, completing schoolwork and homework were the last on a list of school tasks. Instead, other tasks, such as composting and recycling and maintaining good manners, were high on the list. This emphasis was in tune with the school's rule of conduct, STAR (Safe, Thoughtful, and

Responsible). In our first interview, Ms. Dawson illustrated this perspective:

> We'd like to think that we create these well-rounded individuals and send them off to [society], and I think we do. But if most of scholarships are for academic success, then are we really valuing that whole package or are we really saying that we want you to be well rounded, we want you to be good citizens, we want you to be able to work well with other people? But when it comes down it, [it's] what do you get on your tests? It's a mixed message. And I think that's causing [problems for instruction], not just in high schools, but I think it's trickling down to elementary schools too. What is that we really value? And I'm more of a traditional-style teacher when I compare myself now to colleagues. I have certain values. I think that children need to learn certain things in school, and there are certain behaviors that [need to be taught]. But is that really preparing them for their future? I don't know, because their future is going to be so different from [what it is like today].

For the Chinese parents, their perception of what literacy is and its purpose was shaped by their culture as well as their immigrant status in Canada. Literacy throughout Chinese history has served as a vehicle for upward social mobility (G. Li, 2001, 2002). The Chinese parents in the study inherited this belief and viewed literacy as a set of skills and knowledge required for getting ahead in society—getting good grades, going to college, and becoming professionals. Their emphasis on getting ahead, however, was considered narrow focused by the teachers, who did not see going to college and becoming professionals as the sole measure of success. Mrs. Haines commented, "If all of them become professionals, who's going to pump gas [at gas stations]?" In her opinion, success should be measured individually, rather than against uniform social conventions regarding what is considered a successful person.

In addition to the influence of their cultural beliefs, the Chinese families' immigrant status further reinforced the belief that literacy and schooling were the vehicles through which their children could overcome the negative aspects of immigration, such as racism (Ogbu, 1978). Therefore, the parents held a much more pragmatic view of literacy and saw it as the ticket to higher education and a white-collar job. These beliefs were passed on to the children as soon as they entered school. It should be noted that although the parents emphasized academic achievement in literacy, they also invested heavily in making their children well rounded. Almost all children were enrolled in one or more nonacademic classes such as music (piano) and sports (soccer, tae kwon do, kickboxing, and swimming).

The Chinese parents also had a pragmatic expectation of the school as the formal place for their children to learn English literacy as they themselves were not native English speakers. As a language minority in Canada, the parents (as well as the teachers) were well aware of the disadvantage that confronted the children who were not proficient in English despite being born in Canada. The parents expected the school to help the children overcome this disadvantage.

In addition to these practical expectations, the Chinese parents also regarded the school as the place for formal learning, where academic preparation should take priority over other aspects of learning such as "being a good citizen." This view is also rooted in the Chinese belief that a well-rounded person is first of all a learned person. It is believed that children will be more successful if they acquire academic skills early. In China, schools are overwhelmingly academically oriented. For example, starting from the elementary grades, students spend a considerable amount of time at school and at home on activities related to their schoolwork (Minami, 2000; Parry & Su, 1998; Stevenson & Stigler, 1992). These practices formed a frame of reference for the parents to understand Canadian schooling (Ogbu, 1982). For the parents, the contrast between the two types of schooling often resulted in an "arm wrestle between *desire for* and *doubts about* public education" and a state of "stalemate" between the home and the school (Fine & Weis, 1998, p. 250, italics original).

The teachers and the parents also had fundamentally different perspectives on how literacy should be taught. Since literacy is about becoming a good citizen and a well-rounded person, the teachers believed that literacy was best learned through "learning the world," learning through play, experience, and social interaction, that is, through a student-centered pedagogy. The parents, on the other hand, believed that literacy was best learned through "learning the words," and emphasized learning through teacher-led instruction, homework, and students' disciplined efforts.

The teachers' educational beliefs, rooted in their own educational experiences and personal history, reflected a mainstream Canadian way of teaching and learning. They used language experience and literature-based approaches to literacy instruction. Their approaches were also marked by innovative teaching methods such as drawing, role playing, and drama, as well as an emphasis on play, acquisition of practical life skills, independent problem solving, and fostering student autonomy (C. Zhang, Ollila, & Harvey, 1998).

However, these pedagogical practices were in direct conflict with the Chinese parents' belief in more teacher-centered, discipline-oriented, "back-to-basics" schooling. For English language learning, the Chinese parents had an overriding concern about what Anyon (1981) called "performative level" literacy skills (correct spelling, good pronunciation, and standard grammar, and monitoring and correcting student performance). This would mean that phonics should make up a large part of the language arts curriculum, with corresponding homework assignments that require students to memorize, copy, and imitate texts, rather than parent-child reading as homework. Students would need to use standardized textbooks rather than literature books chosen by teachers from a variety of sources.

Furthermore, both teachers believed in an integrated approach to teaching, where different subject areas such as math, social studies, and language arts are taught as an integral whole. The teachers' integration of different skill areas (for example, reading and writing) and subject areas were also opposite to the Chinese belief that these subjects should be taught separately. Curricular integration may be one of the reasons that Chinese parents saw the school instruction of math and writing as inadequate, thus sending their children to private math tutoring institutions after school.

Another cultural difference was the homework tasks. Although Mrs. Haines and Ms. Dawson assigned homework, the parents seemed either not to consider it homework or considered it insufficient. The parents' attitudes reflected the typical Chinese belief that homework should be a significant part of children's after-school activities (Chen & Stevenson, 1989; Stevenson & Stigler, 1992). Like Chinese parents in previous research (J. Anderson, 1995b; C. Zhang et al., 1998), these Chinese parents also appeared to consider homework as pages from a workbook and pencil and paper drill practices. They did not consider reading stories or parent-child reading as homework. As a result, the parents did not participate in some of their children's reading homework and instead provided more homework themselves or hired tutors to do so. The adverse effects of the parents' perceptions of homework versus that of the teachers became evident in the children's homework performance and attitudes. Billy, Andy, and Jake did not finish some of their readings for literature circle and complained that they had so much homework from different sources that they did not have time to read.

One factor that may have contributed to the conflicting ideologies between the teachers' and parents' literacy practices was that the teachers' perceptions of the children's language development was based on their training in English as a first language (L1) teaching, rather than English as a second language (L2) development. Although the teachers' literacy practices are considered effective ways for English as L1 literacy instruction (Pressley et al., 2001), they are not adapted to the needs of English language learners. As described in chapter 3, both teachers taught the children English as if they were L1 children and did not see any difference between English as L1 and English as L2 learning except for vocabulary. The curriculum they followed was developed primarily for English L1 students (British Columbia Ministry of Education, 2000). To the Chinese parents, who were from an English-as-a-foreign-language (EFL) background and more familiar with a traditional approach (in which spelling, grammar, listening, speaking, reading, and writing are taught explicitly and separately), the teachers' holistic approach may have appeared foreign. Many researchers have shown that uncritical implementation of a progressive approach to literacy instruction with language minority students often failed to consider the influence of different variables (for example, learners' language and cultural backgrounds), and often yielded different (sometimes problematic) results (Reyes, 1992; A. I. Willis, 1995). For the Chinese students who came from traditional cultural backgrounds, as Delpit (1995) suggests, the student-centered, expressive, mainstream pedagogy may not have been the best "learning fit."

Cultural Differences and Parental Involvement

Cultural conflicts were evident in the teachers' perspectives on Chinese parental involvement. The parents were actively involved in their children's learning activities at home, such as supervising their homework, direct teaching, providing tutors, and investing in extracurricular activities. Very few parents, however, were involved in learning activities at school. For example, only one parent, Mrs. Chung, volunteered for a field trip for Mrs. Haines's class. And only one parent, Mrs. Lou, who voluntarily withdrew Andy from the ESL list, was involved in what Epstein (1989) calls "governance and advocacy." The Chinese parents' approach to involvement, however, was not invited or supported by the teachers.

The teachers' perceptions indicated a different cultural understanding of the term "involvement" from that of the Chinese parents. They expected the parents to come to the classrooms to help the children with academic matters such as reading and writing, like the white middle-class parents in Lareau's (1989, 2000) study, and they invited the parents to the classroom so that the parents could learn how to read to their children. Although the parents were actively involved in their children's learning in a variety of ways at home, they did not see involvement at school as part of their responsibility. Furthermore, because of their non-English speaking backgrounds, the parents did not think that they were qualified to read and help children in school. As a result, they interpreted the teachers' call for parental involvement as avoiding their teaching responsibilities.

The parents' cultural backgrounds also influenced their understanding of parental involvement at school, a culture where parents generally do not visit or become involved in classroom teaching. Instead, many involved themselves in their home style of caring (such as eating and toileting) that was neither academically related nor helpful for developing independence in the children. The teachers' banning of the Chinese parents from helping with eating and so on at school may have resulted in a misunderstanding of the teachers' intentions. This consequently may have fostered an unwillingness by the parents to participate in classroom activities or even to communicate with the teachers.

Mrs. Haines and Ms. Dawson also had different concepts of parental involvement at home. First, they believed that the parents should spend quality time reading or modeling reading to their children at home. This practice of reading to the children is mostly a white, middle-class practice that is not shared in many other cultures (J. Anderson, 1995; Taylor, 1983; Valdés, 1996). For the Chinese parents, teaching spelling, vocabulary, and math, tutoring classes, and supervising homework were much more important than reading to the children at home as they did not consider reading to their children as homework. Although some parents did read to and with the children at home (for example, Sandy and Billy, Jake, and Anthony's parents), their concept of "reading" was not "just plain reading"—a more experience approach to reading as held by the teachers (Braunger & Lewis, 1997, p. 54); rather, it was studying the texts and learning every new word and phrase—a basal-text approach to reading. Many parents did not like reading to their children as some could not read English themselves. Even if they could, they did not want their children to acquire their accents.

Second, Mrs. Haines and Ms. Dawson believed that the children should be encouraged to play and socialize with other children after school instead of attending different academic classes. They believed that the parents' regimented home literacy practices and high expectations, coupled with their indulging attitude toward their children's social behaviors, stifled their development and deprived them of their real childhood. Mrs. Haines, for example, attributed the difficulties of the four children (Sandy, Alana, Anthony, and Kevin) to improper family practices. These perceptions were not shared by the Chinese parents, who lacked confidence in the quality of the school instruction and considered school homework insufficient and school methods to be lacking rigor. The Chinese parents also had extremely high expectations of their children and were willing to make financial investments (for example, sending them to private lessons) and personal sacrifices (taking care of the children) to compensate for the children's lack of school learning (Chao, 1996; Siu, 1994; S. Y. Zhang & Carrasquillo, 1995).

The teachers perceived these kinds of parental investments and sacrifices as counterproductive to the children's natural cognitive development, overprogramming, and therefore not academically or cognitively beneficial. The teachers' perceptions in turn reinforced their beliefs in a more expressive pedagogy that aimed to foster more well-rounded learning and emphasizing "letting the children just be children." They believed that this pedagogy was healthier for the Chinese children, who were under too much pressure to succeed. Unfortunately, the teachers' beliefs and concerns were not effectively communicated to the parents. Consequently the Chinese parents in turn continued their remedial practices at home. To hold onto what they each believed to be the best pedagogy, the two parties engaged in a cold war in and out of school.

Social Class, Pedagogization of Literacy, and the Politics of Difference

As described in chapters 2 and 3, the parents and the school positioned themselves differently in society. The teachers' (especially Mrs. Haines's) observations of the reversed socioeconomic positions between the Chinese community and the mainstream suggested that the higher socioeconomic status of the new Chinese community challenged the traditional status quo of the majority, white middle-class versus the lower SES Chinese minority. Their perceived reverse racial prejudice indicated a changing power relation between the white majority and the Chinese minority (P. S. Li, 1998). This changing power relationship placed the parents in a "contradictory location" within the white dominant power hierarchy (McCarthy, 1995). Although the parents were a racial majority in the community and in a similar socioeconomic class to the teachers, they were still in a subordinate power position. In their view, discrimination from the mainstream Canadian society was still a barrier to their children's advancement in education.

Although the school represents the mainstream, white middle-class ideology, the power relations between the parents and the school were contested in the battles over best practices for the Chinese children. The teachers believed that their holistic approaches to literacy could best help the students learn and that the parents' preferences for traditional practices were counterproductive. Unconsciously, the well-intentioned teachers enforced the "pedagogization of literacy," which defines literacy and its instruction solely in terms of school-based notions of teaching and learning while marginalizing other forms of literacy, such as those held by the Chinese parents (J. C. Street & B. Street, 1991).

The teachers' perspectives on the Chinese community suggest that the teachers positioned themselves as sources of mainstream knowledge, "windows on Canadian society." Although they worked hard at communicating to the parents about their educational beliefs and practices, the parents still did not seem to accept and understand them. The parents' campaign for traditional schools, their unwillingness to participate in school activities or school homework, and their preference for after-school classes seemed to suggest that they not only had fundamentally different beliefs about literacy learning, but also actively resisted the school practices. The teachers were unwilling to compromise their beliefs and used a variety of measures to educate the parents about their beliefs and practices (for example, inviting the parents to the classroom to learn how to read to their children). The teachers' effort to change the parents further intensified the parents' creative resistance to school practices (McLaren, 1998).

The teachers' "pedagogization of literacy" was also reflected in their approach toward the students' first language and literacy in school. The two teachers were under tremendous pressure to ensure the children's school success, especially in English literacy, for which they were held accountable. They also faced the challenge of a large number of ESL students from a single ethnic group who continued speaking their first language in school. To provide the students with the necessary English environment, the teachers believed that consistent exposure to English provides the best (and only legitimate) avenue for students to acquire English language skills (E. E. Garcia, 1990; Minami & Ovando, 2004; Valdés, 1998). Although they had positive attitudes toward maintaining the children's first language, both teachers, together with the other faculty, maintained that many students failed to learn English because they spoke too much Chinese at school, had little exposure to English at home, and had no English-speaking children to socialize with in and out of school (mainly because of too much exposure to Chinese speaking children). This conception prevented the teachers from encouraging the children to make use of their first language to understand classroom literacy activities and instruction, or providing support to transfer their skills and comprehension in their first language (Chinese) to reading and writing in English. Thus, the teachers had failed to understand the role of Chinese in the development of English literacy and biliteracy, and their good intentions had resulted in a form of subtractive schooling that did not value the students' cultural identity and heritage—the very language that they speak (Fillmore & Meyer, 1992; Minami & Ovando, 2004). The absence of such an understanding can be psychologically and emotionally harmful to the minority students as the underlying ideological force maintains the mainstream cultural hegemony and reinforces the existing inequalities of power, race, ethnicity, and language (Macedo, 1994).

Another practice of pedagogization of literacy was also evident in the conflicts over parental involvement. As described in the previous section, the relationship between the teachers and the parents seemed to follow a school-to-home unidirectional model (Christenson & Sheridan, 2001; Fine, 1993). To help the children achieve, the teachers hoped to foster a continuity of their own expectations and values across school and home. However, rather than seeing the cultural capital of the families (for example, parental investment and support) as strengths and building on the families' different values and practices, the teachers aimed at changing the parents' values and practices to conform to those of the school. As mentioned above, these assumptions and attitudes were unfortunately conveyed to the parents through their actions and consequently affected the relationship with them.

Although their values and practices may contribute to success, the teachers did not initially aim to foster an understanding among the parents of these values and practices. Nor did the teachers aim to have a full understanding of the parents' values, practices, concerns, and needs. This lack of understanding may have contributed to their misconceptions about the families' literacy practices (for example, Mrs. Haines's understanding of Kevin's idiosyncratic behavior as a result of family pressure and Ms. Dawson's understanding of Mrs. Wong's indifference toward Jake's homework). The misconceptions may have affected the teachers' advice about how the parents should change their values and practices. For example, when advising Anthony's parents to drop classes, if Mrs. Haines had understood that Anthony was enrolled not only in math classes, but also in several other extracurricular classes, she might have suggested that Anthony drop some extracurricular classes (such as kickboxing, swimming or soccer), rather than dropping the academic class that the parents cared about most, math. This kind of advice, though legitimate, may have further reinforced the parents' misconception that the school did not care about students' academic development.

Although the Chinese parents desired public school education, they challenged the teachers' pedagogization practice. The parents' middle-class status, however, had given them not only the confidence to request changes in school (for example, changes in the seating arrangement, more homework, and abolition of combined classes), but also the resources to pursue their beliefs outside of school when they were dissatisfied with the school practices. That is, when their own cultural capital was not accepted and utilized by the school, the parents invested their cultural resources in their children's learning outside school through their own actions and decisions (Lareau, 2000). Since the parents were not willing to compromise their beliefs and continued to act on these beliefs with their own resources outside of school, the result was a "silenced dialogue" (Delpit, 1995) between the teachers and the Chinese parents.

The Chinese parents' opposition to school practices represents a new power structure that has significant implications for minority education. Unlike other immigrant minorities (for example, Punjabi and Hispanic immigrants in the United States), who perceive the mainstream to be different from, but not in opposition to themselves

(Ogbu, 1978), the Chinese parents in this study seemed to perceive the mainstream as being in opposition to themselves. In addition, unlike many other immigrant groups who adopted the "accommodation without assimilation" strategy (Gibson, 1988), the Chinese parents seemed to have adopted a "nonaccommodation" approach, especially toward educational practices—they not only put different demands on the school, but also used their own resources outside school to reenforce their own cultural capital and counteract the school's cultural capital. That is, the Chinese parents as a subculture were actively contesting the dominant cultural space of school (McLaren, 1998).

In many ways, the Chinese parents in this study are very similar to the white middle-class parents, the Brownstoners, in Sieber's (1981) study, who were engaged in long-standing political struggles in and outside school to transform the school practices to conform to their middle-class upbringing, values, and beliefs about education. However, unlike the Brownstoners, the Chinese parents did not have support or cooperation from the school, and their efforts did not bring them success in changing the school practices and enforcing their own beliefs in the school setting. Thus, their cultural capital was not being activated in school as it was for the Brownstone children. In Bourdieu's (1977) terms, the cultural capital that the Chinese children acquired at home (habitus) was not translated (through formal schooling) into the cultural competence that sanctions social and educational advantage. In fact, the battles between the school and home cultural capital may have contributed to the Chinese children's academic difficulties. The Chinese parents' creative resistance to the mainstream pedagogy may have reinforced the school's hegemonic practice in that their very resistance outside the school actually helped the school in sustaining its dominant practices and placed the teachers and parents further in opposition to each other (McLaren, 1998; P. E. Willis, 1977). The further fragmentation between school and home cultural discourses in fact presented the children with fewer options for access to dominant-culture literacy. As a result, the children may have been doubly disadvantaged in that they lacked the cultural capital valued by the school and at the same time possessed a habitus that further distanced them from school and discouraged them from exerting themselves in school (Nespor, 1991).

The teacher-parent relationship cycle suggests that the challenges the mainstream teachers experienced teaching Asian English-language learners in a changing sociocultural and socioeconomic context are

multifaceted and complex. The cultural conflicts, as well as the underlying power struggles between the teachers and the parents, played a
key role in shaping the educational experiences of minority children.

Cultural Conflicts and School Achievement: Understanding the Children's Experiences

Each of the focal children experienced different kinds of difficulties in
school. In the lower grades, the students exhibited different kinds of
struggles: Sandy and Anthony developed passive and negative attitudes toward learning, Kevin was coping with his nervous behavior
and difficulty in writing, and Alana experienced social isolation and
slow progress in English. In the higher grades, Billy, Andy, and Jake
were all below grade level in literacy performance, and Tina experienced not only social isolation, but also academic difficulty in content
areas. The children's literacy experiences in and out of school suggested that the battles between school and home had significant consequences on their everyday living and academic achievement. The
battles not only contributed to the children's academic difficulty (for
example, in acquiring English literacy), but also resulted in negative
influences on the children's cognitive and affective development (low
motivation, identity crisis, and negative attitudes toward learning).

Cultural Mismatches, Pedagogical Differences, and Literacy Learning

The children's stories confirm that the cultural mismatch between the
school and home literacy practices was a contributing factor to their
struggles with literacy. The pedagogical differences, for example, had
become a double barrier for students to overcome both in school and
at home. Failure to make transitions between two different approaches
resulted in a more difficult learning environment.

At home, the students were socialized in a pedagogy that was
characterized by direct instruction and a bottom-up approach to reading. The parents believed that reading meant decoding words, and
that it should be taught in a hierarchical fashion, with drill practice
and rote memorization. Their overemphasis on teaching decoding
skills in sequence may have resulted in making their children work on
the basic skills at the lower end of the continuum and limiting their
development in comprehension and exposure to connected text

(G. E. García, Pearson, & Jiménez, 1994). Billy's and Jake's parents, for example, emphasized checking the meaning of every new word, which decreased the children's interest and motivation to read.

This word-by-word decoding practice may have been problematic for the children at school because school reading tasks were more semantically oriented (for example, literature circle storybook readings), and the students had to read multiple pages or chapters and make connections between pages. In Ms. Dawson's classroom, the children's lack of interest in reading the literature circle novels suggests that the chosen materials may have been problematic. One factor might have been that the novels such as *Silver Wing, George's Marvelous Medicine,* and *Stone Fox* were too difficult for their reading proficiency. Research on second-language reading suggests that the difficulty level of reading material should be slightly below the reader's proficiency level (that is, at an i-1 level, with no more than five or six new words per page), so that students are motivated to read (Day & Bamford, 1998). The readings selected for literature circles may have been beyond the students' levels as Billy, Jake, and Andy complained that there were too many new words in the readings.

At school, the children were socialized into student-centered literacy practices in which direct instruction was minimal. This lack of direct instruction may have been problematic for children such as Alana, Sandy, and Anthony, who were used to a direct instructional approach at home, thus contributing to their learning struggle. In Mrs. Haines's class, students had to become familiar with a language experience approach in which no direct instruction of language was offered. As Mr. Ma pointed out, "If the child can absorb the method, it's good. If the child can't adapt to the method, then the child will suffer." In Ms. Dawson's vocabulary activities (such as quizzes and grammar worksheets), the content was mostly decontextualized. Little instruction was offered to explain some of the concepts or reading strategies. For example, Ms. Dawson handed out worksheets on suffixes and prefixes for the students to work on individually, but did not explain how different stems or prefixes work together to make words, nor did she give examples to illustrate their use. As reviewed earlier, Chinese students tend to be structure-oriented learners who require more reinforcement and more direct instruction. Without further explanation, students like Billy and Jake, who do not understand the concepts of prefixes or suffixes before they are presented in class, are unlikely to improve their understanding of them through such independent tasks. This lack of direct explanation was also reflected in Ms.

Dawson's comments on the students' literature circle tasks. Often she pointed out that the students needed to use up the page, but did not provide the necessary scaffolding to the students (for example, Billy, Andy, and Jake) to explain how to expand their writing to fill up the page. Lack of direct instruction often contributed to the students' tendency to be off task. For example, during their group discussions in the literature circle, Andy, Jake, Billy, and Tina often were left alone and failed to stay on task. Instead, the students focused more on disciplinary issues such as who forgot to do homework or bring books.

The culturally different definitions of homework between school and home also affected the students' learning, particularly their attitude toward schoolwork. At home, the children engaged in a large amount of homework from their tutoring classes and were educated by the parents about the importance of the homework from these out-of-school sources. The students also acquired the perception that reading homework from school was not important. In Mrs. Haines's class, for example, students did not have time to finish their assigned homework because they had too much other homework. In Ms. Dawson's class, the students did not have time to read because of too much homework from other sources. Students' apathy toward school homework may also have affected their perception of school learning as being less important than their out-of-school classes and therefore lowered their motivation to try their best at school (for example, Anthony and Sandy passively resisted learning at school). The children who had more rigorous classes outside school might have regarded school as less academically oriented, as did their parents. For example, Billy and Andy took tutoring classes very seriously but did not demonstrate a similar attitude toward learning in school.

Another pedagogical influence was reflected in the cultural relevance of the materials the children read at school. The books chosen in the two classrooms all featured white, middle-class characters or neutral themes such as animals, and thus seemed detached from the students' cultural backgrounds. As Ms. Dawson observed, the children in her class seemed to have a hard time relating to the characters in the books. The children's detachment may have resulted in their lack of interest in reading, and their inability to write meaningful responses and make analytical comments (G. E. Garcia, Pearson, & Jimenez, 1994; McCarthey, 1997). In Mrs. Haines's classroom, although a few ethnic holidays were included, such as Hanukkah and the Chinese New Year, very few reading materials were related to the students' cultural backgrounds.

This lack of cultural relevance in the curriculum suggests that the teachers adopted "tourist" conceptions of cultural diversity (Derman-Sparks, 1989). The students' cultural backgrounds or knowledge from their homes were not used to facilitate their literacy learning or to advance their knowledge in key concepts, principles, and critical literacy skills (for example, skills to understand their own social positioning in the society as minority groups). The teachers did not incorporate students' cultural knowledge into the curriculum or use cultural diversity as a means for knowledge construction and empowerment (Banks, 2002, 2004). This cultural irrelevance may have further widened the gap between school and home and lessened the students' sense of belonging in what they call the "English school."

"The Dark Side of Parental Involvement"

Although parental involvement has been considered to have a positive influence on students' academic achievement, researchers such Lareau (1989, 2000), Lightfoot (1978), and Walberg (1987) point out that along with the advantages, the interdependency between school and home also produce distinct disadvantages for students as well as their families and teachers. Some of these disadvantages include stress for children, tensions within the families, and tensions within schools. The costs for the children could also be cognitive and affective. I agree with the teachers' beliefs that some aspects of the parents' involvement did the children more harm than good. For example, Anthony's parents' spoon feeding and Mrs. Ling's overprotective measures were not conducive to fostering the children's independence. Similar to the children in Lareau's study, some of the children in this study also showed signs of stress and negativity toward learning. For example, Billy and Andy had too much homework to do and did not have time to read or do schoolwork; Anthony was not willing to step out his safety zone; Sandy was passively resistant toward learning; and Tina was fearful and worried about making mistakes.

Similarly, the children's failure to excel had caused tensions and distress in their families. Billy and Sandy's parents, for example, were very disappointed and frustrated with their children's school problems and often became angry and forced them to study. While they blamed the school system for ruining their two children, Andy's parents also blamed themselves for their late discovery of after-school tutoring and other support.

Some types of parental involvement had also put the children in adverse learning situations. As discussed earlier, the parents' creative resistance sometimes deprived them of opportunities and access needed for acquiring English literacy. Mrs. Lou, for example, withdrew Andy from the ESL list so that he would have more English exposure in a regular classroom; the decision, however, may have reduced needed language support. Another example is Anthony's parents, who wanted him to borrow and read preselected information books, rather than respecting his interests and choices. As a result, they avoided libraries.

Modes of Incorporation, School Context, and English (L2) Learning

As discussed in chapter 1, different modes of incorporation and integration into host communities such as contexts of reception in the society (for example, discrimination from the mainstream), the location of the school (low SES neighborhoods), and ethnic solidarity (social networks within ethnic groups) can all affect the immigrant child's adaptation and academic achievement (Portes & McCleod, 1995; Portes & Rumbaut, 1990, 1996). For the Chinese children in the study, the most direct influence on their language learning was their ethnic solidarity, which affected their language environment. Although ethnic networks provided the families with invaluable resources for facilitating school achievement and first-language maintenance, it also had some disadvantages. Living in ethnic solitude, most of the Chinese families had little contact with the mainstream society. Although their children were enrolled in a variety of activities outside school, the activities were mostly within the ethnic network. At school, these children had very few native English-speaking peers.

Like many ESL students who are in situations where English learners outnumber native English speakers, the children in this study faced the challenge of having access to rich, meaningful input from more capable peers (Valdés, 2001; Vygotsky, 1978). Thus, they had fewer opportunities to interact with speakers of fluent English and to be exposed to different forms of English. For most of the children in the study, their only contacts with non-Chinese speakers and the English language were at school or through TV at home. This lack of contact with native speakers of English may have been a factor contributing to the children's difficulty in acquiring both conversational and academic English. As Valdés (2001) points out, "They are surrounded by speakers of imperfect English who are themselves learners of English. Given their lack of access to native-like English, students may not develop a full mastery of the standard forms of English" (p. 150).

For some children, their lack of access to English was further complicated by their lack of interaction with the few non-Chinese children at school. Many socialized only with children who spoke their language. Andy, Billy, and Jake, for example, played only with Cantonese speakers and most often in Cantonese. In this sense, ethnic solidarity and the Chinese students' in-group tendencies may have had double disadvantages to their English language learning, a skill necessary for upward social mobility.

Their unique situation also provided challenges for the teachers who were accountable for the children's English literacy achievement. Although the teachers had made deliberate efforts to make the students use more English, their efforts did not extend to creating opportunities for more exposure to the language, providing more meaningful input of the language, or encouraging interactions with non-Chinese-speaking peers. In a sense, the teachers' efforts, such as the English-only policy, may have had a negative impact on the children.

English-Only, First Language Use, and Identity Formation

One of the most controversial issues in second-language education is the place of students' first language. Suárez-Orozco and Suárez-Orozco (2001) point out that rather than viewing immigrant children's linguistic knowledge as potential assets to be cultivated, many view it as a threat to the integrity of the English language and as a symbolic refusal to be assimilated into the mainstream culture. Contrary to this myth, many researchers have concluded that the use of the child's first language does not impede the acquisition of English; instead, it should be used as a resource for children to learn English (August & Hakuta, 1997; Cummins, 1989; Valdés, 1998).

In this study, although the teachers realized the significance of the children's first language, they did not seem to encourage the children to make use of Chinese to understand classroom literacy activities and instruction. In fact, the teachers considered that speaking their first language in the classroom had resulted in slow progress for the students in English reading and writing, and had consequently adopted an English-only policy in their classrooms. Although it was a logical solution given the children's lack of access to English language out-side of school, this practice may have had some negative effects on the children's literacy development in that no support was provided for them to transfer their skills and comprehension in their first language to reading and writing in English (Moll & Diaz, 1993). For children who are not yet proficient in English literacy, building on their strengths in their first language may be significant to their mastery of English literacy. For example, research suggests that linguistic minor-ity students' first language can be used in cognitively challenging ways to focus on the acquisition of content knowledge and from the content develop the understanding and use of the second language (Hernandez, 1993; Shade, Kelly, & Oberg, 1997).

The teachers' English-only practices may also have had a negative influence on the children's affective development. For example, Sandy was not yet fluent in English, but had to follow the English-only rule, which may have contributed to her lack of interest and friends in the classroom and her negative attitude toward learning. The English-only rule had also alienated new students, such as Alana and Tina, from others because they were not able to express themselves in Eng-lish. For other children such as Jake and Andy, the policy may also have deepened their low confidence in their English-language ability, and that in turn may have fostered their passive attitude toward learn-ing the language.

The English-only practices (together with other perceived con-texts of reception, such as discrimination) may also have resulted in the different workings of the children's identity formation. Since chil-dren's sense of self is profoundly shaped by the reflections mirrored back to them by people around them, the school's attitudes toward the children's first language and literacy in the school setting may have become powerful cues from which the children remade their identities (Suárez-Orozco & Suárez-Orozco, 2001). These identities, in turn, influenced the children's desire for and decisions about personal investment in their literacy learning (Pierce, 1995).

The Chinese children in the study seemed to have displayed two dichotomous identity tendencies. One tendency, displayed by Anthony, Kevin, and Tina, indicated a growing distance from their ethnic language and culture. This tendency, termed "ethnic flight" by Suárez-Orozco & Suárez-Orozco (2001), "often comes at a significant social and emotional cost" (p. 104), though it can help a person suc-ceed by mainstream standards. From early on, these children learned to hide the fact that they understood Chinese and even refused to speak it in their homes. For these children, as Wong Fillmore (1991b) poignantly illustrates, learning a second language means losing their first language.

Another tendency, ethnic affiliation, displayed by students like Billy, Andy, and Jake, indicated a resistance to social alignment with the school practices (Gilmore, 1991). These children developed adversarial identities toward the mainstream language and culture, particularly the school's sanction against their first language in school (Suárez-Orozco & Suárez-Orozco, 2001). Similar to the working-class students in Paul Willis's (1977) study, these children actively engaged in classroom resistance to the English-only policy and persisted in their first-language use and therefore maintained their Cantonese speaker identity. These remakings of identity also came with social and emotional cost. For these children, their resistance may have further prevented them from learning the official knowledge and the code of power that are necessary for doing well in school and realizing their parents' career expectations for them. Therefore, unless more positive attitudes can be fostered, these adversarial identities may in the long run be self-defeating and counterproductive (Nieto, 1991, 2002).

Literacy Underachievement, Cultural Interpretations, and Assessment

Another adverse influence on the children's academic achievement was related to the parents' and teachers' different perspectives on what caused the children's difficulties with school. Their different interpretations on the sources of the children's problems and literacy underachievement often led to different measures to solve the problems they identified. Without mutual understanding and collaboration between the two, their uncoordinated effort may have resulted in further discontinuities for the children.

In grade 1/2, Mrs. Haines attributed the children's difficulties to the families' inappropriate practices. In terms of Sandy's negativity, Mrs. Haines thought that it might be family pressure and indulgence; For Anthony and Kevin, it was family overprogramming; and for Alana, it was the families' lack of involvement. Based on these perceptions, Mrs. Haines suggested that the families focus on less on academic preparation and more on socialization and play. For Anthony, she even recommended that the parents attend counseling. In class, she tried hard to relax the students by emphasizing risk taking and learning through play. The parents attributed the children's difficulties to school practices that focused on too much play, too much freedom, and not enough academic learning. In order to make up for what school was not doing, they decided to focus more on academic learning at home. The parents' and the teachers' different measures therefore further reinforced the school-home conflicts.

In the higher grades, the differences between the teachers and parents were rooted in their cultural interpretation of school difficulties—innate ability versus effort. In Chinese culture, it is believed that innate ability is given at birth and cannot be changed, but through continuous effort, people with low innate ability can achieve the same as people who are "born smart." In the West, it is believed that a child's low innate ability determines school performance (G. Li, 2003; Stevenson and Stigler, 1992; S. Y. Zhang & Carrasquillo, 1995). These different cultural interpretations of school failure were evident in the parents' and the teachers' different understandings of the children's struggles with literacy.

The Chinese parents suggested several external reasons for their children's underachievement, such as the combined class, methods of instruction, and insufficient homework. The teachers, on the other hand, suggested more internal factors such as the children's innate ability, their use of their first language, and their personality. Although it is natural for parents and teachers who come from different backgrounds to have different perceptions of children's reading difficulties, their differences have an impact on how the learners are perceived and on the ways the parents and teachers seek to facilitate their learning at school and at home (McDermott & Varenne, 1995). In the case of Billy, Andy, and Jake, for example, their parents believed that their literacy difficulties were due to external factors and therefore took remedial actions such as after-school tutoring. Such actions to reinforce the children's learning were not in tune with the teachers' suggestions for modified programs based on their assessment that the children's failure was a result of their innate ability.

Related to the innate ability versus effort approach to understanding the children's underachievement was the issue of assessment. Assessment is a highly complex process that requires systematic evaluation of different variables. For the teachers, who viewed difficulties as innate to the children, there was a danger of overdiagnosis of learning disabilities. For the parents, who viewed difficulties as an effort issue, there was a danger of underdiagnosis of children who actually had learning disabilities. For Billy and Andy, who performed at grade level in math and other subjects and who experienced the "fourth-grade slump," difficulty with English literacy might not have been the result of a learning disability. For Jake, who had experienced great difficulty since first grade, a learning disability and delayed diagnosis of his condition may have compounded the problem. Whatever the case, the learners' problems needed to be adequately assessed following government guidelines for identification, assessment, and programming of ESL learners with special needs (Fowler & Hooper, 1998). Inaccurate assessment, whether overdiagnosis or underdiagnosis, may affect the type of support that the teachers and parents aimed to provide for the children, which in turn may have affected the students' optimal development.

School-Home Communications

As discussed previously, the different cultural values between school and home had become an impediment to the children's academic learning at school and home. These differences, which could complement each other, were not communicated between the parents and teachers. Both operated under their own assumptions about their practices without sufficient understanding of each other's values and concerns. This lack of communication often resulted in complex school-home relations laden with tensions and misunderstandings.

Although both sides were concerned about the children's development and took different measures to help them, their understanding of the causes of the children's difficulties were never communicated to each other. The parents seemed to have little understanding of the school's practices, such as why a combined class was used, what was considered normal school homework, or what instructional methods were being used in the classroom. The teachers, on the other hand, had little information about the students' home life, the parents' beliefs, and their efforts to support their children's education. The initiatives used to communicate with parents were often unidirectional and aimed at educating parents to conform to school practices. This kind of well-intentioned strategy often resulted in further resistance and misunderstanding among the parents. What was missing was the open, two-way communication that is the foundation of a genuine school-home partnership in which parents and teachers work together

to identify a mutually advantageous solution in light of problems
(Christenson & Sheridan, 2001; Weiss & Edwards, 1992). The misunderstanding around whether Jake's parents checked his homework,
for example, reflected a lack of this kind of two-way communication.
As the information in this book suggests, this deficiency was counterproductive to understanding (and assessing) the focal children's learning difficulties and facilitating their development.

Conclusion

In this chapter, I have provided an interpretation of the meaning of
the literacy and culture battles in relation to the school-parent relations and the children's school achievement. I have discussed the
cultural conflicts concerning literacy and its instruction, parental
involvement, and the politics of difference underlining the battles
between school and home. These conflicts and their political implications had a significant impact on the children's learning in and out of
school. In understanding the children's difficulties with schooling, I
have discussed different factors, such as the pedagogical differences
between school and home, well-intentioned parental involvement,
modes of incorporation, school policy and the children's remaking of
identity, school and home approaches to students' underachievement,
and last but not least, the lack of school and home communications.
How might these understandings inform the ways we envision and
transform educational practices for language-minority students?
What are the implications of these cultural and political conflicts for
teachers, schools, parents, and students? In the next chapter, I detail
some of the implications for change by revisiting the broader issues
of culture and difference.

CHAPTER SEVEN

=========

Learning from the Battles

Toward a Pedagogy of Cultural Reciprocity

This study has represented a journey toward an understanding of the education of immigrant children in unique, contemporary social spaces. Unlike the widely researched, lower SES minority children, the Chinese children were from middle-class backgrounds and attended a white middle-class school where they substantially outnumbered children of other backgrounds. Their parents "educationalized" their learning at home through after-school classes and they held values about literacy education that aligned with conservative phonics instruction, an approach criticized as "bad teaching" by many North American educators, including the two focal teachers who believed in a more holistic approach to literacy. This study has showed how the teachers and the parents, coming from different sociocultural backgrounds, differed in their social positioning and in their beliefs and perspectives about literacy and schooling. It has also demonstrated that their different beliefs and perspectives shaped and constructed their children's qualitatively different school and home learning experiences. These experiences revealed that culturally contested pedagogy and the differential power imbalance between school and home had had a significant impact on the children's learning and development and had become a risk factor to their achieving academic success.

To help these children overcome this risk factor is a dauntingly challenging task. The teachers were placed in a difficult position: they were faced with a large number of ESL students from one cultural background with little professional preparation or support. Moreover, they were confronted with the problem of dealing with parents who opposed their holistic, progressive approaches to literacy instruction. Their dedication to providing quality education to the children inevitably led them to battle against the parents' approaches to literacy, which they perceived as stifling the children's natural learning and creativity. However, like many teachers in similar situations, they had few opportunities to consider the implicit values of their own middle-class background and to explore and observe students' lives out of school contexts (McCarthey, 1997, 1999), nor had they been able to critically reflect on the social relations between school and home. Without being informed of the students' individual and sociocultural backgrounds or an understanding of their own practices and the intricate social relations, the teachers' battles could only lead to more misconceptions and misunderstandings, further intensified by the conflicts between school and home.

The parents were also placed in a difficult situation. While the teachers viewed the difficulties the children experienced as the *result* of inappropriate parental involvement, the parents viewed their actions and involvement as a *response* to school practices that did not meet their expectations. Like all immigrants, they faced the challenge of not only learning to adapt to life in Canadian society themselves, but also learning how to help their children adapt to a different school system. Coming from a culture that highly valued academic learning, the parents were dissatisfied with the school practices, especially when their children failed to acquire literacy skills necessary for "making it" in the future. Their dissatisfaction with school practices led to their effort to battle against school practices and encouraged remedial interventions at home using their own resources. Although their middle-class status afforded them advantages to survive economically in Canada and resources to help their children, several factors—such as their own limited English language ability, their minority status, their lack of educational experiences in Canada, and their social isolation from the mainstream society—prevented them from having an adequate understanding of Canadian school practices. Their lack of informed knowledge of Canadian schooling also became a catalyst for conflicts between school and home.

So can the enduring battles between the "natural enemies" (Lareau, 2000; Waller, 1932) be resolved? What have we learned from the experiences of the teachers, parents, and students? How can we help teachers be responsive to minority cultures, learn what they do not know about minority beliefs, and accommodate what they do not

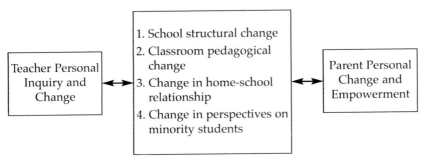

Fig. 7.1. *A discourse of change for a pedagogy of cultural reciprocity.*

believe in? How can we help parents learn what they do not know and accommodate the school practices that they do not believe in? How can we help teachers and parents create better ways to communicate and work together for the benefit of children?

The conflicts and complexities of minority schooling uncovered in this study reveal that there is a need to rewrite the discourse of literacy and difference. Giroux (1991) suggests that this rewriting process involves reconstructing the politics of literacy and culture to engage the broader issue of how learning is truly attentive to the problems and histories that construct the actual experiences that students (as well as teachers and parents) face in their everyday lives. It requires changes not only in school settings such as in school structures, classroom practices, and policies, but also in home settings such as in literacy intervention practices. To rewrite the dichotomous school-home discourses as evidenced in this study, I build on Winters's (1993) notion of "reciprocal enculturation" and propose a new dialogic discourse, a model of change that I call a *pedagogy of cultural reciprocity*, in which different practices, values, traditions, understandings, and ideologies are reconfigured and acquired by both school and home agencies (figure 7.1). Winters suggests that teachers and parents can adopt a "reciprocal enculturation" stance whereby new cultural patterns are acquired by both school and family systems as they develop and mature and each can be endowed with new energy that changes parent-school relations. In this new discourse, I envision both teachers and parents as change agents. In order to achieve cultural reciprocity, they need to first reflect on their own respective cultural beliefs and pedagogical traditions, and learn from each other's cultural knowledge. They also need to work toward change in school settings including school structural change, and change in classroom pedagogical practices, in school-home relations, and in understanding students' development.

In the following pages, I will elaborate on the tenets of change by revisiting the broader issues of difference discussed in the first two chapters of this book: (1) culturally responsive teaching; (2) the great debate between traditional teacher-centered, code-emphasis education and progressive student-centered, meaning-emphasis education; (3) parental involvement and parent-school relations; and (4) understanding the actual experiences of minority learners in the process of change.

Revisiting Culturally Responsive Teaching: Implications for Teacher Personal Change and School Structural Change

As described in previous chapters, the paradox between the teachers and the parents in this study, unlike any other addressed in previous research, is that the teachers embraced a more progressive pedagogy while the parents desired a more traditional style of schooling—a pedagogy that is often considered by some educators to have put minority students at a disadvantage (Anyon, 1981; Finn, 1999; Snow et al., 1991). The teachers were therefore put in a difficult position: if they became responsive to the Chinese parents, they might have been doing a disservice to the children; if they did not, they might have run into the danger of disempowering the children. This paradox goes back to the questions I raised in the introduction of this book: How responsive should teachers be to the minority culture? Can they teach what they do not know or do not believe in? If we believe that we need to educate minority children in their own interests (Freire, 1970), the answer to these questions may be that teachers need to refine their pedagogical practices to address students' needs and families' expectations (for example, by including the good and powerful literacy skills necessary for upward social mobility). To do so, teachers need to adopt a multicultural education stance toward literacy instruction and they must first learn what they do not know, such as cultural differences, and then address the underlying power relationships.

This study has demonstrated that teaching English language learners from diverse backgrounds requires teachers to pay special attention to recognizing and valuing minority culture differences. With the increasing changes in demographic patterns among the

North American school population, cultural differences between school and home practices and values will continue to be a challenge for mainstream teachers to overcome to ensure minority academic achievement. The tensions and dissensions between the two teachers and the Chinese parents in this study also shed light on the underlying power issues in teaching students of different cultural backgrounds in a new socioeconomic context. There is a need for teachers to rethink the curriculum and adjust their instructional practices to ensure an equity pedagogy that accommodates particular cultural ways of learning (Banks, 2002, 2004). To do so requires that teachers not only learn about students' cultures and backgrounds, but also recognize how students' cultural knowledge is differentially situated and represented in the official knowledge of the school curriculum (McLaren, 1995). Based on their knowledge of students' backgrounds and their interpretation of the curriculum, teachers will be able to make culturally sensitive decisions on how to adapt instruction to the interactional, linguistic, and cognitive styles of the minority students and empower students intellectually, emotionally, and politically (Au, 1993; Ladson-Billings, 1994; Nieto, 2002). Achieving these tasks can be tremendously difficult for teachers, especially when they do not believe that parents' cultural practices are helping the children's learning.

Teachers' and parents' differential understandings of learners suggest that teachers need to become familiar with the expectations and cultural beliefs of parents about their children's education if they differ from their own expectations and beliefs. Such familiarity may help teachers better understand and assess students' behavior and performance, as well as better adjust classroom instruction to accommodate the children's specific needs. Familiarity with parents' beliefs can also help teachers create conditions for learning that match students' cultural experiences, and find culturally appropriate ways to inform parents about their own educational beliefs and instructional practices that may help reduce parents' misunderstanding of mainstream schooling.

This study shows that many conflicts were attributed to teachers' misconceptions or insufficient first-hand information about the students' cultural practices. The teachers' experiences with the Chinese students indicate that they need to find effective ways to collect student social and cultural data outside school, as we cannot teach when we do not know who we are teaching. For the teachers who were committed to providing the best education to their students, this is the first step toward being able to be responsive to the students' cultures. Teachers can use a variety of ways to learn about students' individual and sociocultural backgrounds and their out-of-school literacy practices. For example, teachers can use home visits as a very effective way of finding out information about students and their families. They can also use well-planned conferences and questionnaires, and they can create opportunities for students to write their own narratives and interweave their own home experiences (McCarthey, 1997; Voss, 1996). In a sense, they are "action researchers" and "cultural workers" for their students and families.

Like all action researchers and cultural workers, teachers need to be aware of their cultural biases and positioning when they seek to understand diverse points of view from parents and families. In order to gain an impartial perspective on students' backgrounds, they need to take the stance that "their own personal appropriation of truth is merely one of many possibilities, not the *only* one" (Howard, 1999, p. 106). That is, teachers need to approach minority culture differences through a multiple-literacies stance that seeks to investigate, celebrate, and validate students and their families' multiple literacies and cultural resources in order to inform students' learning (Auerbach, 1995; G. Li, 2002; Moll & Greenberg, 1990). As McLaren (1995) suggests, this stance will enable teachers to recognize the importance of encouraging spaces for the multiplicity of voices in our classrooms and of creating a dialogical pedagogy with minority parents.

However, it is not enough for educators to simply understand the cultural differences of schooling and parenting of minority children to ensure equitable education. Rather, an understanding of the politics of difference—the underlying power relationships between the teachers and schools, and the families and communities—is crucial for successful minority education. This kind of understanding requires teachers, who are in a more powerful position, to do a special kind of listening to the parents' and community's voices—to see from the parents' point of view (Delpit, 1995). Unless the parents' voices are heard and legitimized in the classroom, true dialogue between the mainstream teachers and the Chinese parents will not likely begin.

The need to legitimize the parents' voices in this context, however, means that the mainstream teachers have to reassess their dominant status and even their own beliefs and histories. Many researchers who look at white teachers in a multicultural society suggest that the first step for the teachers is to be critical from within, that is, to critically examine their own ideological stance so as to unravel the "dynamics of dominance" in their own personal and professional lives, and raise their awareness of the politics of cultural differences (Howard, 1999; Spindler & Spindler, 1994). This "inner work of multicultural teaching" is essential for establishing a healthy parent-school relationship as we cannot fully and fruitfully engage in meaningful dialogue across the differences of race and culture without doing the work of personal transformation (Howard, 1999, p. 3).

This inner working will help teachers to foster new beliefs and attitudes toward culturally different families. To hear and legitimize parent voices requires that teachers "accept parents as the first and most important teachers of their children, and most important, *use the strengths and resources parents already have, especially their culture and language*" (Nieto, 1991, p. 264, italics original). In addition, teachers need to be aware that all families have strengths, and parents have important information and crucial perspectives about their children. More importantly, cultural differences should be viewed as assets rather than deficits (Banks, 2004; Nieto, 2002). The Chinese families' preference for a traditional approach to literacy instruction and their practices at home, for example, should be viewed as assets to phonics and vocabulary instruction at school, rather than the causes of the students' learning difficulties. The old view that parents who speak another language or come from another culture are unable to provide appropriate environments for their children can lead to condescending practices that reject the parents' skills and resources: "Practices such as top town classes on parenting, reading, nutrition, and hygiene taught by 'experts' are often the result of this kind of thinking. When parents are perceived to have skills, strengths, and resources that can aid their children, the results are different. There is nothing wrong with information to help parents with the upbringing and education of their children if and when it is given with mutual respect, dialogue, and exchange. Otherwise, it can become another heavy-handed and patronizing strategy that does little to inspire confidence and trust" (Nieto, 1991, p. 264).

Teacher education or professional development programs need to provide forums and opportunities such as courses in multicultural education to help teachers engage in this critical examination of their own attitudes and beliefs (Sleeter, 1992). These courses can become a venue for teachers to step outside their classrooms to not only discuss their own perspectives but also to understand how schools as institutions work in shaping their practices and student achievement. As Cairney and Ruge (1998) argue, "The existing power relations in education at any level will not be 'interrupted' until teachers are able to step out of their classrooms to allow themselves to see the social relations (who can say what to whom, etc.) that perpetuate inequality of access and authority (i.e., who has opportunities to learn and whose knowledge is validated)" (p. 8).

Teacher education and professional development also need to help teachers face the challenge of a changing educational environment by providing continued support in planning instruction and curriculum while facilitating their understanding of the politics of difference. Educational experiences such as university ESL courses and other forms of professional development can provide teachers with more opportunities to "explore beliefs, pose questions, and gain new knowledge, skills, and attitudes with regard to ESL students" (Clair, 1995, p. 190). These experiences can also help inform teachers that children's first language has a positive influence on the success of second-language learning, and that the development of that first language not only leads to faster acquisition of English, but also builds students' self-confidence and positive attitudes toward school (Cummins, 1996; Cummins & Swain, 1986; E. E. Garcia, 1990). This understanding will help mainstream teachers to broaden their repertoire of teaching strategies to better serve English language learners who are culturally and linguistically different from native-English-speaking children (Carrasquillo & Rodríguez, 2002; Fránquiz & Reyes, 1998). For example, teachers can select level-appropriate and culturally relevant reading materials to build on students' experiences and employ strategies to help these learners effectively transfer their first language skills to their second language. Thus, professional development together with knowledge of students' individual and cultural backgrounds can provide teachers with skills and strategies to adjust classroom instruction and accommodate students' divergent needs and interests.

In addition to teachers' personal and professional transformation, being culturally responsive should also be a schoolwide effort. Relying on changes in a few teachers is far from enough to be truly responsive to minority cultural differences. Corson (1992a) proposes that change must also occur at the structural level of the school. For example, school leadership could implement language policies designed to create a schoolwide culture that is more responsive to the needs of minority children. At Taylor Elementary, for example, school leaders could hold interactive forums or seminars to discuss the unofficial English-only policy, and work with teachers and students to implement language policies that "respond effectively to the acquired cultural interests of the minority community" (Corson, 1992a, p. 488). Perhaps a policy that calls for a "mutual sociolinguistic accommodation" would be more suitable. Mutual accommodation would produce greater school achievement because both teachers and students need to modify their behaviors in the direction of a common goal: academic success with cultural integrity (Nieto, 1991). Nieto (1991) explains that in practice, mutual adaptation means that "schools use the language and culture of students in teaching and that students use the language and culture of the school in learning. This practice can mean using the native language in instruction, designing instruction so that it takes into account the various preferred communication styles of students and accepting and using the experiences that students have in their home and communities as the basis for their learning" (p. 268).

Although Canadian bilingual education usually refers to French and English education, with such a high ethnic concentration, schools could move to bilingual education in Chinese and English. A two-way bilingual education that validates both English and Chinese as languages of instruction and aims to develop bilingual proficiency and academic achievement might be very beneficial to foster students' bicultural and biliteracy development (Nieto, 2002; Minami & Ovando, 2004). Such programs had been proven to be significant in facilitating Asian students' literacy learning as well as the development of positive crosscultural attitudes and behaviors among students (Thomas & Collier, 1997; Pang, Kiang, & Pak, 2004). In this type of bilingual program, Chinese students and English monolingual students are placed together in a bilingual classroom to learn each other's language and work academically in both languages. To implement such programs might be quite difficult and take time, given the current educational realities in Canada. The school, however, could take its first step by offering Chinese language courses. These language courses could not only affirm students' cultural identity but also bring culturally different instructional practices to the teachers.

Another structural change to respond to students' cultural differences is to recruit and welcome a diversity of teachers and staff, especially teachers who share the cultural backgrounds of the students. Nieto (1991) suggests that when faculty members are diverse, multilingual, and multicultural, all students see themselves reflected. Faculty diversity not only can change students' and parents' perceptions of and attitudes toward the school, but also help the school deal with cultural misunderstandings and conflicts. More importantly, minority staff can model relations of equal status using discourse norms appropriate to minority children (Corson, 1992a). At Taylor Elementary, the absence of teachers and staff from their own cultural backgrounds prevented the students from seeing the school as their own. Instead, they saw it as the Canadians' school. When talking about their dissatisfactions with the school, the parents in the study all said that if there were bicultural teachers from their own backgrounds, communication with the school would be much easier for them, as the bicultural teachers would understand what they wanted.

Last, a significant structural change could be made by eliminating combined classes. According to the teachers, the decision to combine classes was based on Vygotsky's (1978) notion of socioconstructivist learning. This choice, however, had caused a rift between school and home as it was antithetical to the parents' beliefs. Since teachers can provide scaffolding and support for learning in single-grade classrooms, responding to parents' requests might be beneficial for establishing a trusting relationship with the parents.

In sum, to achieve cultural reciprocity and be responsive to the cultural beliefs that they do not share, it is necessary for teachers to undertake personal transformation in looking at their own beliefs and practices and understanding the parents' beliefs. It is also necessary for the school to reorganize its policies and practices to ensure an empowering environment for the Chinese students. Both teachers and mainstream schools need to move beyond a contributions approach to cultural diversity (one that focuses on heroes and holidays) and adopt a transformative multicultural-education approach (one that involves changing the structure of the curriculum). Such a stance will not only help the teachers connect across the cultural borders, but also help mainstream schools to advance the interests and needs of minority groups (Banks, 2002; Giroux, 1992).

Revisiting the Great Debate: Implications for Change in Classroom Practices

The learners' disparate home and school literacy practices suggest that although research has generated knowledge about the negative effects of cultural discontinuity on minority children, this knowledge has not reached some teachers, such as Mrs. Haines and Ms. Dawson. Cultural mismatch is still a risk factor that remains largely unaddressed in instruction. This study suggests that to establish a pedagogy of cultural reciprocity, it is necessary to reiterate the significance of understanding and building on minority students' cultural background and home literacy experiences in literacy instruction.

If we accept that minority cultural differences are strengths and resources that parents already have, then in what ways can teachers use these strengths and resources in the classroom? In other words, in what ways can teachers meet the challenge of being responsive to cultural differences, and create more practical solutions and instructional approaches to accommodate the educational needs of culturally diverse students and their families? In this case, in what ways can the progressive teachers accommodate the Chinese families' preference for traditional approaches to instruction?

As reviewed in chapter 1, effective literacy instruction is characterized by the balanced teaching of skills, literature, and writing; scaffolding and matching of task demands to student competence; encouragement of student self-regulation; and strong crosscurricular connections. Simply stated, both phonics and meaning-based instruction need to be used to maximize students' (especially minority students') learning. The two teachers in this study had already implemented many innovative, meaning-based methods of instruction that have been proved to be important to language minority students' literacy development. For example, they integrated materials across subject areas; they used a rich variety of materials including manipulatives, different trade books, and authentic literature; and they facilitated students' learning through different activities such as field trips, hands-on experiences, writers' workshops, and literature circles; and followed students' individual developmental pace. These innovative practices provided students not only with opportunities to explore literacy but also with much-needed exposure to the rich resources of children's literature. Building on these effective practices, teachers can continue to experiment with alternative approaches that accommodate the needs of minority students. They need to respect the fact that students come from different pedagogical traditions, and take into consideration in their instruction these culturally specific pedagogical practices. Such consideration may entail some substantial reshaping of the form and content of curriculum and instruction, for example, from a Eurocentric or monolithic curriculum to a multicultural education.

Gay (2000) suggests that teachers can respond to cultural diversity in many different ways, as culturally responsive teaching is comprehensive and multidimensional. Building on what they are already successful in, teachers can accommodate minority students' needs by incorporating "culturally mediated cognition, culturally appropriate social situations for learning, and culturally valued knowledge in curriculum content" (Hollins, 1996, p. 13). These aspects can be incorporated into a wide range of classroom practices such as instructional techniques, assessment, classroom climate, learning contexts, and school-home relationships (Gay, 2000). In responding to the Chinese parents, for example, the teachers need to take into consideration the parents' values, which include systematic phonics and vocabulary instruction, direct teaching of strategies and skills, high academic expectations, and a large amount of homework.

In both Mrs. Haines's and Ms. Dawson's classes, although there were elements of phonics and vocabulary instruction, those were not taught systematically, nor in conjunction with other reading activities. Research on effective reading instruction for English language learners has shown that vocabulary must be taught in context and students' comprehension of new vocabulary must be constantly checked. In addition, students must also be provided with opportunities for meaningful use of new vocabulary (Gersten & Jiménez, 1994). Mrs. Haines's phonics instruction was used mainly for the sake of placating the parents, and in Ms. Dawson's class, the worksheets were not well devised or properly used to strengthen knowledge or skills taught. The difficulties of the learners in reading and vocabulary seemed to indicate a need for systematic phonics instruction that is planned, deliberate in application, embedded in meaningful contexts, and proceeds in an orderly manner (British Columbia Ministry of Education, 2000). Learners, especially ESL learners, need to develop not only phonemic awareness of spoken words and knowledge of spelling, but also independent ability to recognize syntactic structures that permit interpretive decoding (Adams, 1990).

Students need to learn not only the performative level functional literacy skills, but also higher-level literacy skills that involve using print to make sense of the world (Minami & Ovando, 2004). In addition to teaching phonemic and phonological skills, teachers also need to incorporate explicit teaching of strategies and skills to help students develop higher-order dimensions of reading. Snow et al. (1991) suggest that primary literacy instruction must include "goal-specified, teacher-led lessons in which basal readers and workbooks are utilized, work attack strategies are explicitly taught, both literal and inference comprehension questions are posed, and ample opportunities for practice are provided. Approaches like these focus children's attention closely on the text and may help children formulate generalizations about the reading process" (p. 166).

Since many of the children struggled with writing, more attention needs to be directed to explicit instruction of writing skills and strategies. In process writing, writing techniques are often introduced through short lessons at the beginning of each writing workshop, and skills and techniques that need improvement are often followed up in subsequent workshops and conferences (Atwell, 1987). In Mrs. Haines's class, although the students had ample opportunities to write about their readings or events, very little instruction in writing skills and strategies (prewriting, composing, editing, and revision) were offered. Often children followed the models provided on the blackboard and copied the words and sentences. As a result, most of the children's writings were only one or two sentences in length. Similarly, in Ms. Dawson's class, many of the students' writings were short, and effective writing skills and strategies were not explicit taught. These writing skills and strategies, however, are crucial to children's writing development. The instruction of these skills and strategies should begin in the primary grades and students should be provided with opportunities to practice writing longer passages through independent and collaborative engagement (Hillock, 1986; Snow et al., 1991). Graves (1985) points out that young writers experience several developmental stages in the process of becoming a writer, including mastering spelling, motor-aesthetic problems (hand writing and appearance of the page), writing conventions, topic information, and revision. Teachers need to know the general sequence of childhood development and need to teach children necessary skills through scaffolded instruction to help them successfully overcome these writing blocks.

In addition to adding explicit reading and writing instruction, teachers can also develop a culturally responsive curriculum through a variety of other measures. For example, they can incorporate a variety of teaching strategies, such as providing direct and indirect instruction, structured and unstructured learning situations, and contextualized vocabulary learning so that teaching methods accommodate the Chinese students' different learning styles. Teachers can also select multicultural reading materials that are appropriate to the learners' levels of proficiency so that the students can appreciate the readings and can draw on their own experiences. Level-appropriate and culturally relevant reading materials will also increase students' motivation to read and interest in writing about the readings. For learners who struggle with second-language literacy, it is beneficial to encourage them to make sense of second-language learning by using their first language. Teachers can explore strategies to help these learners to effectively transfer their skills in their first language to their second language. In writing, for example, teachers can allow students to use Chinese vocabulary if they get stuck with words or phrases they can't express in English.

Another significant implication related to classroom practices is the need for teachers to raise academic expectations and standards, especially in core subject areas such as math. Lowering expectations or setting standards that are not challenging can be detrimental to academic achievement (Banks, 2002; Nieto, 1991). Although the expectations and standards in the two classrooms were not low by Canadian standards, the parents perceived that there was a discrepancy between Canada and their home countries and saw that as problematic. The parents' concerns were not without basis, as a recent international report by National Center for Education Statistics (2003) also indicated that math education in Canada and the United States, was behind many Asian countries and regions such as Singapore, Hong Kong, Taipei, and Japan. Because the parents perceived that math education was not rigorous enough, they decided to seek outside help, which resulted in heavy burdens on students. If the school raises its expectations and standards, and builds teaching on what students can already do in math, it will greatly help students achieve maximum learning success. Raising expectations and standards, however, does not mean homogenizing instruction, but creating new and different learning opportunities for students (Banks, 2004; Nieto, 1991). Teachers will still need to use a variety of approaches, innovative methods, and a multitude of materials to achieve these standards.

Related to increasing expectations and standards, there is also a need for teachers to make changes in homework assignments. The teachers' and the parents' misconceptions about what is considered as homework as well as the amount of homework assigned seemed to cause great conflict between school and home. The teachers considered parent-child shared reading as homework, while the parents considered the children's individual practice on their school work as homework. Teachers may first need to establish better communication with the parents about homework. For example, they can use specific assignment books or homework journals paired with family understandings of the procedures (Christenson & Sheridan, 2001). Second, they may need to assign a variety of homework. They can assign shared reading or other homework that involve parents' participation as well as homework related to the phonics instruction or math instruction in the classroom. In addition, teachers may also need to consider a slight increase in the amount of homework. These varied kinds and amounts of homework may accommodate the value and attention that the parents and the students place on the homework assigned and may not seek other sources for homework. If time and resources allow, teachers can even set up a parent-teacher homework hotline or an after-school homework center to provide support to both parents and students (Christenson & Sheridan, 2001).

Last, the teachers' classroom practices need to address the problem of students' lack of access to rich, meaningful language input from more capable peers. Since young children learn through various literacy encounters in their everyday lives, particularly when there is active engagement with someone more skilled than themselves (Hallet, 1999; Vygostky, 1978), it is important for teachers to make deliberate efforts to maximize such encounters and engagement. They need to find ways (for example, effective grouping and the buddy system that was used in the lower grades at Taylor Elementary) to bring about interactions between mainstream and minority students, and between more capable peers and less fluent or proficient learners (Valdés, 2001). At the school level, as I mentioned in the previous section, a two-way interlocking bilingual program might be able to create a school environment that would be linguistically rich in both English and Chinese.

In sum, building on their own pedagogical practices, teachers can accommodate minority students' instructional needs in a variety of ways, such as including more systematic phonics instruction, explicit instruction in literacy skills, and homework. The recommendations, however, do not suggest abandoning or dismantling the teachers' student-centered, progressive instruction to follow the parents' traditional approach. Rather, I suggest that teachers and schools give thoughtful consideration to the implementation of a progressive pedagogy in light of the social, cultural, and linguistic needs of English language learners who come from very different belief systems (Kutoba, 1998; Reyes, 1992; A. I. Willis, 1995). As Henrichsen (1989) asserts, in crosscultural contexts, educational innovation can be effective only when it is conversant with the traditional pedagogical values of the minority community. In order for a progressive pedagogy to be effective, teachers need to create an equity pedagogy that respects the parents' traditional educational practices (Banks, 2002, 2004). Teachers need to modify their progressive instructional approaches to include more direct instructional intervention, such as discernible structure to literacy lessons, concrete examples of instruction in context, adequate mediation and feedback, clear teacher monitoring of students, and teacher modeling (Franquiz & Reyes, 1998; Jiménez & Gersten, 1999). As Gersten and Jiménez (1994) suggest, with some refinement and restructuring the teachers can strengthen their pedagogical practices and increase the Chinese students' chance of success with progressive literacy instruction.

Revisiting Parental Involvement: Implications for Change in Parent-School Relationships

All parents in this study demonstrated active involvement at home, including parenting and child rearing, communicating with the school about their concerns and needs, and supporting, supervising, and investing in their children's academic learning. However, very few of the parents were involved in school settings—few of them volunteered in school, went to meetings, or participated in school activities.

The teachers and the parents had culturally different understandings of parental involvement at home and in school. The parents considered parental involvement at home to consist of monitoring or supervising homework and investing in their children's learning, for example through tutoring classes. They might also provide direct teaching if they could; however, they expected that their children would complete their homework independently and seek help only if they encountered difficulties. In terms of school involvement, the parents seemed to experience barriers reflecting differences in language, values, goals, methods of education, and definitions of appropriate roles (Moles, 1993). The teachers, on the other hand, viewed parental involvement as a shared activity, a task that should be completed through parent-child interactions at home. The teachers expected the parents' academic involvement at school and considered the parenting roles the parents' brought to school to be inappropriate.

Although the parents viewed themselves as incapable of assuming teacher roles in the classroom and considered that inappropriate, their creative resistance to school practices seemed to suggest that they were interested in being involved in a variety of educational issues, such as choosing instructional methods, setting the configuration of classes, assigning the amount of homework, attending ESL classes, and assessing students' performance. The parents' attempt to get involved in these issues demonstrated their desire to take ownership of decision making in school settings (Chavkin, 1989; Fine, 1993).

These different patterns of behavior suggest that the school needs to expand the meaning of parental involvement to consider cultural differences and power relationships between school and home. Without acknowledging the cultural values and practices of minority parents as legitimate, we may run into the danger of imposing mainstream parenting which will result in the denial of the families' cultural identity and strengths, and force conformity to mainstream values and expectations (G. Li, 2002). In order to avoid patronizing the parents, more dialogue about different cultural ways of parental involvement between school and home need to be undertaken.

Although the teachers had tried to involve the parents in the classroom, their efforts had focused on improving parenting skills (for example, Mrs. Haines's effort to have the parents learn how to read to their children) rather than improving home-school communication (Sleeter, 1992). For teachers, one effective way would be to approach the parents with a mind open to new learning (Springate & Stegelin, 1998). Teachers could use individuals from the culture (such as Mrs. Yep) as guides to learn from parents about their literacy practices. Approaching the parents with a desire to learn, rather than with the intention to change them, would significantly empower the parents and make them more willing to participate in dialogues with the school. Moreover, teachers could involve the parents by incorporating some of the parents' opinions in the classroom to show their sincerity and respect for the parents' concerns. For example, the teachers could include some explicit writing and grammar instruction in their literature or experience-based approach, and could further involve the parents in choosing books to use for such purposes. Teachers could also empower parents by organizing writing instruction that includes assignments that not only produce literacy-related interactions in the home, but also involve parents and other community members in the writing process, for example, a writing module on bilingualism that involves interviewing parents and community members (Moll, 1999). These kinds of gestures help the parents come to trust the school's intention of accommodating their cultural beliefs and sharing decision making on curriculum and instruction. In addition, such opportunities to interact with people who affect learners (especially families and community members) around school-based learning goals can have a positive influence on classroom environments (Bransford, Brown, & Cocking, 1999).

Teachers could also reach out to the community, rather than always asking the parents to come to school. Teachers could do home visits to get to know the parents' concerns on a personal level. Though this may be time consuming and hard for the teachers to achieve, it is the most powerful and effective way for teachers to get to know the students' home literacy practices and to build trust with parents (McCarthey, 1997). Teachers could also visit the private tutoring institutions that the children attended in order to gain firsthand experiences of what the parents want for their children. Learning about the practices that the parents value would significantly facilitate the teachers' understanding of the parents' concerns and beliefs and their repertoire of strategies for accommodating the parents' needs. If necessary, teachers (and the school) then could use community resources or parents as consultants to explore ways of making these accommodations. By constantly involving parents to address school concerns, the teachers and the parents will become true partners and collaborators in finding culturally relevant and educationally beneficial ways to achieve a common goal, that is, to provide quality education for the children.

In addition to the teachers' efforts to involve parents, the school can also take an active role in promoting parental involvement. In fact, without the requisite support and institutional sanction at the administrative level, it is hard for teachers to achieve success in involving parents (Christenson & Sheridan, 2001; Winters, 1993). School leadership can help to establish appropriate guidelines and strategies for involving parents through schoolwide programs. In Taylor Elementary, for example, the school could use the Parent Advisory Council (PAC) not just for fundraising, but also for involving parents in different aspects of school activities, such as helping with reforming the curriculum and participating in school decision making on structure. The school could also use the PAC to promote parents' and teachers' mutual understanding of each other's practices and designing long-term plans for communication between school and home.

The discontinuity between home and school suggests that developing a genuine school-home partnership is critical in addressing minority children's developmental needs. Both the teachers and the parents invested a fair amount of time and effort to ensure the children's academic progress, but their efforts were not coordinated.

Rather, their actions were sometimes contradictory because of their assumptions about each other's practices, for example, the issue of homework. This divide was counterproductive to the children's development. A connection needs to be built between parents and teachers and the school so that they can work together to ensure the success of English language learners.

The call for parent-school cooperation is not new. Many researchers and practitioners have developed ideas and programs that enable teachers to collaborate successfully with parents (e.g., Epstein & Dauber, 1991). Again, application of this knowledge was not evident in the education of the Chinese children. In fact, there was little dialogue between the parents and the teachers about the children's learning difficulties and their different understandings of their problems. There is an urgent need to start this dialogue so that further cooperation can be possible. Teachers and schools who are in a powerful position can initiate the dialogue by inviting parents to share their perspectives.

This study suggests that conventional ways of communicating with parents who are from different cultural backgrounds and who do not speak English, such as parent-teacher conferences and report cards in English, may not work. Teachers who do not speak the parents' first language may need to make use of bilingual resources in the school district or the parent community to ensure two-way communication with the parents. They can use a variety of nonconventional channels such as informal home-response journals in the parents' home language or formal home-school programs (see Edwards, Pleasants, & Franklin, 1999; Lazar & Weisberg, 1996). By communicating in different ways with parents in their native language about their beliefs and concerns, teachers can establish a reciprocal cultural exchange, and work with parents as collaborators to best facilitate children's educational needs.

Schools also need to establish specific channels of communication to address the major concerns and questions of parents, families, and teachers, such as curriculum and students' academic progress. For example, Christenson and Sheridan (2001) suggest that to promote understanding of school practices, teachers can provide grade- or course-level curriculum guides to parents, or hold an interactive forum with parents to discuss standards, assessment, and the testing process, as well as how parents can support the standards. Teachers can also provide parents with monthly progress and growth reports with sign-off sheets.

In sum, teachers can create a variety of methods to ensure two-way communication with parents and to involve parents in joint planning of instruction in the classroom. These methods and initiatives will help teachers and parents learn from each other and build strong, genuine parent-school partnerships.

Implications for Change in Understanding English Language Learners

Previous research has indicated that for minority children from different cultural backgrounds (such as Hispanics, African Americans, and Native Americans and Canadians), discontinuities (both cultural and political) between school and home are a risk factor in their literacy development. The present study contributes to this body of knowledge by providing insight into the literacy discontinuities of Chinese Canadian learners who are often stereotyped as high achievers, and overlooked in literacy research. In order to establish a pedagogy of cultural reciprocity, it is important to break away from these stereotypes and examine the literacy development of learners from a new perspective that is based on the learners' complex, multilayered realities.

The "model-minority" myth connotes being high achieving and being assimilated into the mainstream. The eight focal children in the study, each with their distinct learning difficulties and identities, did not fit the model-minority stereotype that often ignores differences between and within groups (Kim & Yeh, 2002; G. Li, 2003). Like many other Asian children who are underachieving in school, they were under the "stereotype threat" that shaped their identity formation and expected performance (Steele, 1999). As Chun (1995) points out, the model-minority stereotype often exerts pressure on students to assimilate within an inflexible mold of the mainstream and to achieve success through exemplary conduct and behavioral conformity. As discussed in chapter 6, the children displayed two dichotomous identity tendencies: ethnic flight (strong identification with the mainstream culture and shame of ethnic culture) and ethnic affiliation (adversarial resistance to the mainstream culture). The children were under tremendous pressure to assimilate and make identification choices from early on. The children who had chosen a nonaccommodation, nonconformity stance, for example Andy, Billy, and Jake, had suffered from "the hidden, yet injurious" costs of learning the language and culture of power that was essential to their making it in the mainstream society (Chun, 1995). The children who had chosen ethnic flight, for example Sandy, Anthony, and Tina, were already struggling with psychological and emotional issues that often accompany a sense of lost identity (Kim & Yeh, 2002). Like many other Asian children, the Chinese children experienced anxiety about meeting performance that was expected of Asian students. The pressure to excel, regardless of their individual development, had resulted in high stress and adversarial effects on their learning.

Besides the psychological cost, there is also an academic cost of model minority stereotypes, which often results in serious neglect in schools of the needs of Asian students. Research has revealed that public schools have failed not only to address the psychological and emotional concerns of Asian children, but also to provide them with services and support (Chun, 1995; Kim & Yeh, 2002). The stereotypes, which disguise within-group variability, often hide the instructional needs of particular groups or individuals and mislead policy makers (Barrozo, 1987; G. Li, 2003). The focal students' instructional needs in acquiring English literacy (for example, a need for explicit instruction of skills and strategies) and their collective needs to become biliterate in English and Chinese were not addressed by the teachers, the school, or the policy makers.

These psychological and academic costs suggest that it is necessary to look at the children independently of the model-minority molds. As the children's stories demonstrate, although all the focal learners shared some similarities, they varied in many respects, such as in literacy performance, in-class behavior, their dispositions toward reading and writing, and their family circumstances. This variability suggests that they were "multidimensional" learners (Ivey, 1999, p. 190). This multidimensionality requires educators and researchers to explore the different experiences that are specific to each individual learner in order to have an informed understanding of each learner and the learner's particular developmental needs.

Furthermore, the multivocal perspectives on learners' literacy development suggest that learners are complex social beings who struggle not only with rudimentary reading and writing skills, but also with issues such as how they are perceived and consequently how different members of society intervene in their lives. For these children, school success or failure in literacy is dependent upon a complex combination of home and school issues that may vary from child to child, as literacy is deeply embedded in the social practices and relationships of schools and homes (Cairney & Ruge, 1998). Therefore, an understanding of these learners requires us to move beyond a surface-level analysis of their literacy abilities (for example, comparing the underachieving children with the successful "model minorities"). Instead, we need to associate their literacy performances with deeper levels of reasoning that explore complex sociocultural values illustrated by different social members in the children's literacy contexts. That is, we need to understand how the children learn not only from a sociocultural perspective, but also from an acculturative perspective that examines their interactions with others and the larger context, such as the school and the mainstream society (Kim & Chun, 1994). This understanding will help parents, teachers, and researchers overcome the tendency to blame certain families or individuals for the children's school failure, and come to an educated, comprehensive understanding of these learners.

Implications for the Chinese Immigrant Parents

This study shows that the Chinese parents were a powerful influence on the children's academic learning. Although they differed in their individual experiences and educational backgrounds, they were all active supporters of their children's education. Their middle-class status afforded them not only a good learning environment (for example, higher SES schools), but also resources to invest in their children's learning, such as after-school classes. Their middle-class status, however, did not exempt them from social isolation from mainstream society and from a lack of communications with the school. In addition to the cultural distance from the school and the mainstream, another important factor is the parents' English language ability (G. Li, 2002). Several parents, for example, were not able to attend parent-teacher conferences or failed to understand school practices due to their inability to speak English. Therefore, it is necessary for immigrants to learn the language of power and to be able to communicate through their own words rather than other people's words (Delpit, 1995; Purcell-Gates, 1996). The more they learn, the better they can help with their children's learning, participate in school activities, and invest in their integration into the host society (G. Li, 2002).

   In addition to learning the language of power, Chinese parents also need to learn to adapt their strategies of involvement to ensure their children's success. First, the parents need to adjust their creative actions against school practices. As discussed in chapter 6, the parents' actions at home may have in fact widened the distance between school and home and consequently limited the children's access to the official knowledge of school. Therefore, it is important for parents to understand that their creative resistance to school practices may have an adverse impact on their children's learning. They need to gain a critical awareness of how the school system works and learn to help their children negotiate more access to the official knowledge of the system. Second, the parents need to reconsider their noninvolvement in the school setting. From a critical point of view, the parents' absence in the school setting has a dual penalty: "a missed opportunity to influence the school in positive and important ways and experience in the gratification that accompanies contribution, and a missed exposure to knowledge and the chance to learn new skills" (Winters, 1993, p. 30). Third, since most of them did not have schooling experiences in Canada nor much contact with mainstream society, their understanding of Canadian schooling might be limited. Though it is important for them to use schooling practices in their home country as a frame of reference to make sense of their children's school experiences, they need to critically examine their own beliefs and pedagogical practices. For example, they need to understand that focusing solely on the children's rudimentary skills without holistic development may be counterproductive to their high academic expectations.

Like the teachers, the parents also need to approach the school with a learning attitude to better understand how the Canadian school system works, for example, the culture of the school including curriculum and resources (Delgado-Gaitan, 1990). It is important for them to understand that though differences exist between the teachers' and their own beliefs, it is necessary to work with classroom teachers to understand the differences and find joint solutions to bridge these differences for the benefit of the children's learning. As I have argued elsewhere (G. Li, 2003), immigrant parents need to make an effort to establish a partnership with schools so that their children's educational needs can be better communicated to the schools in order for the schools to act effectively as cultural brokers for their children. To do this, immigrant families need to become involved in their children's education not only in the home milieu, but also in school settings. In addition to support at home (for example, spending time with their children while working on homework, supervising their TV viewing, and exposing them to different literacy activities such as going to the library and museums), parents can increase their presence and participation in school. They can serve as volunteers, participate in school activities, and meet more frequently with the teachers. This kind of active involvement will help fight against the political nature of school practices that have a profound impact on their children's educational experiences.

In addition to this kind of parental involvement, the parents can also become involved in decision making on issues concerning their first-language maintenance and second-language learning. They can join the school to push for a bilingual Chinese-English program. In such a program, their first language will become "a recognized political voice" through which they can gain more access to the schooling process (Corson, 1992b, p. 65). This access will allow the Chinese parents to take more charge of the schooling process and to ensure that their values and beliefs are included in the process. They will become experts, advisers, and decision makers in their children's education, like the white middle-class parents, the Brownstoners, in Sieber's (1981) study.

In sum, the Chinese immigrant parents can be active agents of change in reshaping their children's educational experiences. Through gaining knowledge about the mainstream school, self-empowerment, and active involvement in school and home, they can, together with the teachers, build a pedagogy of cultural reciprocity for their children.

Final Thoughts

In this book, I have presented mainstream teachers' and Chinese parents' perspectives on literacy and education as well as the literacy experiences of the focal children in school and at home. Furthermore, I have discussed different factors that contributed to the cultural and pedagogical battles between school and home. The stories of the teachers, the parents, and the students suggest that teaching, learning, and living in a new socioeconomic context is indeed a highly contested process in which the roles of school and home are constantly renegotiated and redefined. Literacy and schooling are indeed contested public spheres characterized by ongoing struggles for control and contradictions among the competing cultural orientations (Gay, 1995).

The ongoing struggles between school and home suggest that teaching and learning in such contexts is a complex, multifaceted process in which different agencies, practices, values, viewpoints, understandings, and ideologies came into play. As Valdés (2001) points out, it is "not a straightforward and unproblematic practice, but a contested site in which there is a struggle about the role and the future of immigrants in our society" (p. 159). This process provides us with "a plural consciousness in that it requires understanding multiple, often opposing ideas and knowledges, and negotiating these knowledges, not just taking a simple counterstance" (Mohanty, 1991, p. 36). Through understanding this process, we engage in more informed and critical reflections on the broader issues of literacy education as it occurs today in and out of our classrooms. As we enter the brave new world of social and cultural diversity, such critical reflections will help us to challenge the official discourses of power and cultivate pedagogies of reciprocity in which different cultural values and pedagogical traditions are adopted and incorporated for an equitable education for students of diverse backgrounds.

Achieving a plural consciousness and cultivating a pedagogy of cultural reciprocity, however, requires us to abandon the binary oppositions that prevail in the dominant educational canon. McLaren (1995) argues that binaries create a dependent power hierarchy that legitimates certain cultural realities and marginalizes others. The complexity and multidimensionality of the lived realities of the teachers, the parents, and the students in this study challenge our notions of these binary oppositions as majority versus minority, progressive versus traditional, and dominance versus resistance. I conclude with a brief discussion of these binary oppositions.

First, the traditional white majority/immigrant minority binary opposition has been problematic to our understanding of the education of immigrant children. Immigrant minorities, such as the Chinese in this study and Hispanics in the United States are the majority who are outside of the sphere of political dominance, and are not part of the dominant class (Macedo, 1994). The "majority" is the "minority" (such as the white teachers) in a power position. Instead of altering the terms' semantic values to define the power hierarchy, we may need to break the binary to view whiteness as an ethnicity, not as a defining cultural frame (Howard, 1999; McLaren, 1995). Viewing the majority (the Chinese) and the minority (whites) from such a plural consciousness, we envision a new "cultural imaginary" (McLaren, 1995, p. 59) in which genuine learning of each other's cultural values and traditions is possible, hence opening up the promise for dialogue and for creating a pedagogy of cultural reciprocity.

Another binary opposition problematic to this dialogue is the debate between progressive and traditional pedagogies. Like many others, the teachers and parents in this study saw the two pedagogies as mutually exclusive. This polarized view seemed to block the possibility of searching for some common ground between the two paradigms. With the increasing diversity in our classrooms and communities, the dominance of one paradigm is no longer possible or desirable. Research on exemplary instruction for English language learners (e.g., Jiménez & Gersten, 1999), minority groups (Ladson-Billings, 1994), and mainstream classrooms (Pressley et al., 2001) suggests that rather than seeing the two different pedagogies as polarized and mutually exclusive, they may be complementary and can coexist in the classroom to address the divergent instructional needs of students from different sociocultural backgrounds and pedagogical traditions. Viewing the two paradigms from outside the framework of binary opposition therefore allows us to explore new spaces for reciprocity between the two pedagogies.

Finally, I propose a new perspective on the dominance/resistance dichotomy that was central to the parents' and the teachers' ongoing struggles. Rather than seeing dominance/resistance as bad and negative, I see it as signifying a crisis within the dominant system (McLaren, 1998). Conflicts and resistance, though sometimes counterproductive as demonstrated in this study, can be seen as a catalyst for change. As Marx asserts, without conflict, there is no progress. The parents' resistance, as well as the teachers', therefore can be seen as a beginning step for establishing a pedagogy of cultural reciprocity.

In closing I want to reiterate that establishing a pedagogy of cultural reciprocity involves change and the willingness to change on the part of both teachers and parents. Without the initiatives of the teachers and the participation and cooperation of immigrant parents, educational transformation and change will be fruitless. I hope the lived struggles of the teachers, the parents, and the students in this study have planted the seeds for opening up dialogues to engage both teachers and parents in working for change.

References

Adams, M. J. (1990). *Beginning to read: Thinking and learning about print.* Cambridge, MA: MIT Press.

Adamson, B., & Lai, W. A. (1997). Language and the curriculum in Hong Kong: Dilemmas of triglossia. *Comparative Education, 33*(2), 233–246.

Alvermann, D. E., Dillion, D. R., & O'Brien, D. (1996). On writing qualitative research. *Reading Research Quarterly, 31,* 114–120.

Anderson, J. (1995a). How parents perceive literacy acquisition: A cross-cultural study. In E. G. Sturtevant & W. Linek (Eds.), *Generations of literacy* (pp. 262–277). Commerce, TX: College Reading Association.

Anderson, J. (1995b). Listening to parents' voices: Cross-cultural perceptions of learning to read and write. *Reading Horizons, 35,* 394–413.

Anderson, J., & Gunderson, L. (1997). Literacy from a multicultural perspective. *The Reading Teacher, 50*(6), 514–516.

Anderson, K. J. (1991). *Vancouver's Chinatown: Racial discourse in Canada, 1875–1980.* Montreal: McGill-Queen's University Press.

Anyon, J. (1981). Social class and school knowledge. *Curriculum Inquiry, 11*(1), 3–42.

Ashworth, M. (1979). *Immigrant children and Canadian schools.* Toronto, ON: McClelland & Stewart.

Ashworth, M. (2001). ESL in British Columbia. In B. Mohan, C. Leung, & C. Davison (Eds.), *English as a second language in the mainstream: Teaching, learning, and identity* (pp. 93–106). New York: Longman.

Atwell, N. (1987). *In the middle: Reading, writing, and learning with adolescents*. Portsmouth, NH: Heinemann.

Au, K. H. (1993). *Literacy instruction in multicultural settings*. Fort Worth, TX: Harcourt Brace.

Au, K. H. (1998). Socio constructivism and the school literacy learning of students of diverse backgrounds. *Journal of Literacy Research, 30*(2), 297–319.

Au, K. H., & Jordan, C. (1981). Teaching reading to Hawaiian children: Finding a culturally appropriate solution. In H. Trueba, G. Gutherine, & K. Au (Eds.), *Culture and the bilingual classroom: Studies in classroom ethnography* (pp. 139–152). Rowley, MA: Newbury House.

Auerbach, E. R. (1993). Reexamining English only in the ESL classroom. *TESOL Quarterly, 27*(1), 9–32.

Auerbach, E. R. (1995). The politics of the ESL classroom: Issues of power in pedagogical choices. In J. W. Tollefson (Ed.), *Power and inequality in language education* (pp. 9–33). Cambridge, UK: Cambridge University Press.

August, D., & Hakuta, K. (1997). *Improving schooling for language minority children: A research agenda*. Washington, DC: National Academy Press.

Bakhtin, M. M. (1981). *The dialogic imagination: Four essays by M. M. Bakhtin*. Austin, TX: University of Texas Press.

Banks, J. (1993). The canon debate, knowledge construction, and multicultural education. *Educational Researcher, 22*(5), 4–24.

Banks, J. (2002). *An introduction to multicultural education*. Boston, MA: Allyn & Bacon.

Banks, J. (2004). Multicultural education: Historical development, dimensions, and practice. In J. Banks & C. A. M. Banks (Eds.), *Handbook of research on multicultural education* (2nd ed., pp. 3–29). New York: Jossey-Bass.

Barrozo, A. C. (1987). *The status of instructional provisions for Asian ethnic minorities: Lessons from the California experience*. Paper presented at the annual meeting of the American educational Research Association, Washington, DC.

Berenstain, S., & Berenstain, J. (9187). *The day of the dinosaur*. New York: Random House.

Beck, I. L., Perfetti, C. A., & McKeown, M. G. (1982). Effects of long-term vocabulary instruction on lexical access and reading comprehension. *Journal of Educational Psychology, 74*, 506–521.

Becker, H. S., Geer, B., Hughes, E. C., & Strauss, A. L. (1961). *Boys in white: Student culture in medical school.* Chicago: University of Chicago Press.

Bourdieu, P. (1977). Cultural reproduction and social reproduction. In J. Karabel & A. H. Halsey (Eds.), *Power and ideology in education* (pp. 487–511). New York: Oxford.

Bransford, J. D., Brown, A. L., & Cocking, R. R. (1999). *How people learn.* Washington, DC: National Academy Press.

Braunger, J., & Lewis, J. (1997). *Building a knowledge base in reading.* Newark, DE: International Reading Association.

British Columbia Foundation Skills Assessment. (2001). *District results report: Grade 4.* Victoria, BC: BC Ministry of Education.

British Columbia Ministry of Education. (2000). *The primary program: A framework for teaching.* Victoria, BC: Author.

British Columbia Ministry of Education. (2001). *British Columbia Foundations Skills Assessment Results Report.* Victoria, BC: Author.

British Columbia Ministry of Educaton Special Programs Branch. (2001). *English as a second language standards.* Victoria, BC: Author.

British Columbia Stats. (2001). *2001 census data.* Retrieved Feb. 24, 2004, from http://www.bcstats.gov.bc.ca/

Bunting, E. (1994). *Smoky night.* Chicago: Harcourt.

Cairney, T. H., & Ruge, J. (1998). Community literacy practices and schooling: Towards effective support for students. Retrieved May 30, 2003, from http://www.gu.edu.au/school/cls/clearinghouse/content_1998_community.

Carger, C. (1996). *Of borders and dreams: A Mexican-American experience of urban education.* New York: Teachers College Press.

Carless, D. R. (1998). A case study of curriculum implementation in Hong Kong. *System, 26,* 353–368.

Carrasquillo, A. L., & Rodríguez, V. (2002). *Language minority students in mainstream classrooms* (2nd ed.). Toronto: Multilingual Matters.

Carron, G., & Châu, T. G. (1996). *The quality of primary schools in different developmental contexts.* Paris: UNESCO.

Chall, J. S. (1967). *Learning to read: The great debate.* New York: McGraw Hill.

Chall, J. S. (1983). *Learning to read: The great debate* (2nd ed.). New York: McGraw Hill.

Chall, J. S. (1996). *Learning to read: The great debate* (3rd ed.). New York: McGraw Hill.

Chall, J. S. (2000). *The academic achievement challenge*. New York: Guilford Press.

Chall, J. S., Jacobs, V. A., & Baldwin, L. E. (1990). *The reading crisis: Why poor children fall behind*. Cambridge, MA: Harvard University Press.

Chao, R. K. (1996). Chinese and European American mothers' beliefs about the role of parenting in children's school success. *Journal of Cross-Cultural Psychology 27*(4), 403–423.

Chavkin, N. F. (1989). Debunking the myth about minority parents. *Educational Horizons, 67*(4), 119–123.

Chen, C., & Stevenson, H. W. (1989). Homework: A cross-cultural examination. *Child Development, 60*, 551–561.

Chinese Around the World. (1996). *Canadian community faces racial conflict*. Retrieved April 25, 2001, from http://huaren.org/diaspora/n_america/canada/doc/0196–01.html.

Chow, B. (2004). *Primary education. GlobalBeat Hong Kong*. Retrieved January 26, 2004, from http://jmsc:hku.hk/newmedia/primary.htm

Chow, L. (2000). *Chasing their dreams: Chinese settlement in the northwest region of British Columbia*. Prince George, BC: Caitlin Press.

Christenson, S. L., & Sheridan, S. M. (2001). *Schools and families: Creating essential connections for learning*. New York: Guilford Press.

Christian, D. (1994). *Two-way bilingual education: Students learning through two languages*. Santa Cruz, CA: National Center for Research on Cultural Diversity and Second Language Learning.

Chun, K. (1995). The myth of Asian American success and its educational ramifications. In D. T. Nakanishi & T. Y. Nishida (Eds.), *The Asian American educational experience: A source book for teachers and students* (pp. 95–112). New York: Routledge.

Citizenship and Immigration Canada. (2002). *Demographics*. Retrieved March 1, 2003, from http://www.cic.gc.ca/

Clair, N. (1995). Mainstream classroom teachers and ESL students. *TESOL Quarterly, 29*, 189–196.

Coleman, P. (1998). *The pressure for choice: An analysis of a series of "traditional school" proposals made to school boards in B. C.* Vancouver, BC: Society for Advancement of Excellence in Education.

Compton-Lilly, C. (2003). *Reading families: The literate lives of urban children*. New York: Columbia University.

Cope, B., & Kalantzis, M. (2000). Multiliteracies: The beginning of an idea. Introduction to B. Cope & M. Kalantzis (Eds.), *Multiliteracies: Literacy learning and the design of social features* (pp. 3–8). London: Routledge.

Corson, D. J. (1992a). Minority cultural values and discourse norms in majority culture classrooms. *The Canadian Modern Language Review, 48,* 472–496.

Corson, D. J. (1992b). Bilingual education policy and social justice. *Journal of Educational Policy, 7*(1), 45–69.

Cousins, L. (1989). *Jack and Jill.* New York: Penguin Books.

Cummins, J. (1984). *Bilingualism and special education: Issues in assessment and pedagogy.* Clevedon, England: Multilingual Matters.

Cummins, J. (1986). Empowering minority students: A framework for intervention. *Harvard Educational Review, 56,* 18–36.

Cummins, J. (1989). *Empowering minority students.* Sacramento, CA: California Association for Bilingual Education.

Cummins, J. (1996). *Negotiating identities: Education for empowerment in a diverse society.* Ontario, CA: California Association for Bilingual Education.

Cummins, J., & Sayers, D. (1995). *Brave new world: Challenging cultural illiteracy through global learning networks.* New York: St. Martin's Press.

Cummins, J., & Swain, M. (1986). *Bilingualism in education: Aspects of theory, research, and practice.* New York: Longman.

Dahl, R., & Blake, Q. (1991). *George's marvelous medicine.* New York: Puffin Books.

Dahl, R., & Blake, Q. (1995). *The magic finger.* New York: Viking.

Dai, B., & Lu, J. (1985). Reading reform in Chinese primary schools. *Prospects, 15*(1), 103–110.

Davidman, L., & Davidman, P. T. (1997). *Teaching with a multicultural perspective: A practical guide.* New York: Longman.

Day, R., & Bamford, J. (1998). *Extensive reading in the second language classroom.* Cambridge, U.K.: Cambridge University Press.

Delgado-Gaitan, C. (1990). *Literacy for empowerment.* New York: The Falmer Press.

Delpit, L. D. (1988). The silenced dialogue: Power and pedagogy in educating other people's children. *Harvard Educational Review, 58*(3), 280–298.

Delpit, L. D. (1991). A conversation with Lisa Delpit. *Language Arts, 68,* 541–547.

Delpit, L. (1995). *Other people's children: Cultural conflict in the classroom.* New York: New Press.

DePalma, A. (1997, February 14). *For many from Hong Kong, Vancouver is a way to station.* Retrieved May 11, 2002, from http://www.huaren.org/diaspora/n_America/Canada/news/021497 –01.html

Derman-Sparks, L. (1989). *Anti-bias curriculum: Tools for empowering young children.* Washington, DC: National Association for the Education of Young Children.

Edwards, P. A., Pleasants, H. M., & Franklin, S. H. (1999). *A path to follow: Learning to listen to parents.* Westport, CT: Heinemen.

Epstein, J. L. (1989). On parents and schools: A conversation with Joyce Epstein. *Educational Leadership, 47*(2), 24–28.

Epstein, J. L. (1992). School and family partnerships. In. M. Alkin (Ed.), *Encyclopedia of Educational Research* (6th ed., pp. 1139–1151). New York: McMillan.

Epstein, J. L. (1995). School/family/community partnerships: Caring for the children we share. *Phi Delta Kappan, 76,* 701–712.

Epstein, J. L. (2001). *School, family, and community partnerships: Preparing educators and improving schools.* Boulder, CO: Westview Press.

Epstein, J. L., & Dauber, S. L. (1991). School programs and teacher practices of parent involvement in inner-city elementary and middle schools. *The Elementary School Journal, 91*(3), 289–305.

Erickson, F. (1993). Transformation and school success: The politics and culture of educational achievement. In E. Jacob and C. Jordan (Eds.), *Minority education: Anthropological perspectives* (pp. 27–52). Norwood, NJ: Ablex.

Fillmore, L. W., & Meyer, L. M. (1992). The curriculum and linguistic minorities. In P. W. Jackson (Ed.), *Handbook of research on curriculum: A project of the American Educational Research Association* (pp. 626–658). New York: Macmillan.

Fine, M. (1993). [Ap]parent involvement: Reflections on parents, power, and urban public schools. *Teachers College Record, 94*(4), 682–710.

Fine, M., & Weis, L. (1998). *The unknown city: Lives of poor and working-class young adults.* Boston: Beacon Press.

Finn, P. J. (1999). *Literacy with an attitude: Educating working-class children in their own interests.* Albany: State University of New York Press.

Fowler, J., & Hooper, H. R. (1998). *ESL learners with special needs in British Columbia: Identification, assessment and programming.* Victoria, B.C.: British Columbia Ministry for Education, Skills, and Training.

Fránquiz, M. E., & Reyes, M. D. L. L. (1998). Creating inclusive learning communities through English language arts: From Chanclas to Canicas. *Language Arts, 75*(3), 211–220.

Freeman, Y. S., & Freeman, D. E. (1992). *Whole language for second language learners.* Portsmouth, NH: Heinemann.

Freire, P. (1970). *Pedagogy of the oppressed.* New York: Seabury Press.

Gage, N. L., & Berliner, D. C. (1992). *Educational psychology* (5th ed.). Boston: Houghton Mifflin.

Gannett, R. S. (1987). *Elmer and the dragon.* New York: Random House.

Garcia, E. E. (1990). Educating teachers for language minority students. In W. R. Houston, M. Haberman, & J. Sikula (eds.), *Handbook of research on teacher education* (pp. 717–729). New York: Macmillan.

Garcia, G. E., Pearson, P. D., & Jimenez, R. T. (1994). *The at-risk situation: A synthesis of reading research.* Champaign: IL: Centre for the Study of Reading.

Gardiner, J. R., & Sewall, M. (1980). *Stone fox.* New York: Crowell.

Gay, G. (1995). Mirror images on common issues: Parallels between multicultural education and critical pedagogy. In C. E. Sleeter & P. L. McLaren (Eds.), *Mulitculutral education, critical pedagogy and the politics of difference* (pp. 155–189). Albany: State University of New York Press.

Gay, G. (2000). *Culturally responsive teaching: Theory, research, and practice.* New York: Teachers College Press.

Gee, J. P. (1989). Literacy, discourse, and linguistics: Introduction. *Journal of Education, 171*(1), 5–17.

Gee, J. P. (1996). *Social linguistics and literacies: Ideology in discourses.* London: Taylor & Francis.

Geertz, C. (1973). *Thick description: Toward an interpretive theory of culture.* In C. Geerts (Ed.), *The interpretation of cultures* (pp. 3–30). New York: Basic.

Gersten, R. M., & Jiménez, R. T. (1994). A delicate balance: Enhancing literacy instruction for students of English as a second language. *The Reading Teacher, 47*(6), 438–449.

Gersten, R. M., & Woodward, J. (1992). *Defining expert instruction for the language minority student in the intermediate grades.* Eugene, OR: Eugene Research Institute.

Gibbon, A. (1999, June 7). *Vancouver's Chinese community: Ethnic Chinese and 'ethnic Canadians' culturally distinct, demographically similar.* Statistics Canada, 1996 Census: Some *Globe and Mail* calculations, 1–7. Retrieved May 11, 2002, from http://www.huaren.org/diaspora/n_America/Canada/doc/060799-01.html

Gibson, M. A. (1988). *Accommodation without assimilation.* Ithaca, NY: Cornell University Press.

Gilmore, P. (1991). "Gimme room": School resistance, attitudes, and access to literacy. In C. Mitchel & K. Weiler (Eds.), *Rewriting literacy: Culture, and the discourse of the other* (pp. 57–76). New York: Bergin & Garvey.

Giroux, H. (1983). *Theory and resistance in education: A pedagogy for the opposition.* South Hadley, MA: Bergin & Garvey.

Giroux, H. (1988). *Teachers as intellectuals: Toward a critical pedagogy of learning.* Asheville, NC: Greenwood.

Giroux, H. (1991). Series introduction: Literacy, difference, and the politics of border crossing. In C. Mitchell & K. Weiler (Eds.), *Rewriting literacy: Culture and the discourse of the other* (pp. ix–xvi). Toronto: OSIE Press.

Giroux, H. (1992). *Border crossing: Cultural works and the politics of education.* New York: Routledge.

Giroux, H., & Simon, R. (1989). Popular culture and critical pedagogy: Everyday life as a basis for curriculum knowledge. In H. Giroux & P. McLaren (Eds.), *Critical pedagogy, the state and cultural struggle* (pp. 236–252). Albany: State University of New York Press.

Goetz, J. P., & LeCompte, M. D. (1984). *Ethnography and qualitative design in educational research.* New York: Academic Press.

Goldstein, T. (2003). *Teaching and learning in a multicultural school: Choices, risks, and Dilemmas.* Mahwah, NJ: Lawrence Erlbaum.

Goodman, K. S. (1967). Reading: A Psycholinguistic guessing game. *Journal of the Reading Specialist, 6,* 126–135.

Goodman, Y. M. (1977). Acquiring literacy is natural: Who skilled cock robin? *Theory Into Practice, 16*(5), 309–314.

Goodman, Y. M. (1986). Children coming to know literacy. In W. H. Teale & E. Sulzby (Eds.), *Emergent literacy: Reading and writing* (pp. 1–14). Norwood, NJ: Ablex.

Graves, D. (1985). Blocking and the young writer. In M. Rose (Ed.), *When a writer can't write* (pp. 1–18). New York: Guilford Press.

Gunderson, L. (2000). Voices of the teenage diasporas. *Journal of adolescent and adult literacy, 43*(8), 692–706.

Gunderson, L. (2001). Different cultural views of whole language. In S. Boran & B. Comber (Eds.), *Critiquing whole language and classroom inquiry* (pp. 242–271). Urbana, IL: National Council of Teachers of English.

Gunderson, L., & Anderson, J. (2003). Multicultural views of literacy learning and teaching. In A. I. Willis, G. E. Garcia, R. Barrera, & V. J. Harris (Eds.), *Multicultural issues in literacy research and practice* (pp. 123–144). Mahwah, NJ: Lawrence Erlbaum.

Guthrie, J., McGouch, K., Bennett, L., & Rice, M. (1996). Concept-oriented reading instruction: An integrated curriculum to develop motivations and strategies. In L. Baker, P. Afflerbach, & D. Reinking (Eds.), *Developing engaged readers in school and home communities* (pp. 165–190). Hillsdale, NJ: Erlbaum.

Gutierrez, K., Rymes, B., & Larson, J. (1995). James Brown versus. Brown v. The Board of Education: Script, Counterscript, and Underlife in the classroom. *Harvard Educational Review, 65*(3), 445–471.

Hallet, E. (1999). Signs and symbols: Environmental print. In J. Marsh & E. Hallet (Eds.), *Desirable literacies: Approaches to language and literacy in the early years* (pp. 52–67). London, UK: Paul Chapman.

Harry, B. (1992). *Cultural diversity, families, and the special education system: Communication and empowerment.* New York: Teachers College Press.

Hawkins, J. N., & Stites, R. (1991). Strengthening the future's foundation: Elementary education reform in the People's Republic of China. *The Elementary School Journal, 92*(1), 41–60.

Heath, S. B. (1983). *Ways with words: Language, life, and work in communities and classrooms.* New York: Cambridge University Press.

Henrichsen, L. E. (1989). *Diffusion of innovations in English language teaching: The ELEC effort in Japan, 1956–1968.* New York: Greenwood Press.

Herandez, J. S. (1993). Bilingual metacognitive development. *The Educational Forum, 54*(4), 350–358.

Hillock, G. (1986). *Research on written composition.* Urbana, IL: National Council of Teachers of English.

Hoffman, M., & Binch, C. (1991). *Amazing grace.* New York: Dial Books for Young Readers.

Hollins, E. R. (1996). *Culture in school learning: Revealing the deep meaning*. Mahwah, NJ: Erlbaum.

Hoover-Dempsey, K. V., Bassler, O. C., & Brissie, J. S. (1987). Parent involvement: Contributions of teacher efficacy, school socioeconomic status, and other school characteristics. *American Educational Research Journal, 24*, 417–435.

Howard, G. (1999). *We can't teach what we don't know: White teachers, multiracial schools*. New York: Teachers College Press.

Hudson-Ross, S., & Dong, Y. R. (1990). Literacy learning as a reflection of language and culture: Chinese elementary school education. *The Reading Teacher, 44*(2), 110–123.

Hull, G., & Schultz, K. (Eds.). (2002). *School's out!: Bridging out-of-school literacies with classroom practice*. New York: Teachers College Press.

Huss-Keeler, R. L. (1997). Teacher perception of ethnic and linguistic minority parental involvement and its relationships to children's language and literacy learning: A case study. *Teaching and Teacher Education, 13*(2), 171–182.

Irvine, J. C., & York, D. E. (1995). Learning styles and culturally diverse students: A literature review. In J. Banks & C. A. M. Banks (Eds.), *Handbook of research on multicultural education* (pp. 484–759). New York: MacMillan.

Ivey, G. (1999). A multicase study in the middle school: Complexities among young adolescent readers. *Reading Research Quarterly, 34*(2), 172–192.

Jacob, E., & Jordan, C. (1993). Understanding minority educational anthropology: Concepts and methods. In E. Jacob & C. Jordan (Eds.), *Minority education: Anthropological perspectives* (pp. 15–26). Norwood, NJ: Ablex.

Jiménez, R. T., & Gersten, R. (1999). Lessons and dilemmas derived from the literacy instruction of two Latina/o teachers. *American Educational Research Journal, 36*(2), 265–301.

Juel, C. (1988). Learning to read and write: A longitudinal study of 54 children from first through fourth grades. *Journal of Educational Psychology, 80*(4), 437–447.

Juel, C., Griffith, P. L., & Gough, P. B. (1986). Acquisition of literacy: A longitudinal study of children in first and second grades. *Journal of Educational Psychology, 78*, 243–255.

Ketchum, P. J. (1997). *Grade 5 spelling skills and drills*. Pittsburg, PA: Hayes Publiching Co.

Kim, A., & Yeh, C. J. (2002). *Stereotypes of Asian American students.* New York: Eric Clearing House on Urban Education.

Kim, U., & Chun, M. B. J. (1994). Educational "success" of Asian Americans: An indigenous perspective. *Journal of Applied Developmental Psychology, 15*, 329–343.

King, J. (1994). The purpose of schooling for African American children: Including cultural knowledge. In E. Hollings, J. King, & W. Hyman (Eds.), *Teaching diverse populations: Formulating a knowledge base* (pp. 25–60). Albany: State University of New York Press.

Klotz, H. (1999, October 27). *Chinese: English Canada's second language.* With files from Jennifer Pritchett, *Ottawa Citizen,* 1–3. Retrieved May 11, 2002, from http://www.huaren.org/diaspora /n_America/Canada/news/021497–01.html

Knowles, V. (1997). *Strangers at our gates: Canadian citizenship and immigration policy, 1540–1997.* Toronto: Dundurn Press

Kurelek, W. (1998). *A prairie boy's summer.* Plattsburg, NY: Tundra Books.

Kutoba, R. (1998). Voices from the margin: Second and foreign language teaching approaches from minority perspectives. *Canadian Modern Language Review, 54*(3), 394–412.

Ladson-Billings, G. (1990). Reading between the lines and beyond the pages: A culturally relevant approach to literacy teaching. *Theory Into Practice, xxxi*(4), 312–320.

Ladson-Billings, G. (1994). *The dream keepers: Successful teachers of African American children.* San Francisco: Jossey-Bass.

Langer, J. A. (Ed.). (1987). *Language and literacy and culture: Issues of society and schooling.* Norwood, NJ: Ablex.

Lareau, A. (1989). *Home advantage: Social class and parental intervention in elementary education.* New York: Flamer Press.

Lareau, A. (2000). *Home advantage: Social class and parental intervention in elementary education* (2nd ed.). New York: Rowman & Littlefield.

Lave, J., & Wenger, E. (1991). *Situated learning: Legitimate peripheral participation.* Cambridge: Cambridge University Press.

Lazar, A. M., & Weisberg, R. (1996). Inviting parents' perspectives: Building home-school partnerships to support children who struggle with literacy. *The Reading Teacher, 50*(3), 228–237.

Lee, S. (1996). *Unraveling the "model minority" stereotype: Listening to Asian American youth.* New York: Teachers College Press.

Li, G. (1995). College English education should transfer from static teaching to dynamic teaching. *Journal of College English Teaching and Testing, 13*(3), 9–14.

Li, G. (1998, February). Building cultural continuity between home and school: A socio-cultural perspective on language and literacy and its implications for tomorrow's teachers. *Proceedings of WESTCAST'98 conference, Western Canadian Association for Student Teaching.* Victoria, BC: University of Victoria.

Li, G. (2000). Literacy and identity: An ethnographic study of a Filipino family. *McGill Journal of Education, 35*(1), 1–27.

Li, G. (2001). Literacy as situated practice: The world of a pre-schooler. *Canadian Journal of Education, 26*(1), 57–76.

Li, G. (2002). *"East is east, west is west"? Home literacy, culture, and schooling.* New York: Peter Lang.

Li, G. (2003). Literacy, culture, and politics of schooling: Counternarratives of a Chinese Canadian family. *Anthropology & Education Quarterly, 34*(2), 184–206.

Li, P. S. (1997). *Making of post-war Canada.* Cambridge, MA: Oxford University Press.

Li, P. S. (1998). *The Chinese in Canada.* Ontario: Oxford University Press.

Lightfoot, S. L. (1978). *Worlds apart.* New York: Basic Books.

Lopez, M. E. (1999). *When discourses collide: An ethnography of migrant children at home and in school.* New York: Peter Lang.

Louie, V. (2001). Parents' aspirations and investment: The role of social class in the educational experiences of 1.5- and second-generation Chinese Americans. *Harvard Educational Review, 71*(3), 438–474.

Lucas, T., Henze, R., & Donato, R. (1990). Promoting the success of Latino language-minority students: An exploratory study of six high schools. *Harvard Educational Review, 60*(3), 315–340.

Macedo, D. (1994). *Literacies of power: What Americans are not allowed to know.* Boulder, CO: Westview Press.

Makhoul, A. (2000). *Richmond school district builds on a strong foundation.* Ottawa: Caledon Institute of School Policy.

McCarthey, S. J. (1997). Connecting home and school literacy practices in classrooms with diverse populations. *Journal of Literacy Research 29*(2), 145–182.

McCarthey, S. J. (1999). Identifying teacher practices that connect home and school. *Education and Urban Society, 32*(1), 83–107.

McCarthy, C. (1993). *Race, identity, and representation in education.* New York: Routledge.

McCarthy, C. (1995). The problem with origins: Race and the contrapuntal nature of the educational experience. In C. E. Sleeter & P. McLaren (Eds.), *Multicultural education, critical pedagogy, and the politics of difference* (pp. 245–245). Albany: State University of New York Press.

McDermott, R., & Varenne, H. (1995). Culture as disability. *Anthropology & Education Quarterly, 26*(3), 324–348.

McKay, S., & Wong, S. (1996). Multiple discourses, multiple identities: Investment and agency in second-language learning among Chinese adolescent immigrant students. *Harvard Educational Review, 66*(3), 577–608.

McLaren, P. (1995). White terror and oppositional agency: Towards a critical multiculturalism. In C. E. Sleeter & P. McLaren (Eds.), *Mulitculutral education, critical pedagogy and the politics of difference* (pp. 33–70). Albany: State University of New York Press.

McLaren, P. (1998). *Life in schools: An introduction to critical pedagogy in the foundations of education.* New York: Longman.

Mead, G. H. (1938). *Philosophy of the act.* Chicago: University of Chicago Press.

Mikulecky, L. (1990). Literacy for what purpose? In R. L. Venezky, D. A. Wagner, & B. S. Ciliberti (Eds.), *Toward defining literacy* (pp. 24–34). Newark, DE: International Reading Association.

Miller, C. (2000, December 20). Disappointed parents show frustration at raucous meeting: Board gives traditional school failing grade. *The Vancouver Courier,* Dec. 20, p. 13.

Minami, M. (2000). Crossing borders: The politics of schooling Asian students. In C. J. Ovando & P. McLaren, (Eds.), *The politics of multiculturalism and bilingual education: Students and teachers caught in the cross fire* (pp. 188–207). Boston: McGraw Hill.

Minami, M., & Ovando, C. J. (2004). Language issues in multicultural contexts. In J. A. Banks & C. A. M. Banks (Eds.), *Handbook of research on multicultural education* (2nd ed., pp. 567–588). New York: Jossey-Bass.

Minichiello, D. (2001). Chinese voices in a Canadian secondary school landscape. *Canadian Journal of Education, 26*(1), 77–96.

Mohanty, C. T. (1991). Cartographies of struggle: Third world women and politics of feminism. Introduction to C. T. Mohanty, A.

Russo, & L. Torres, (Eds.), *Third world women and the politics of feminism* (pp. 1–47). Bloomington, IN: Indiana University Press.

Mok, I. A. C., & Morris, P. (2001). The metamorphosis of the "virtuoso": Pedagogical patterns in Hong Kong primary mathematics classrooms. *Teaching and Teacher Education, 17*(2001), 455–468.

Moles, O. C. (1993). Collaboration between schools and disadvantaged parents: Obstacles and openings. In N. F. Chavkin (Ed.), *Families and schools in a pluralistic society* (pp. 2–20). Albany: State University of New York Press.

Moll, L. C. (1994). Literacy research in community and classroom: A sociocultural approach. In R. B. Ruddell, M. R. Ruddell, & H. Singer (Eds.), *Theoretical models and processes of reading* (pp. 179–207). Newark, DE: International Reading Association.

Moll, L. C. (1999). Writing as communication: Creating strategic learning environments for students. In E. R. Hollins & E. I. Oliver (Eds.), *Pathways to success in school: Culturally responsive teaching* (pp. 73–84). Mahwah, NJ: Lawrence Erlbaum.

Moll, L. C., & Diaz, S. (1993). Change as the goal of educational research. In E. Jacob & C. Jordan (Eds.), *Minority education: Anthropological perspectives* (pp. 67–82). Norwood, NJ: Ablex.

Moll, L. C., & Greenberg, J. (1990). Creating zones of possibilities: Combining social contexts for instruction. In L. C. Moll (Ed.), *Vygotsky and education: Instructional implications and applications of sociohistorial psychology* (pp. 319–348). Cambridge: Cambridge University Press.

Morris, P. (1997). School knowledge, the state, and the market: An analysis of the Hong Kong secondary curriculum. *Journal of Curriculum Studies, 29*(3), 329–349.

Morris, P., & Lo, M. L. (2000). Shaping the curriculum: Contexts and cultures. *School Leadership & Management, 20*(2), 175–188.

National Center for Education Statistics. (2003). *Trends in international mathematics and science study.* Retrieved January 26, 2005, from http://nces.ed.gov/timss/timss03tables.asp?Quest=1&Figure=1

Nespor, J. (1991). The construction of school knowledge: A case study. In C. Mitchell & K. Weiler (Eds.), *Rewriting literacy: Culture and the discourse of the other* (pp. 169–196). Toronto, ON: OSIE Press.

Nieto, S. (1991). *Affirming diversity: The sociopolitical context of multicultural education.* New York: Longman.

Nieto, S. (2002). *Language, culture, and teaching: Critical perspectives for a new century.* Mahwah, NJ: Lawrence Erlbaum.

Ogbu, J. U. (1978). *Minority education and caste: The American system in cross-cultural perspective.* New York: Academic Press.

Ogbu, J. U. (1982). Cultural discontinuities and schooling. *Anthropology & Education Quarterly, 13*(4), 290–307.

Olsen, L. (1997). *An invisible crisis: The educational needs of Asian Pacific American youth.* New York: Asian American/Pacific Islanders in Philanthropy.

Pai, Y. (1990). *Cultural foundations of education.* New York: Merill.

Paine, L. W. (1990). The teacher as virtuoso: A Chinese model for teaching. *Teachers College Record, 92*(1), 49–81.

Pang, V. O. (1990). Asian American children: A diverse population. *Educational Forum, 55,* 49–66.

Pang, V. O., Kiang, P. N., & Pak, Y. K. (2004). Asian Pacific American students: Challenging a biased educational system. In J. A. Banks & C. A. M. Banks (Eds.), *Handbook of research on multicultural education* (2nd ed., pp. 542–563). New York: Jossey-Bass.

Pang, V. O., & Sablan, V. A. (1998). Teacher efficacy: How do teachers feel about their abilities to teach African American students? In M. E. Dilworth (Ed.), *Being responsive to cultural differences* (pp. 39–54). Thousand Oaks, CA: Corwin Press.

Parry, K., & Su, X. (1998). *Culture, literacy, and learning English: Voices from the Chinese classroom.* Portsmouth, NH: Boynton/Cook.

Penfield, J. (1987). ESL: The regular classroom teacher's perspective. *TESOL Quarterly, 21*(1), 21–39.

Peng, S. S., & Wright, D. (1994). Explanation of academic achievement of Asian American students. *Journal of Educational Research 87*(6), 346–352.

Perfetti, C. A. (1984). Reading acquisition and beyond: Decoding includes cognition. *American Journal of Education, 92,* 40–60.

Phillipson, R. (1988). Linguicism: Structures and ideologies in linguistic imperialism. In T. Skutnabb-Kangas & J. Cummins (Eds.), *Minority education: From shame to struggle* (pp. 339–358). Clevedon, England: Multilingual Matters.

Pierce, B. N. (1995). Social identity, investment, and language learning. *TESOL Quarterly, 29*(1), 9–31.

Pierson, H. D. (1998). Societal accommodation to English and Putonghua in Cantonese-speaking Hong Kong. In M. C. Pennington (Ed.), *Language in Hong Kong at century's end* (pp. 91–112). Hong Kong: Hong Kong University Press.

Pintrich, P. R., & Schrauben, B. (1992). Students' motivational beliefs and their cognitive engagement in classroom academic tasks. In

D. H. Schunk & J. L. Meece (Eds.), *Student perceptions in the classroom* (pp. 149–183). Hillsdale, NJ: Erlbaum.

Portes, A., & Hao, L. (1998). E Pluribus Unum: Bilingualism and loss of language in the second generation. *Sociology of Education, 71*(4), 269–294.

Portes, A., & MacLeod, D. (1995). Educational progress of children of immigrants: The roles of class, ethnicity, and social context. *Sociology of Education, 69,* 255–275

Portes, A., & Rumbaut, R. C. (1990). *Immigrant America: A portrait.* Berkeley: University of California Press.

Portes, A., & Rumbaut, R. C. (1996). *Immigrant America: A portrait* (2nd ed.). Berkeley: University of California Press.

Portes, A., & Schauffler, R. (1996). Language and the second generation: Bilingualism yesterday and today. In A. Portes (Ed.), *The new second generation* (pp. 8–29). New Work: Russell Sage Foundation.

Pressley, M. (1998). *Reading instruction that works: The case for balanced teaching.* New York: Guilford Press.

Pressley, M., Whaton-McDonald, R., Allington, R., Block, C. C., Morrow, L., Tracey, D., Baker, K., Brooks, G., Cronin, J., Nelson, E., and Woo, D. (2001). A study of effective first-grade literacy instruction. *Scientific Studies of Reading, 5*(1), 35–58.

Purcell-Gates, V. (1996). *Other people's words: The cycle of low literacy.* Cambridge, MA: Harvard University Press.

Ran, A. (2001). Travelling on parallel tracks: Chinese parents and English teachers. *Educational Research, 43*(3), 311–328.

Read, C. (1971). Preschool children's knowledge of English phonology. *Harvard Educational Review, 41*(1), 1–34.

Reyes, M. de la Luz. (1991). A process approach to literacy using dialogue journals and literature logs with second language learners. *Research in the Teaching of English, 25*(3), 291–313.

Reyes, M. de la Luz. (1992). Challenging venerable assumptions: Literacy instruction for linguistically different students. *Harvard Educational Review, 62*(4), 427–446.

Rogers, T., Tyson, C., & Marshall, E. (2000). Living dialogues in one neighborhood: Moving towards understanding across discourses and practices of literacy and schooling. *Journal of Literacy Research, 32*(1), 1–24.

Ryan, B. A., & Adams, G. R. (1995). The family-school relationships model. In B. A. Ryan & G. R. Adams (Eds.), *The family-school connection: Theory, research, and practice* (pp. 3–28). Thousand Oaks, CA: Sage.

Schieffelin, B. B. (1986). Introduction. In B. B. Schieffelin & P. Gilmore (Eds.), *The acquisition of literacy: Ethnographic perspectives.* Norwood, NJ: Ablex.

Shade, B. J., Kelly, C., & Oberg, M. (1997). *Creating culturally responsive classrooms.* Washington, DC: American Psychological Association.

Shannon, P. (1989). *Broken promises.* Cambridge, MA: Bergin & Garvey.

Shannon, P. (1990). *The struggle to continue: Progressive reading instruction in the United States.* Portsmouth, NH: Heinemann.

Sieber, R. T. (1981). The politics of middle-class success in an inner-city public school. *Journal of Education, 164*(1), 30–47.

Simon, R. (1987). Empowerment as a pedagogy of possibility. *Language Arts, 64*(4), 370–382.

Siu, S. F. (1994). Taking no chances: A profile of a Chinese-American family's support for school success. *Equity and Choice 10*(2), 23–32.

Skutnabb-Kangas, T. (1983). *Bilingualism or not: The education of minorities.* Clevedon, England: Multilingual Matters.

Sleeter, C. E. (1992). *Keepers of the American dream: A study of staff development and multicultural education.* Washington, DC: Falmer Press.

Sleeter, C. E., & McLaren, P. (1995). Exploring connections to build a critical multiculturalism. Introduction to C. E. Sleeter & P. McLaren (Eds.), *Mulitculutral education, critical pedagogy and the politics of difference* (pp. 5–32). Albany: State University of New York Press.

Snow, C. E., Burns, S., & Griffin, P. (1998). *Preventing reading difficulties in young children.* Washington, DC: National Academy Press.

Snow, C. E., Barnes, W. S., Chandler, J., Goodman, I. F., & Hemphill, L. (1991). *Unfulfilled expectations: Home and school influences on literacy.* Cambridge, MA: Harvard University Press.

Spiegel, D. L. (1992). Blending whole language and systematic direct instruction. *The Reading Teacher, 46*(1), 38–44.

Spindler, G., & Spindler, L. (1982). *Doing the ethnography of schooling: Educational anthropology in action.* Berkeley: University of California Press.

Spindler, G., & Spindler, L. (1994). Introduction to G. Spindler & L. Spindler (Eds.), *Pathways to cultural awareness: Cultural therapy with teachers and students* (pp. xiv–xxi). Thousand Oaks, CA: Corwin Press.

Springate, K. W., & Stegelin, D. A. (1998). *Building school and community partnerships through parent involvement.* Columbus, Ohio: Merrill.

Stahl, S. A. (1992). Saying the "p" word: Nine guidelines for exemplary phonics instruction. *The Reading Teacher, 45*(8), 618–625.

Stanovich, K. E. (1986). Mathew effects in reading: Some consequences of individual differences in the acquisition of literacy. *Reading Research Quarterly, 21*, 360–406.

Stanovich, K. E. (1990). A call for end to the paradigm wars in reading research. *Journal of Reading Behavior, 22*, 221–231.

Statistics Canada. (2001). 2001 Census of Canada. Retrieved January 30, 2005, from http://www12.statcan.ca/english/census01/home/index.cfm

Steele, C. M. (1999). A threat in the air: How stereotypes shape intellectual identity and performance. In E. Y. Lowe (Ed.), *Promise and dilemma: Perspectives on racial diversity and higher education* (pp. 92–128). Princeton, NJ: Princeton University Press.

Steffenhagen, J. (2001, April 6). Basics reading program "amazing": The reading debate. *Vancouver Sun*, B1–B4.

Stevenson, H. W., & Stigler, J. W. (1992). *The learning gap: Why our schools are failing and what we can learn from Japanese and Chinese education.* Toronto, ON: Summit Books.

Street, B. (1993). The new literacy studies. Introduction to B. Street (Ed.), *Cross-cultural approaches to literacy* (pp. 1–22). New York: Cambridge University Press.

Street, B. (1995). *Social Literacies: Critical approaches to literacy in development, ethnography and education.* London: Longman.

Street, J. C., & Street, B. (1991). The schooling of literacy. In D. Barton & R. Ivanic (Eds.), *Writing in the community* (pp. 106–131). Newbury Park, CA: Sage.

Suárez-Orozco, C., & Suárez-Orozco, M. (2001). *Children of immigration.* Cambridge, MA: Harvard University Press.

Suzuki, B. (1995). Education and the socializations of Asian Americans: A revisionist analysis of the "model minority" thesis. In D. T. Nakanishi & T. Y. Nishida (Eds.), *The Asian American educational experience: A source book for teachers and students* (pp. 113–132). New York: Routledge.

Taylor, D. (1983). *Family literacy: Young children learning to read and write.* Portsmouth, NH: Heinemann.

Taylor, D., & Dorothy-Gaines, C. (1988). *Growing up literate: Learning from inner-city families.* Portsmouth: NH: Heinemann.

Teale, W., & Sulzby, E. (1986). *Emergent literacy: Reading and writing.* Norwood, NJ: Ablex.

Tharp, R. G., & Gallimore, R. (1988). *Rousing minds to life.* Cambridge, UK: Cambridge University Press.

Thomas, W. P., & Collier, V. P. (1997). *School effectiveness for language minority students.* Washington, DC: National Clearing House for Bilingual Education.

Toohey, K. (2000). *Learning English at school: Identity, social relations and classroom practice.* Clevedon, England: Multilingual Matters.

Townsend, J. S., & Fu, D. (1998). A Chinese boy's joyful initiation into American literacy. *Language Arts, 75*(3), 193–201.

Trueba, H. T., Jacobs, L., & Kirton, E. (1990). *Cultural conflict and adaptation: The case of Hmong children in American society.* New York: Falmer Press.

U. S. Census Bureau. (2001). *Population profile of the United States.* Retrieved May 11, 2002, from http://www.census.gov/population/www/pop-profile/profile.html

U.S. Department of Education. (2002). *No child left behind act of 2001: Executive summary.* Retrieved May 21, 2004, from http://www.ed.gov/admins/lead/account/nclbreference

Valdés, G. (1996). *Con Respeto: Bridging the distance between culturally diverse families and schools: An ethnographic portrait.* New York: Teachers College Press.

Valdés, G. (1998). The world outside and inside schools: Language and immigrant children. *Educational Researcher, 27*(6), 4–18.

Valdés, G. (2001). *Learning and not learning English: Latino students in American schools.* New York: Teachers College Press.

Valenzuela, A. (1999). *Subtractive schooling: U. S.-Mexican youth and the politics of caring.* Albany: State University of New York Press.

Voss, M. M. (1996). *Hidden literacies: Children learning at home and at school.* Portsmouth, NH: Heinemann.

Vygotsky, L. S. (1978). *Mind in society.* Cambridge, MA: Harvard University Press.

Walberg, H. J. (1987). Home environment and school learning: Some quantitative models and research syntheses. In E. J. Griffore & R. P. Boger, (Eds.), *Child reading in the home and school* (pp. 105–120). New York: Plenum.

Waller, W. (1932). *Sociology of teaching.* New York: Wiley.

Walsh, C. E. (1991a). *Literacy as praxis: Culture, language, and pedagogy.* Norwood, NJ: Ablex.

Walsh, C. E. (1991b). *Pedagogy and the struggle for voice: Issues of language, power, and schooling of Puerto Ricans.* New York: Bergin & Garvey.

Wang, X. (2003). *Education in China since 1976.* Jefferson, NC: McFarland.

Ward, W. P. (1978). *White Canada forever: Popular attitudes and public policy toward orientals in British Columbia.* Montreal: McGill-Queen's University Press.

Ward, W. P. (1990). *White Canada forever: Popular attitudes and public policy toward orientals in British Columbia* (2nd ed.) Montreal: McGill-Queen's University Press.

Weis, L. (1990). *Working class without work: High school students in a deindustrializing economy.* New York: Routledge.

Weiss, H. M., & Edwards, M. E. (1992). The family-school project: Systematic interventions for school improvement. In S. L. Christenson & J. C. Conoley, (Eds.), *Home-school collaboration: Enhancing children's academic and social competence* (pp. 215–243). Silver Spring, MD: National Association of School Psychologists.

Wells, G. (1986). *The meaning makers: Children learning language and using language to learn.* Portsmouth, NH: Heinemann.

Wells, G. (1989). Language in the classroom: Literacy and collaborative talk. *Language and Education, 3*(4), 251–273.

Wertsch, J. V. (1991). *Voices of the mind: A sociocultural approach to mediated action.* Cambridge, MA: Harvard Education Press.

Wigfield, A. (1997). Children's motivations for reading and reading engagement. In J. T. Gurthrie & A. Wigfield (Eds.), *Reading engagement* (pp. 14–33). Newark, DE: International Reading Association.

Willis, A. I. (1995). Reading the world of school literacy: Contextualizing the experience of a young African American male. *Harvard Educational Review, 65*(1), 30–49.

Willis, P. E. (1977). *Learning to labor: How working class kids get working class jobs.* Westmead, England: Saxon House.

Winters, W. G. (1993). *African American mothers and urban schools: The power of participation.* New York: Lexington Books.

Wong Fillmore, L. (1982). Language minority students and school participation: What kind of English is needed? *Journal of Education, 164*(2), 143–156.

Wong Fillmore, L. (1991a). Second language learning in children: A model of language learning in social context. In E. Bialystok (Ed.), *Language processing in bilingual children* (pp. 49–69). London, UK: Cambridge University Press.

Wong Fillmore, L. (1991b). When learning a second language means losing the first. *Early Childhood Research Quarterly, 6*, 323–346.

Xu, H. (1999). Young Chinese ESL children's home literacy experiences. *Reading Horizons, 40*(1), 47–64.

Yao, E. L. (1985). Adjustment needs of Asian immigrant children. *Elementary School Guidance and Counseling, 19*(3), 222–227.

Zhang, C., Ollila, L. O., & Harvey, C. B. (1998). Chinese parents' perceptions of their Children's literacy and schooling in Canada. *Canadian Journal of Education, 23*(2), 182–190.

Zhang, S. Y., & Carrasquillo, A. (1995). Chinese parents' influence on academic performance. *New York State Association for Bilingual Education Journal, 10*, 46–53.

Zhou, M., & Bankston III, C. L. (1996). Social capital and the adaptation of the second generation: The case of Vietnamese youth in New Orleans. In A. Portes (Ed.), *The new second generation* (pp. 197–220). New Work: Russell Sage Foundation.

Index

Jiménez, R. T., 25, 26, 222
Juel, C., 24

Kim, A., 226, 227
Klotz, H., 40
Knowledge: assumptions about, 184;
background, 27; beliefs on nature of,
184; construction process, 29, 30; cultural, 21, 199, 209, 211; culturally
valued knowledge in, 218; from ethnic
homes, 6; lexical, 24; linguistic, 201;
personal, 21; school recognition of, 6;
spelling-sound, 24; validation of, 21
Knowles, V., 42
Kutoba, R., 221

Ladson-Billings, G., 5, 211
Langer, J. A., 5, 18, 35
Language: as asset to be cultivated, 201;
conversational fluency in, 51; counterscript, 19; counterword, 19; cultural
variations in, 5; development, 189; differences, 8; effect of ethnic solidarity on
learning, 200; English-only method of
learning, 68–72, 201–203; first, 201–203;
hetereoglossic voices and, 38; home, 8,
29, 37; importance of retaining first language, 69, 141, 201–203; inequalities of,
193; learning, 19, 20, 35–37; learning
use of, 19; loss of, 5; orthographic code
of, 22; ownership of, 20; phonics, 22;
position in social world and, 19; proficiency, 51; reform, 46; school, 8; social,
19; of students, 215; turning against
first language, 128, 130, 147, 202, 203;
in university admissions, 2; use of
code-switching in, 107, 111, 139; use of
first language to facilitate learning of
English, 29, 201–203; whole, 22, 84
Lareau, A., 6, 7, 31, 190, 194, 199, 208
Lave, J., 20
Lazar, A. M., 225
Learning: attentiveness to actual experiences of students, 209; attitudes
toward, 29; avoidance of, 113; complexities of, 3; contexts embedded in, 35; in
cross-cultural context, 8; dependence
on continuity between school and
home, 35; embedded, 73; facilitation of,

83; field-dependent, 150; goals for, 20;
holistic approach to, 86; integrated
process of, 81; language, 20, 35–37;
learners' participation as negotiation of
meaning, 19; literacy, 1–16; meaning-
based, 73; motivation for, 20; nonparticipation in, 29; personal investment in,
20; resistance to, 111, 120, 148, 149, 196;
rote, 111; socioconstructivist, 216;
styles, 219; surface, 73; through repetition, 111
Lee, S., 8
Li, G., 5, 6, 8, 9, 32, 34, 67, 93, 103, 104,
186, 212, 223, 227, 228, 229
Li, P. S., 4, 36, 40, 41, 42, 192
Lightfoot, S. L., 31, 199
Ling family: background information,
59*tab*; concern with grammar instruction, 85; parents, 85; Xiao-min, 61
Literacy, 20; acquisition, 35–37; after-
school programs, 87–95; belief systems,
19; building on students' cultural backgrounds in, 217; changes in classroom
practice and, 216–222; continuum of
instructional approaches for, 26; cultural beliefs and, 8; cultural conflict
and, 63–100; cultural differences and,
185–196; cultural variations in practices
of, 5; culture and, 18; debates over best
method of instruction in, 22–27; defining, 17, 18; development of, 20; differing perspectives of home/school, 184;
differing sets of conventions of, 33; differing views of acquisition and meaning of, 32; as discursive practice, 17;
dominant-culture, 195; early grade
instruction, 25; education, 207; ethnic
solidarity effect on acquisition of, 36;
experiences, 196; higher-level skills of,
218; holistic approach to, 207; home
practices, 7; instruction, 17–38; instruction in language-experience approach,
72–77; learning, 1–16; legitimization of,
6; marginalization of certain forms of,
192; minority family practices, 6;
modes of incorporation and acquisition
of, 35; motivation to achieve, 20, 37;
multicultural education stance toward,
210; multiple, 212; need for multiple

ing and, 31, 32; levels of, 30; Lou family, 162–166; Ma family, 129–132; parents' perceptions of, 190; regarded by parents as teacher avoidance of teaching responsibilities, 190; in school learning activities, 189; school tension and, 199; social class and, 32; socioeconomic status and, 31; Tang family, 141–144; teacher expectations of, 190; variations in types of, 5; Wong family, 170–173

Parents: acceptance as most important teachers of children, 213; as change agents, 209; communication concerning homework, 220, 221; legitimization of voices of, 212, 213; listening to, 212; strengths and resources of, 213

Parents, Chinese. *See also* individual families: aloofness to teachers from, 63, 64; antithetical beliefs to those held by mainstream school systems, 35; belief in back-to-basics schooling, 188; belief in education as childrens' way to avoid discrimination, 67; blaming schools for childrens' performance, 72; challenges to school and teacher practices by, 6, 7, 9, 33, 34, 38, 63–100, 194; changes in involvement with school, 222–226; combined class concerns, 43, 72, 78, 86, 155, 164–165, 204; concern over increase in complexity of curriculum in higher grades, 148; concern over math teaching, 80; conflict with Canadian teachers, 8, 9; in contradictory location within dominant power hierarchy, 192; cultural differences in school involvement, 17–38; definitions of "well-educated" by, 92; dissatisfaction with school practices, 145; dress code concerns, 43; educational expectations of, 6; educationalization of learning at home by, 207; educational values of, 11; effect of cultural values on children's education, 33–35; engagement of children in daily literacy activities, 34; error correction concerns of, 86; expectations of, 9, 34, 185, 187; feeling that there is too much play in school,

78; field-trip concerns, 88; freedom of choice concerns, 72, 79, 122; holding school accountable for student performance, 148, 154, 162–166, 187, 203–205; home visits to, 212; homework concerns, 43, 119, 122, 142, 188, 198; implications of pedagogy of cultural reciprocity on, 228–230; investment in children's education by, 34; involvement in school, 95–99; learning activities at home, 108–112, 117–123; linguistic expectations, 67; literacy beliefs differing from mainstream parents, 34; maintenance of Chinese as priority, 65; middle-class status of, 9; model minority image of, 9; need for understanding of teachers' approach to education, 26; nonaccommodation approach toward educational practice, 195; obstacles to school involvement, 95–99; overindulgence by, 90; passive cooperation from, 145; perspectives on literacy and education, 64–100, 186, 187; perspectives on student difficulties, 154–155, 162–166, 172–173, 203–205; preference for traditional teacher-centered approach, 2, 22–27, 26, 77, 79, 88, 185, 187, 188, 192; provision of structured, formal educational experiences by, 34; resistance to cooperation with school, 11; resocialization into mainstream parenting styles, 6; school discipline concerns, 43; as subculture contesting dominant cultural space of schools, 195; unwillingness to adapt to new schools, 2; view on learning to speak English, 71–72; views of new sociocultural context, 64–67; views on after-school classes, 91–95; views on Canadian schools, 2, 43; views on discrimination, 67; views on language-experience methods of instruction, 77–80; views on literature-based approach to literacy, 85–86; wish for uniforms, 78; within-ethnic class differences, 34; writing concerns, 86, 132

Parry, K., 187